WILDERNESS SURVIVAL

WILDERNESS SURVIVAL

Living Off the Land with the Clothes on Your Back and the Knife on Your Belt

Mark Elbroch and Michael Pewtherer

RAGGED MOUNTAIN PRESS | McGRAW-HILL

Camden, Maine • New York • Chicago • San Francisco • Lisbon
London • Madrid • Mexico City • Milan • New Delhi
San Juan • Seoul • Singapore • Sydney • Toronto

The McGraw·Hill Companies

4 5 6 7 8 9 DOC DOC 9 8

Library of Congress Cataloging-in-Publication Data
Elbroch, Mark.
  Wilderness survival : living off the land with the clothes on your
back and the knife on your belt / Mark Elbroch and Michael Pewtherer.
    p. cm.
  Includes index.
  ISBN 0-07-145331-8 (pbk. : alk. paper)
  1. Wilderness survival—United States. 2. Outdoor life—United
States. I. Pewtherer, Michael. II. Title.
  GV200.5.E44 2006
  613.6'9—dc22   2006001789

Questions regarding the content of this book should be addressed to
Ragged Mountain Press
P.O. Box 220
Camden, ME 04843
www.raggedmountainpress.com

Questions regarding the ordering of this book should be addressed to
The McGraw-Hill Companies
Customer Service Department
P.O. Box 547
Blacklick, OH 43004
Retail customers: 1-800-262-4729
Bookstores: 1-800-722-4726

All photos and illustrations by the authors.

CONTENTS

ACKNOWLEDGMENTS

My early adventures in primitive skills were shared with many; foremost among them are Kalya Sanford, Mike Pewtherer, Jonathan Talbot, Ricardo Sierra, Frank Grindrod, Josh Kaufman, and Casey, Hanneman, Catherine, and the so many others I shared time with while I worked with Hawk Circle Programs, and who supported and shared in my enthusiasm and learning in the field. Several particular hills, a valley filled with wild edibles, a wild stream and a swimming pond were essential in my learning and enjoying primitive skills so many years ago—a very special thank you to the lands which sustained us while we practiced, learned, fumbled and laughed at ourselves; these places remain a quiet place inside me where I turn in times of need and sanctuary. Thanks also to the wild flora and fauna.

The core people who provide me with enduring and consistent support include Keith Badger, Nancy Birtwell, Fred Vanderbeck, and my family. My grandfather introduced me to nature and birds many years ago among the hedgerows and fields of Suffolk, England. Since then, every member of my family has not only suffered with, but also supported and encouraged my obsessive interests in wildlife, birding, and tracking. My parents support me in every way possible, as does my grandmother Liz Gorst. And a special appreciation for my Uncle Rob, also known as Christopher, who shares a special insight into survival after years in Africa.

Thanks also to Jonathan Eaton at Ragged Mountain for this opportunity, and Anne Hawkins for her enthusiasm and negotiation of the contract. Of course, a heartfelt thanks to Mike Pewtherer as well, for sharing in such a life-changing adventure and our continuing friendship.

MARK ELBROCH

I would like to thank my wife Diane for her endless patience and willingness to transcribe and proofread many of my notes and essays and Mark Elbroch for his friendship and help in this work. A big thanks goes out to Sylvan Incao, my childhood friend who first set me on the path to the skills contained in this book and to Ricardo Sierra who taught me so much and provided a sound platform from which I could begin in earnest my journey with the "skills." I would also like to thank my parents for their constant support and their faith that I would find my way both into and out of the woods around our home. The following people also deserve thanks for their contributions both large and small: Jonathan Talbott, the Hawthorne Valley Association for their stewardship of "my" woods, Conrad Vispo, Keith Badger, Frank Grindrod, Jon Young, Tom Brown Jr., Kevin Reeve, Craig Holdrege, Henry Glick, Joshua Kaufman, Daniel Grey, Michael Schuldt, and all those people who have found, and those yet to find, value and comfort in living with the earth.

MIKE PEWTHERER

Introduction

MARK ELBROCH

Mike Pewtherer, David MacDonald, and I met at Hawk Circle, a learning center started in 1989 by Ricardo Sierra to teach wilderness survival skills to children and adults. Mike had worked with Hawk Circle since its inception, and David and I joined in subsequent years. While exploring woodlands, teaching others, and practicing survival skills, we became firm friends and continually pushed each other's interests, applications, and knowledge of wildlife and wilderness skills.

It was during my three years with Hawk Circle that I was able to transform the many notes I had acquired during courses on survival skills into working reality—to put skills to the test. Practicing with others exponentially increased the speed with which we learned, because each of us brought unique perspectives to new challenges and offered distinctive strengths and interests. Mike saved us days of practice by sharing what he was learning in his experiments with traps, David taught us much about primitive pottery and alternative methods of making cordage and baskets, and I contributed what I could from practicing hand-drill fires and tracking. Our pooled community knowledge grew quickly. To intellectually understand a survival skill is never enough, as countless variables and trials emerge when you enter the landscape, gather raw materials, and attempt to produce results. Practice, and more practice, is essential.

This book has two components. One is Mike Pewtherer's essays on how you can begin to practice survival skills. Mike has been practicing survival skills for seventeen years, and his extensive field experience provides the details that make these essays most useful. The book's other component is a personal journal.

The journal is my own account of a wilderness trip that Mike, David, and I undertook nearly ten years ago in the Northeast. Due to the illegality of practicing primitive hunting and fishing skills (and out of season, too), this is as specific as we will be. It was our longest survival trip to date and was attempted only after each of us had practiced fire making and other skills for many years and had taken several short solo trips into the woods with only knives and our clothes. We selected a location with which we all had varying degrees of familiarity and an environment that provided springs for drinking water.

As you read the journal, it will quickly become apparent that we were not experts. The three of us were in our mid-twenties, and we were each in a transitional period as we attempted to follow our hearts into more focused careers and interests. This adventure was a natural progression in our growth, for if we didn't take the opportunity to apply the survival skills, then why were we practicing them in the first place?

The breaking of laws over the summer did not bother us in the least. Speaking for myself, at that time in my life I believe I assumed a moral high ground on the matter; I firmly believed that what we were practicing was closer to true conservation ethics than the imposed laws we broke. Naturally, we were more innocent and idealistic then, as is apparent in the journal's language and tone. Clearly, we were seeking something inspiring, or even spiritual, in survival skills that we could not find in American culture.

Our trip was neither well planned nor perfectly orchestrated. Ground rules were never discussed beforehand. Yet I knew that Mike and I wished to "survive" for a period long enough to prove that we were no longer drawing on the fat reserves we'd accumulated in our everyday lives. We wanted to be sure we'd been successful in living away from modern society. Yet I also believe we expected to simply enter the woods, survive and then reappear only at the completion of the experience; but this is not what happened.

Of the three of us, Mike was most focused on skills of survival. He already knew he wanted to devote his life to practicing and perfecting these skills, and he wanted to teach them to others. Mike also sought to test specific skills to see whether they were really useful in a survival situation and to fine-tune their application accordingly. He needed to gain his own stories to share with others.

David, too, harbored an intense desire to master survival skills. Yet David vacillated between practicing skills which would keep him alive in the woods and the finer crafts. He enjoyed and was very skilled at making beautiful things, and spent most of his days making baskets and other products.

For me, I knew this trip would offer closure to my era in wilderness living skills and the start of completely focusing on just one skill—animal tracking. I was more invested in what I might learn from the overall experience than in the individual skills themselves. What would I learn about myself, the natural world, and humanity from living so simply and in a fashion imitating our human ancestors who perfected these skills over untold generations?

Realize that "wilderness" has evolved and forever changed. Pure drinking water has become a luxury; wildlife dynamics and densities have been altered; and exotic fungal, plant, and animal species inhabit nearly every niche of North America. We could never re-create living as was done 500 years ago, so instead we attempted a modern wilderness survival experience. And rather than our adventure be borne of dire need, we *chose* to do what we did. It was a luxury and gift to ourselves.

Our summer was filled with learning and wonder, and I kept pen to paper throughout. I had intended this journal to be written for others, but as I reread it, I noticed that I had written something far more personal. In it, I witness a transition from physically documenting each day to the philosophical ramblings of a mind and spirit with time to reflect. As I lay in stream pools and forest debris, the stress in my neck and shoulders dissipated and my views on the world mellowed. I've learned much about myself from the reliving of the experience.

So the story begins. Try not to judge us too harshly. Rather you are encouraged to laugh with or even at us, and enjoy the lightness of the tale. Mike, David, and I believe survival skills offer many lessons in and of themselves. Whether you read about them or practice them in the field, they provide direct insight into self and planet. Survival skills are primal, and their effects can be experienced by anyone who has an open mind and heart.

Be forewarned that you may find portions of the journal disturbing, controversial, or even disappointing. The three of us visited town on one occasion, and David decided to spend half of nearly every week in society with friends and family. We killed numerous animals—sometimes in a brutal fashion—frequently trespassed, and disregarded hunting and fishing regulations. After years of rumination, my perspectives on what we did have changed, and I'll share them in the epilogue.

This journal is a snapshot of that earlier time. It is an honest, stumbling account of learning through countless mistakes and follies. Above all, it is a story of simplicity. We hope it will inspire you to make a trip of your own.

A Journal of Wilderness Survival

JUNE 25TH

Tomorrow I enter the woods, build a shelter, and sleep ensconced in sticks and leaves. Quite a contrast from this week of bed-and-breakfasts and hotels, a rehearsal dinner, wedding feasts, restaurants, and breweries. I packed on a few extra pounds for the lean times ahead.

I'm sitting in one of the greatest technological creations of all time—a massive metal craft flying from Chicago to Boston. I am eager, anxious, and incredibly nervous about my time in the woods. I expect to suffer a bit—not to a torturous degree by any means—but I will experience a niggling discomfort as I slide from plush, modern living to a rustic life in the woods. I also hope to achieve a clarity that many preach is possible only while living so simply and purely.

We are now a mobile people, so mobile that we have lost the sense of place we gain from learning and experiencing one home over time. We don't know the names of the plants in our yards or the animals that live among us. I move through life missing all but the obvious. I feel the need to slow down, and the remedy might be a lengthy stay in nature.

Survival

What do you picture when you hear the word "survival"?

For many, the image that comes to mind is of a skinny, disheveled person shivering in a damp cave with a few worn skins for clothing. The *American Heritage Dictionary of the English Language* provides the roots of the word survive as coming from the Latin "super," meaning "superior or above," and "vivere," meaning "to live." Thus, one interpretation is "superior living."

Survival need not be a struggle. Most often, survival experiences are spoken of as "man pitting himself against nature." Anytime you work against something rather than with it is a struggle! Swimming against the current, carving against the grain, going up the descending escalator—all are examples of struggles caused by working against the nature of the situation.

In the wilderness, if you're thirsty and you run randomly to the bottom of every valley looking for water, you will become frustrated, discouraged, and likely dehydrated. A better idea would be to first go to a good vantage point to see if any clear indicators of surface water are visible. If there are none, then perhaps you'll look for trees that require a lot of water, such as cottonwoods, willows, and basswoods. Knowing that water is either on or near the surface when these water indicators are present will drastically increase your chances of maintaining morale and health.

Likewise, if you make a beeline to a particular spot in the wilderness, you will probably encounter plenty of resistance—thickets, cliffs, and perhaps swamps or rivers. If you move as the landscape dictates and you go with the flow of the landscape while keeping in mind your goal, your movements will require less energy and will probably be more efficient.

In the wilderness, you must attend to five priorities in a survival situation, and the order in which you attend to them can make the difference between life or death. The following list goes from the greatest priority to the least:

1. *Attitude.* If you look at your situation and panic, or if you merely lament your ill luck, nothing beneficial will happen. However, comprehending your predicament and deciding on a course of action are productive activities, getting you closer to your goals and easing the journey.

2. *Shelter.* Without shelter, nights can be long and sleepless. Exposure to the weather, fair or stormy, can leave you hypothermic, tired, and ineffective when it comes to other survival tasks. In very cold or hot climates, shelter is an obvious need—you can die from exposure in a short time. With shelter, your "batteries" can be recharged. You have a "home," a base from which to make forays for other needs, and a physical and emotional aid.

3. *Water.* Without water, your mental faculties begin to diminish after about three days, and your ability to function decreases quickly from this point. Dark or strong-smelling urine and headaches are clear indicators of dehydration. Drinking unpurified water, however, can result in vomiting and diarrhea, causing a further loss of water. Finding potable water will help keep your head clear and your body healthy.

4. *Fire.* Fire is a higher priority than food for these reasons: Fire improves morale, provides heat to supplement a shelter, purifies water, aids in the making of tools, and makes it possible to dry clothes and supplies. Cooking food, of course, is important as well, as are drying and otherwise preparing food for consumption or storage.

5. *Food.* Even though food is often the first item missed when you have none of the above, it is the only one you can do without for two weeks or more. Gandhi's twenty-one-day fast while in his early sixties is tribute to that.

If you find and/or create everything described in this survival list, you can remain in the wild indefinitely. Although the prioritization should be followed strictly in a survival situation, don't think that while you are looking for a shelter location you should ignore good fire-making materials or foods that present themselves. The list is merely a guide to show you where your main focus should be.

Practice skills independently, but periodically look at the larger picture to see where each skill fits in as part of survival as a whole. Walking out into the woods and making a shelter becomes a different experience entirely when you have no gear or supplies, no backup, and no food or fire. Start slowly. Go camping and take food, knives, canteens, and clothes, but leave your sleeping bag, tent, and matches at home. While you are in the woods with supplies, pretend that you have no water. Try to find some and rock-boil it in a pot. Take your time and substitute modern gear with gear borrowed from the land.

Camping is a lot of fun, so enjoy learning how to let the land support you and practicing various skills. Never get too attached to your survival tools, though. It is a good idea to give away, or return to the land, tools you have made. Don't make just one good canteen and hold onto it forever. Make many, so that canteen making becomes second nature and not a chore. Remember, the loss of anything you can make is a chance to improve on it. The loss of anything you cannot make, however, can be devastating.

REGULATIONS AND THE LAW

Check out your state and local hunting regulations to ensure that you are operating within the law when it comes to practicing survival skills. Here, I'll use the laws in the state of New York as an example.

In an involuntary survival situation, such as being stranded while camping or if your vehicle breaks down in a wilderness area, you are legally permitted to do whatever is necessary to survive. If you voluntarily enter a survival scenario, however, you are expected to obey all laws with regard to trespassing, fire making, camping, and so forth.

In a voluntary survival situation, numerous laws pertaining to hunting and fishing apply. New York state laws on the taking of wildlife with primitive or traditional weapons are full of gray areas. Because New York has a permission-based system, any method of taking game that is not approved in

the hunting and trapping regulations is to be considered illegal. Yet some animals can be taken by "any safe means," which, according to the New York State Department of Conservation and Department of Fish and Wildlife, does not include poisons. In the case of woodchucks, however, poison gas cartridges can be used. When it comes to bow hunting, New York requires a minimum draw weight of thirty-five pounds, and you must have a valid license; spear hunting for deer, however, is illegal, as is the use of snares for any animal.

Fishing requires a license unless you are under the age of sixteen, a resident or direct family member of a resident on an active farm while fishing on that farm, or a Native American from a reservation within New York State. Spearfishing is legal in certain waters for certain fish, such as bullhead, eels, suckers, bowfin, carp, gar, burbot, and freshwater drum. Bait and hook type vary in their legality, depending on the body of water being fished. Some specify single hooks and artificial bait only, whereas others allow treble hooks and live bait. Restrictions on daily limits and minimum sizes also need to be followed. To find out more about fishing laws in your area, check with your local town hall or the game warden.

Enjoy your catch.

Day 1 ⬌

A hectic morning tying up loose ends: bills, letters, messages, etc. I shaved my head and beard. Less to deal with, as well as a ritualistic act of commitment to a lengthy experience. My new patchy appearance isn't appropriate for mingling in modern society. I stashed wedding gear at my apartment, which is being sublet for the month of July. Everything in order, I drove the four hours to meet Mike and David.

As I pulled into our rendezvous spot, the two of them dropped from a tree on the far side of the field. They had met a few days earlier to live in a semi-survival condition—meaning they were floating in and out of the woods, feeding on foods both harvested and bought in town. I had flown west to attend a wedding and hadn't been able to join them until now. I was happy they remembered to meet me.

More chores: dropping off cars and preparing them for an extended sit (disconnecting batteries, etc.), and saying good-byes to families. It was late afternoon before we entered the woods. I wore and carried clothes: shorts, t-shirt, long-sleeved shirt and pants, as well as a knife, a journal, a handful of dog-bane that I'd harvested last fall to make natural string, and a piece of leather I'd tanned several months ago. I planned to make a small bag from the leather to tote things about. I also carried a small metal bowl to help us get started in the first few days.

The lush greenery was intense; the week of rain had brought forth a thick carpet of green from field to forest floor. We arrived at Mike and David's camp in short order, which we planned to abandon the next day. I attempted to patch the vestibule of their shelter to create my own quarters for the coming night. Snapping-turtle jerky lay on a small rack from the prior evening. I expected it to be a rather gruesome culinary experience, but it was quite good. Chewy. Mike told me of the success of his turtle trap.

(continued on page 17)

Traps

How do you hunt multiple locations while at the same time lounging in camp? By using traps. Traps are mechanical hunters with great patience. They never tire, cramp, or lose interest. Hunting requires time and energy and does not guarantee success. Rather than stalking and waiting, your time and energy for trapping are used to locate excellent set areas and check the traps once they are in place. Traps are used to hold or kill an animal without direct manipulation by, and therefore often in the absence of, the hunter. Yet trapping is an art that is only learned through trial and error. Making the traps is the simplest aspect of trapping.

TYPES OF TRAPS

Traps can be classified in terms of: (a) where the energy to catch the animal comes from; (b) why the animal goes to the trap; and (c) the killing or holding mechanism.

The energy required to hold or kill an animal comes from one of three sources: the animal's weight or movement, the contraction of a spring stick (sapling or branch), or the falling of a weight or counter-weight.

The animal trips the trap either because bait is attached to a trigger or there is incidental contact with a trigger or noose due to placement of the trap.

There are three main types of killing or holding mechanisms: (1) snares use strong cordage and a noose or net to hold or kill the prey; (2) deadfall and live-capture traps use a weight or basket in combination with gravity to crush or capture the animal; and (3) pit traps use a concealed hole to hold (or kill by way of stakes in the bottom) game.

Trapping is used primarily when you are staying in one location, because it allows you to become familiar with the area and the game present. It is possible to trap successfully while on the move, but this requires a greater tracking ability to identify sites that will be productive within a twelve- to twenty-four-hour window. Staying in one location while trapping is conducive to setting a trapline—a series of traps set in a loop or circuit that can be checked twice daily. Trapping on the move is better suited to setting a few traps fairly near camp.

BAITS

Look at a feeding area to see what foods are plentiful. For example, if the edge of a clover field is the feeding area of a rabbit, you probably won't have much luck using clover as bait. However, red maple buds or a piece of wild apple may bring success. Good bait is often food that an animal would like to eat but that is not readily available. One option is to leave a number of prospective baits close together in the feeding area overnight, then check in the morning to see which ones have been eaten.

SET LOCATIONS

Animals have a home range within which they sleep, den, and move to and from feeding areas and day beds. The best place to trap an animal with a *baited set* is on the edge of a feeding area. This way the animal is already in a feeding "mind-set" and may be curious about a different food.

Incidental (nonbaited) traps are best set over den entrances and along trails or runs used exclusively by your quarry. (On larger trails, other animals will likely walk through your set and destroy it.) If a rabbit is heading to a clover patch, it is not likely to stop on the way for some wilting clover lying on the ground, but it may not notice a noose placed in the trail.

PEG SNARE

Type: Nonbaited snare.
Materials: Strong cordage and a peg.
Placement: Trail or run, den openings, water entrances.
Directions:
1. Drive a peg into the ground near the trail or run.
2. Tie cordage to the base of the peg.

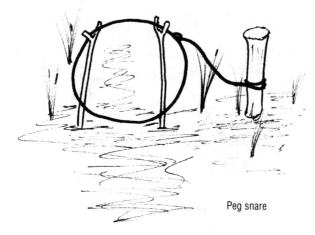

Peg snare

3. Make a noose and set it in the trail. If necessary, support it in the open position with a few twigs or grasses. Make the noose a little larger than the animal's head so that as the animal moves down the trail its head, but not its shoulders, passes through the noose. When the noose tightens from the animal's forward movement, the animal panics and strangles itself.

T-BAR SNARE

Type: Baited snare.
Materials: Flexible sapling, two notched sticks, "T-bar" (a "T"-shaped section of a sapling trunk with a branch growing perpendicular to it), a number of twigs, and strong cordage.
Placement: Near feeding areas.
Directions:

1. Harvest two sticks about ten inches in length and sharpen one end of each stick.
2. An inch from the other end of each stick, carve a notch so that when the pointed ends are in the ground, the top of the notch will be horizontal and capable of preventing the squared ends of the T-bar from moving upward.
3. Cut the horizontal part of the T-bar piece to about six inches in length (for squirrels), with the branch at the center.
4. Trim the vertical leg of the T-bar to two inches in length, and sharpen the end to receive the bait.
5. Square both ends so that they correspond to the notches in the pointed sticks.
6. Tie a noose and a length of cordage to the center of the T-bar, and bring everything to the set area.

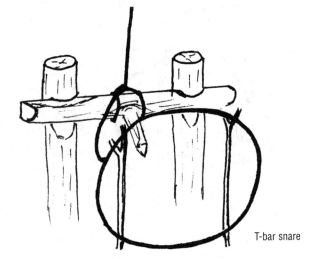

T-bar snare

7. To determine the exact set location, bend a sapling so that the top comes down to within two feet from the ground.

8. Remove a number of the branches to allow the sapling to snap quickly erect. To lend strength and snap to your spring stick, parallel branches or neighboring saplings can be tied to one another so as to work in tandem.

9. With the tip of the sapling two feet from the ground, place your T-bar directly under it.

10. Attach the cordage to the sapling, place the bait on the pointed stick, and set the T-bar in the notches.

11. Place the noose around the T-bar, lifting it off the ground with twigs so that the animal must extend its head through the noose to get the bait.

The force used to remove the bait twists and frees the T-bar from the notches, allowing the sapling to snap upward. This tightens the noose and kills the animal.

The T-bar snare can be set with the bait branch horizontal for an approach from above. In this case, place twigs around the trap as a fence to prevent an animal from going under the noose. The bait branch can also point downward for an approach from the front or back (using two nooses).

KEEPER SNARE

Type: Nonbaited snare.
Materials: Strong cordage and a weight three times or more than that of the target species (rocks or chunks of wood make good weights).
Placement: Trails and runs in wooded areas, den openings, water entrances.
Directions:
1. Set a noose on a trail or over a den opening.
2. Run the cordage from the noose up through a "Y" in a branch and onto another branch above that.
3. Tie a weight to the end of the cordage and place it on the higher branch in such a way that it will fall with a little tug on the snare line.

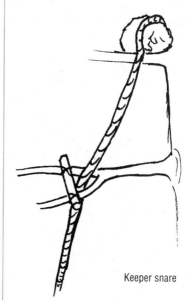

Keeper snare

4. Lash a one-inch-diameter piece of wood across the "Y" just beyond the notch, leaving enough room for the cordage to move without a problem.

When an animal hits the noose, the rock falls off its perch and plummets toward the ground. The animal is pulled swiftly upward until it hits the bottom of the "Y" branch and dies.

FIGURE-FOUR DEADFALL

Type: Baited and nonbaited deadfall.
Materials: Three straight branches (the size varies depending on the target species—mice to deer; a weight three times that of the target species to kill the animal, or a box/basket [with a weight lashed to the top] large enough to hold the animal)
Placement: Trail, run, or feeding area.

Components:
One upright stick, one diagonal stick, and one trigger stick. The bait or trigger stick and the diagonal stick are similar in length, while the upright stick is longer.
Directions:
1. Square the edge of the upright stick about two and one-half inches up, and make a wedged tip.
2. Notch the diagonal stick three or more inches from one end to correspond with the top of the upright; make a wedged point on the other end.
3. Notch the bait or trigger stick to receive the lower end of the diagonal stick; make a corresponding notch on the squared edge of the upright stick.
4. If you are going to use bait, sharpen the end farthest from the diagonal stick. If you are *not* going to use bait, use a branch

Figure-four deadfall

with a few twigs left attached (so that it will not impede the falling of the weight).

5. To set the trap, place the notch of the diagonal stick on the upright. As you put the bait or trigger stick in place, apply pressure on the tip of the diagonal stick, then substitute your hand with either a log or a stone. If the weight tips to either side, drive a guide stake in on either side to allow only upward or downward movement.

5. If the ground is soft, you may need to add a flat rock underneath the trap as a smashing surface.

When the bait is taken, the weight falls, crushing the prey. Note that the greater the angle of the weight, the longer it takes to fall. This increases the chance of the animal escaping. If no large rocks are available, you can attach a basket of small stones to a log to add any needed weight.

When you set this trap on a trail, you can substitute a branch with one end left untrimmed for the bait stick. A passing animal that touches any of the branches will cause the weight to fall and kill the animal. If the branch is too sturdy, it may prevent the weight from doing its job.

SNAPPING-TURTLE TRAP

Type: Baited, live capture.
Materials: Cordage; approximately thirty one-and-one-quarter-inch-diameter sapling pieces eighteen to thirty inches long with a sharpened end, including two "Y" sticks; a few dinner-plate-sized flat stones; rotten fish or other meat for bait; and one thin, straight trigger stick eighteen inches long.
Placement: Lake and swamp shallows about knee-deep.

Snapping-turtle trap

Directions:

1. Create a horseshoe shape with the sharpened stakes, with the mouth open to deeper water.
2. Hammer the sharpened stakes into the bottom of the swamp to ensure that they are firmly embedded.
3. Make the width of the trap about six inches wider than the size of the turtle you want to catch.
4. Have the stakes protrude six inches above the surface, and lash them to one another to prevent splaying due to pressure from the inside. The two stakes on either side of the horseshoe's mouth are "Y" sticks, and they will hold the swinging door.
5. Line the bottom of the trap with flat stones—the bigger the better—to prevent the turtle from digging its way out.
6. To make the door, place one of the sapling pieces in the notch of both "Y" sticks so that it spans the mouth; this will be the hinge.
7. Lash sticks to the hinge four inches apart from one notch or mark to the other.
8. Lash an additional stick across the bottom of the door parallel to the hinge. When the door is placed in the "Y" sticks, it should be able to swing in a full circle.
9. Tie a stone to the inside of the door; the stone must be heavy enough to prevent the door from floating open.
10. Drive a stake into the swamp bottom just in front of the mouth of the horseshoe, and leave enough protruding to prevent the door from swinging outward.
11. Tie some cordage across the open tops of the "Y" sticks to hold the hinge in place.
12. To set the trap, swing the door inward until it is parallel with the surface of the water and prop it open with a thin stick or reed as a trigger.
13. Tie a piece of rotten meat to the back of the horseshoe, and check the trap once a day.

Once the silt has settled from installation of the trap, a snapping turtle, smelling the bait, will swim into the trap. The trigger stick propping open the door will be dislodged as the turtle moves toward the bait. When the door closes, striking the shell, the turtle will move forward toward the bait, allowing the door to close completely. The stake at the entrance prevents the door from swinging open, rocks prevent a digging escape, and the turtle will not be able to climb up and over the walls. You can feed the turtle and keep it alive until you are ready to eat it.

Note: If the horseshoe is not long enough, the door will fall onto the turtle's back without closing completely, and the turtle will escape.

Snapping turtles are strong and fast with their mouths; take great care when dealing with them.

Traps can be made in many variations for different situations. Your imagination is your only limitation.

(continued from page 9)

As the daylight faded, the birds next to the stream were alarming. I moved out onto a gravel bar and sat to wait for them to settle down and become silent. Storm clouds rolled in from the west, soft thunder providing background to the continuous calls of birds. I was feeling a bit dreamy—it took me a few minutes to realize that the raucous din of kingbirds, robins, and catbirds was not about me. No, the intensity and duration of the alarms, combined with the fact that they were made well above the ground, indicated an avian predator. I watched the silhouettes of birds dance and swarm around something hidden in the high branches of the massive sycamore across the stream. I crept down the gravel bar and watched as the great horned owl dropped from her perch and floated down valley to disappear into the wall of forest. I'd disturbed her and the birds suddenly became quiet.

DAY 2

Thunder cracked and lightning cut the black night as we sat around the fire last night. The rain began, yet the hemlock foliage above us kept it at bay—at least in the beginning. I watched raindrops appear as black spots on red coals and quickly fade away. I stayed by the fire quite late, mesmerized by the glow and warmth. There's something about fire…

The storm raged throughout the night, with rain coming down in absolute torrents. The vestibule began to leak early; there were so many leaks that I now refer to the structure as the "sieve." I attempted to curl into the smallest shape possible, yet the number of leaks dripping on me were uncountable. In short time, Mike, who was also in the vestibule, and I were soaked to the bone. David was warm and dry, tucked in the "debris hut" portion of the shelter.

For those who struggle to envision a "debris hut," try to picture a massive pile of leaves. There is an opening, though, just small enough to wiggle inside. The tiny chamber, which is created by a skeletal framework of sticks and the ground, is custom designed to fit the builder. It is more like a leafy sleeping bag than a tent—small, simple, well camouflaged, and effective.

As morning approached, the temperatures chilled, and I felt fingers of cold down my back and across my chest. Sleep was sporadic. I woke again with first light and the crackle of Mike's fire, and I rose to dry my clothes and skin. We began our day passing a bowl of hemlock tea. Not poison hemlock, but made from the foliage of the eastern hemlock tree. While I washed the bowl in the stream below, I spent time with a northern waterthrush, which bobbed its tail rapidly atop a log while suspiciously eyeing me.

Mike escorted me to a white pine that he and David had felled to make containers. I began by making a watertight cooking container, which I tested in a nearby spring. Seams are avoided by folding the bark rather than slitting it, and securing

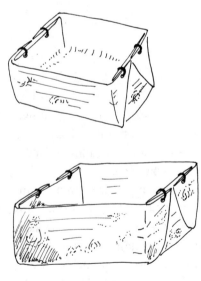

it with rootlets. The design is simple and effective. I allowed the water to sit as I created a second, cylindrical, more "aesthetic" container for fun. The first container held true and flavored the water lightly with pine—wonderful.

I headed down the valley to wander and explore, with hopes of gathering berries and collecting hand-drill materials for fire making. The wind swayed trees and grasses alike, and storm clouds rolled in with incredible speed. I

Waterproof folded-bark container

stood beside a massive white oak, protected from the slanted sheets of rain. I sat down and suddenly realized I was surrounded in arrowwood—a plant I'd only heard was in the area and a useful plant should I decide to make a hunting bow and arrows. The storm had forced me to slow down.

For the second afternoon shower I hid less successfully behind a younger sugar maple. Returning to camp, I worked the leather I had brought into a small bag. A simple design with simple lacing—plain, functional, and beautifully natural.

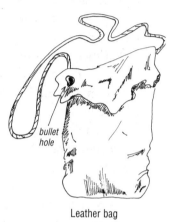

bullet hole

Leather bag

Mike joined me, carrying a massive load of raspberries and early blackberries. We gorged ourselves but still saved one-third for David. Mike had plans to hunt the southern valley and check in on a young woodchuck he'd noticed along the stream. I decided to tag along.

We moved silently through the woods, both armed with throwing sticks. The mud felt invigorating and cool against my feet, but the rain had also unleashed a distracting mass of gnats. We followed the stream a bit, and Mike stopped to explain where the woodchuck had previously been and what our strategic approach should be. After establishing a visual signal to indicate the prey was in sight, we began to stalk downstream. Slowly moving one foot in front of the other, we balanced ourselves carefully in the current. Our feet soon found natural catches by themselves. As I sank into the flow of the stream and surrounding woodland, the distraction of the gnats faded away. In moments like these, I lose track of time altogether.

I'm not sure how far we'd gone, but I noticed a creature whipping downstream along the bank next to us. I chirped softly to signal Mike to stop, and we both watched a mink lope past and disappear over a gravel bar downstream. Mike gestured that he was going to follow her, and I signaled that I was

front   rear

Mink tracks

heading for a mud patch I'd seen her cross. I found perfect tracks—small, perfect tracks.

As I knelt, attempting to absorb every detail of the pattern and tracks, I heard Mike chirp. I looked at him and he mouthed, "coming back." I looked downstream and caught the mink on her way up toward me, a bit higher on the bank. She held an enormous crayfish in her jaws, its massive claws dangling from one side of her mouth and its tail sticking out the other. She passed not five feet from me, her stunning chocolate coat glistening with the flex of her muscles. Dappled sunlight accented her fur as she passed, and I noticed for the first time that her tail was not uniform in color. It was banded, alternating dark chocolate brown and a milk chocolate brown. You learn so much from glimpses of wild creatures.

Mike and I stared at each other, grinning ear to ear. He came over to study the tracks. We stood, more content than imaginable. The mink was hunting downstream and then carrying her entire prey back upstream a considerable distance along a well-traveled route. It seemed to me that she was showing signs of rearing young. I whispered to Mike it was likely she'd return along the same route. As I spoke the words, I watched Mike's eyes bulge, and he nodded upstream over my shoulder. I turned and began to watch the mink progress quickly toward us along her commuter route, the trail in which we stood. Closer and closer she loped, twenty feet, fifteen, ten— she did not slow down. She stopped at our feet and began to sniff around. She locked her eyes on our ankles and then slowly began to look from our feet to our knees to our waists to our chests to our eyes. Then recognition was instant, and she turned and bounded upstream. Wow!

We kept walking downstream, reliving the moment over and over again. We'd have reminisced along the stream all afternoon if we hadn't been rerouted by two stream walkers and a dog—unusual this far off trail. So we moved to investigate two ponds where muskrat activity was high. The ponds were surprisingly small, and the high muskrat population had established an incredible trail network in the surrounding fields, where the muskrats fed on all sorts of herbaceous plants as well as woody plants such as wild roses.

As we approached the second pond, Mike signaled to stop and look. A muskrat was swimming a few feet offshore, exploring the tussocks that lined this side of the pond. The animal was an easy shot with the throwing stick. I don't know why Mike didn't throw. For me, I wasn't ready to take the life of a muskrat. I wasn't really hungry yet, and part of me felt I needed to suffer a bit before I was allowed to kill. Stupid, really. I think I must be afraid of something or some part of myself.

Rather than throw sticks, we watched the muskrat explore, dive, and reappear over and over again. Finally, the animal disappeared into a bank burrow. As we began to circle back toward camp, Mike said, "I never know whether to watch or thump 'em." Eventually, we must "thump" in order to live freely in these woods. What a lesson is in store for me.

We ended the evening with a swim and collection of spices, jewelweed, and lady's thumb. David appeared with more berries and stories of adventures. Jewelweed is amazingly filling.

DAY 3

The night was chilly. Although I had rebuilt the "sieve," I hadn't packed it with leaves. Watertight, but chilly. I had enough leaves to cover my body from pelvis to chest, which was just enough to finish the night without shivering. I rose early to warm by the fire and watch sunlight fill the valley below. The sky was clear of clouds and the sun shone clear and bright.

We decided to have a minnow and crayfish bake in the afternoon. So, off I went to gather materials for a minnow catcher I had been designing in my mind—essentially a shallow basket on the end of a stick. With construction under way, it was a bit ugly, and I rather hoped function would outperform form.

As I wandered back to camp with basket and pole, I discovered an abandoned white-footed mouse nest. A loose ball of inner barks formed the walls and held the sleeping chamber. Hickory nuts lay strewn about beneath the nest and inside as well.

A beaming Mike greeted me upon my arrival. He held a Canada goose aloft. The bird appeared to be fully grown, but incomplete flight feathers had held the young bird grounded. Mike was eager to eat, so we began preparations immediately.

In the short time I was out there, I noticed an enhancement in my taste buds. Possibly I was just paying more attention to what and how often I was eating. But a meal of roast goose, with a side of watercress and spinach-like lady's-thumb electrified my taste buds. And this is survival living? I just hoped we'd be able to maintain the food supply.

The goose had outstanding flavor—no spices were necessary. The liver was the best-tasting liver I'd ever had. Mike even made me try the heart. As we drank the broth and chewed on the greens, David and I managed to persuade Mike to relay his tale of the full hunt, in true native fashion.

He told us he was circling past a small pond and saw a family of geese. The young were large but flightless. As Mike approached, the entire family took to water for safety. Adult Canada geese pair and mate for life, so Mike began to scope out the younger birds. He planned his attack but missed with both throwing sticks. Then he turned to using stones. He said he threw innumerable stones before he managed to stun a bird adequately to reach it and make a swift kill. Oh, we laughed at his persistence!

Some might argue this was not a perfectly executed hunt—we certainly did—yet we reveled in the gift of the goose. We were not sport hunters and knew we had much to learn.

We lounged about a bit during the afternoon, bellies full. Mike and I went to study the mouse nest again. We discovered more mouse signs in the area and a raccoon skull. We also went to check on a skull Mike had seen while running earlier in the week. It turned out to be the skull of a gray squirrel.

Skulls are stunning in form—all similar, yet each intricately different. I just recently learned that you could interpret the relative age of a male fisher by the development of the "ridge," or sagittal crest, along the top of the skull.

We organized a group hike in search of a new campsite. While out exploring, we walked right up to a singing veery, the infamous "underwater flute" of the northeastern woods. We walked to within several feet of the bird. While the muted speckles on his chin and upper chest vibrated with music, the soft rust of his back held still. Able to create two notes simultaneously, the veery's song spiraled and twisted, flowing from perch to thicket. The bird's eyes kept a wary watch over his audience.

Next, we hit the massive raspberry patch at the northern end of the hill. We gorged like bears. I ate and ate, deep in the bush, listening to the rustling of companions doing the same. On we searched, arguing the pros and cons of various locations. Our number-one prerequisite was a spot unlikely to be visited by some lost or wandering human being. Our current camp was in an area where people are known to occasionally fish and hike.

We finally agreed on a spot high up on a ridge—a beautiful spot where an updraft kept smoke and air on the move. Leaf litter, which we needed for shelters, was high, and we were in an area where people rarely, if ever, passed through. We'd found our new home.

David announced a decision he'd been mulling over. He had decided he needed to visit his family and girlfriend once a week. He said he never realized he'd feel so lonely out here, or how much he needed others. We all agreed to be less fanatic. We were here to learn about self and planet, not to punish ourselves. David left immediately.

Day 4

Mike and I slept alone in the "sieve camp." Further work on the shelter resulted in a warm, cozy night, and I listened to a great horned owl screech at dusk and dawn. It was an odd morning. Both Mike and I were struck with an extraordinary lethargy. My head was slightly groggy and my vision a bit altered. Nothing dramatic—just a bit off. I wondered whether it might have been the milkweed flowers we'd gathered in a nearby meadow and eaten the night before. They tasted especially bitter and undercooked, yet we forced them down. I couldn't remember what I had read about the effects of milkweed poisoning, but I did know they needed to be cooked in multiple changes of water to avoid nasea and sickness. Perhaps we hadn't changed the water enough times or the bark containers had absorbed that which we were trying to remove.

We hiked the ridge, which took greater effort than it should have, to start construction of our debris huts. We reached our destination and immediately sat down to recuperate. There seemed no rush, so we chatted, watched wood thrushes sing, and listened to scarlet tanagers in the canopy. This was a special place. The hemlocks were older than the surrounding trees, and a vista was afforded by a steep drop at the edge of camp. A good feeling lingered about the area. We'd done well.

While we sat, David reappeared with news of eating burritos and fruit sorbet, and of an oncoming three-day storm. That was just what we needed to hear to get motivated, and within a few hours we had completed our debris huts. While building, I took frequent breaks, still groggy. But I managed a functional debris hut, equipped with awning and all the trimmings.

So why was I lethargic? There's the milkweed theory, and Mike and I had been discussing possible side effects of transitioning from wedding foods and modern cheer to a hundred-percent wild diet of bitter plants and organic meats. Who knows? Could also be linked to the fact I hadn't had a bowel movement since I arrived. Food went in but hung in limbo.

I was actually looking forward to seeing my poo. I thought that if it looked enough like raccoon or bear scat, I'd start leaving piles along stone walls or next to dominant conifers upon which I would scratch claw marks with my knife. What fun! Our debris huts completed, the three of us built a frame for a central shelter that we would use for cooking and hanging out. We opted for separate debris huts in which to sleep for two main reasons: (1) they require no fire to stay warm and are therefore more energy efficient; and (2) our central shelter is kept separate to create distance between food and our own shelters. My debris hut is made for one, not one plus a raccoon or fox.

(continued on page 30)

Shelter

There are many ways to build shelters and many environments in which to build them. The woodland shelter described here is called the "debris hut," introduced to the modern world by Tom Brown, Jr. The debris hut is a small, easily constructed, snug little "burrow"; if built correctly, it can keep you warm and dry even in the harshest of winter storms.

The debris hut is nothing more than a framework of sticks filled and covered with leaves and other forest debris. The purpose of the leaves is similar to that of wool in a sweater. The leaves, if adequately stuffed into the frame, create an area of dead air space around you. It is then possible for your body to heat up the hut and keep you warm, even when wet.

I have never slept so well as the nights I have spent in my debris huts, but I must warn you that your first few nights may not be so restful. Leaves do not immediately offer the same security that we associate with blankets, but after a night or two, you might find the leaves preferable.

The following are guidelines for locating and building a one-person debris hut.

FINDING A SUITABLE LOCATION

One of the first orders of business is to find a suitable location for your hut. After all, a good shelter in a bad location is a bad shelter.

1. *Resources.* An area without leaf litter will provide a challenge when it comes to building a shelter. Look for an area with lots of leaf litter, such as a flat area in a mixed-wood forest.
2. *Grade.* Sleeping on a slight incline may prove to be a lesson in frustration. Anything beyond

even the slightest incline can leave you cramped and somewhat crumpled on the downhill side of your shelter. Look for a flat area on which to build.

3. *Drainage.* The beautiful, grassy meadow near the creek is likely a floodplain. Find some higher ground on which to build. Look at your proposed shelter area and try to imagine where water will run in a torrential downpour.

4. *Safety.* Always check the areas both overhead and upslope from your shelter. Are there big dead branches or trees that may fall and injure you? Are there large rocks that could roll when the soil below them is eroded by rain, and squash you in your shelter? It is also a good idea to check for rocks or roots that may be uncomfortable to sleep on. Remember, your goal is to survive.

5. *Experience.* If you practice building shelters in varied locations, you'll get a better sense of which materials will work and how much material you'll need. If you're an experienced builder, you'll save yourself a lot of valuable time in an involuntary survival situation; you'll know how to build, and, equally important, you'll know *where* to build. Remember, there's no such thing as a "perfect spot," so don't waste time searching for it.

CONSTRUCTION

Once you have your spot picked out, the initial construction goes pretty quickly. You will be working first with a ridgepole, a support for the ridgepole, ribbing, and small brushy material to cover the ribbing. You will also need to pay attention to the size of your shelter as you build it.

1. *The ridgepole.* The ridgepole is a straight branch or sapling that functions as the primary support for the structure. It should be longer than you are tall by at least two feet and strong enough to hold your weight. Make sure that there are no ants or other critters already using it as a home.

2. *Support for the ridgepole.* Find something about waist high with which to support one end of the ridgepole. A fork in a tree, a branch, or a rock will work, or you can construct something by using a "Y" stick or two. (Be careful—I know of one fellow who broke his arm when his improperly secured support collapsed.)

3. *Measurements.* The following measurements are for cold weather. In warmer times, shelters can be made more spacious inside and use less insulation outside. Your ridgepole should run from your support to the ground. When you lie down

under it on your back, your toes should be a couple of inches below the ridgepole at the lower end. To measure the height of the upper end, roll onto your side. Your upper shoulder should be one hand's length from the bottom of the ridgepole.

4. *Ribbing.* Once the pole is set, start laying ribbing (sticks) against it, creating an A-frame. Gather sticks from thumb thickness to wrist thickness. When you lay them against the ridgepole, it is important that your ribbing does not protrude more than three or four inches above the ridgepole. If the ribbing is too high, you'll invite the possibility of water running down the ribbing or ridgepole and into your shelter. When you are lying on your back, centered under the ridgepole, the ribbing at your shoulders should be one hand's length away on either side. To do this, lie on your back, centered under the ridgepole. Reach your right hand across your chest, and put a twig into the ground one hand's length away from your shoulder. Repeat for the left side. As you apply the ribbing, you can taper it in toward your feet. At this point, you should have something resembling a wooden tent with one open end. Place ribs over one-half of the open end. The other half will serve as your doorway. Another option is to completely block off the end and remove a few of the ribs from the side for a doorway. Different situations require different types of "doors," as I will discuss later.

5. *Shelter size.* Until you have built a number of shelters, it is wise to periodically get in and check for size. If you can't breathe without moving the shelter's frame, you might want to enlarge it. If you have enough room for a social event, you ought to downsize.

6. *Small brushy material.* Now lay small brushy material, such as

Debris hut frame

the thin, upper branches of fallen dead trees, in a crosshatch manner over the ribbing. The purpose is to keep the soon-to-be-applied debris from falling down into the shelter and your eyes.

LEAF GATHERING

The "digging dog" technique of leaf gathering works well. Start well away from your shelter and, using your fingers as a rake, move backward, flinging the leaves between your legs and toward the shelter. In very short order you should have a big pile of leaves (check them for ants before putting them on your shelter). Start gathering leaves—lots and lots of leaves. Keep gathering leaves; do not stop. Cover the entire shelter with mounds of leaves, then pack them. The most effective packing technique is to actually slide the leaves down along the ribs. Basically, you reach up to the top of the pile and bring your hands downward in the same direction as the ribbing. It is shockingly disappointing to see how far leaves

will compact in this manner. Continue with the piling and packing until the leaf layer is about four feet thick for winter use.

In summer, an arm's length thickness seems to do the trick. You can't cheat here. You could loosely pile leaves to four feet and then freeze all night—not the greatest idea in the world. Once the ribs are covered with leaves, lay loose bark or dead branches over the shelter to keep the leaves from blowing away.

STUFFING THE INSIDE

Now it's time to stuff the inside. Some people like to be picky here, removing all the sticks and other lumpy debris from their leaf pile before stuffing their shelter full of it; others pick out the undesirables as they find them while attempting to sleep. Once the inside is packed properly, you should have trouble getting into your shelter the first time due to the quantity of leaves. I always start barefoot and slowly worm my way in until I am all the way into the shelter. I then begin

Finished debris hut

WILDERNESS SURVIVAL

rolling around to pack the leaves giving me more space to—you guessed it—stuff it with more leaves! I also use my legs to push and compress the leaves into the shelter as much as possible. It is amazing how compressed all those leaves become in a short period of time. Therefore, it's better to gather more than you think you will need now, while you are in leaf-gathering mode, than at one in the morning when you're too cold to sleep. In cold weather, this step is vital. Do it right and don't skimp.

It is a good idea to keep your eyes closed as you enter and exit the shelter. In this way, you can avoid any falling debris. I also give the ridgepole a good kick before entering; this knocks most of the loose material out of the "ceiling" and decreases the chance of it falling in my eyes.

DOORS

There are a number of ways to construct a door for this type of shelter, one of which is the plug. This door type consists of two disks, usually made by loosely "weaving" green branches in the shape of the door opening. Leaves are sandwiched between the two disks (like a cookie), then are lashed together with more green branches or cordage. When you crawl backward into the shelter, you simply pull the plug into the opening (it should be a tight fit) and leave it there for the night.

Another option, and the one I prefer, is to have a "door pile," which is simply a heap of leaves that you compress with your arms and pull in after yourself. Once pressure is released, the pile of leaves expands, nicely filling the opening.

OPTIONS FOR THE DEBRIS HUT

There is no end to how elaborate a debris hut can be. I often settle for the basic hut with an awning over the door, or maybe a little area in which I can crouch and work on rainy days. If I'm in a bit of a rush, I'll just pile some leaves together and burrow in.

Debris hut with awning

This is a fine shelter if you can manage to sleep in one position. Unfortunately, movement will dislodge all the leaves and you will wake up cold within a few minutes.

POINTERS

Keep a *big* pile of spare leaves outside your shelter; in this way, in the event of a leak, you have the patching material ready. You will also find that, after a few weeks in one shelter, the bedding leaves will become pulverized into powder. Therefore, you must periodically pull out the bedding leaves, heap them on top of the hut, and get fresh ones for the inside.

For your first attempt, you may want to substitute a sleeping bag for the bedding leaves, then move to just leaves over time. This will allow you to become familiar with sleeping inside the debris hut.

Please understand that exposure is a real danger in the outdoors. Practice shelter building in warm weather with backups until you have a firm grasp and understanding of the debris hut.

Good luck, and sweet dreams.

(continued from page 25)

We hiked throughout the afternoon in search of animal signs, hunting areas, and new places to explore. We found a massive raspberry patch on the hill to the northwest of camp. As we circled back, we walked the stream to gather crayfish for dinner.

Crayfishing is wonderful fun and a very social event indeed. Each in turn, we swore loudly when crayfish outwitted our attack approaches or clamped down on fingers. Curses were quickly followed by roars of laughter. Ah, the therapy of laughter! We also learned why the crayfish were fleeing for the tussocks. As we felt along the base of the grass clumps, we found holes. Deep where fingers could not be watched, crayfish congregated—but now, no longer safe from their pursuers. Holes varied in size and depth, but all were one-stop shopping for crayfish. That is, of course, if you didn't mind the occasional pinch.

We also harvested lamb's-quarters, a green leafy plant, on our way back, following the stream down toward the sieve camp. We decided to eat at the old camp, as we needed water for cooking and had not brought containers to carry it up the hill. We were in good cheer and arrived to find that one of Mike's friends had stopped by and left us a six-inch trout. We ate that, too. Apparently, before I arrived, Mike had told a friend where this camp stood. Another reason to move.

Day 5

We awoke to a hard rain, and I discovered a small leak on one leg in the reconstructed "sieve." Hopefully, my new shelter atop the ridge to the north had fared better than this one. We had prearranged to meet in an old abandoned shack, should we wake to rain. I was the first to arrive, chilly and soaked thoroughly. It wasn't long before David and Mike arrived and a fire was drying our clothes and warming our bodies. We huddled under the tiny roof, just large enough for us and a small fire. We worked on projects. I coal-burned a spoon and worked on cordage for snares.

Pounding basswood for fibers

(continued on page 38)

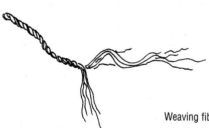

Weaving fibers into cordage

Making Camp

The layout of your camp is important. For example, you want to make sure your latrine area is downhill from your camp and well away from any water source to avoid contamination. Also, having your food storage and cooking areas separate, clean, and away from your sleeping quarters is a good way to avoid animal visitors both large and small. A common mistake among camping parties is gathering firewood and food close to camp, slowly depleting their closest supplies. Keeping a buffer zone—an area surrounding your camp in which you don't harvest food or firewood—is a precaution that can save your life. In the event of an injury, heavy snows, or other movement inhibiting factors, you will have a good supply of materials and food nearby.

There are numerous other details to make camp life a little easier, if not downright luxurious. Tongs, hand vises, hide scrapers, digging sticks, and fire pits (with all the attachments) can really improve life outdoors.

FOOD STORAGE

One way to protect your stores is to toss a line over a high branch, tie a food satchel to it, and haul it aloft. As long as the satchel is high enough without being too close to the branch above, or to the tree trunk, it should be out of reach of most critters.

Another way to keep food safe is in a storage pit. Dry areas are best for long-term storage, but any soil type will work for short-term storage.

One type of pit can be made by digging a hole in the ground about two feet deep, two feet wide, and as long as needed. Four inches from the top of the hole, widen the pit all the way around by four inches to create a "shelf." Line the pit up to the bottom of the "shelf" with stone, and pack the seams with a raw clay or mud and grass mixture. Make a small fire inside to drive out any moisture.

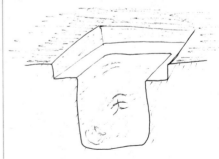

Storage pit

For the lid, cut sapling trunks the width of the hole plus eight inches for the "shelf" on each side. Lash the trunks together until you have a lid that can be rested on the "shelf" over the hole.

For handles, a piece of sapling with two branches growing out of it can be lashed to two opposing corners of the lid. Paste over the lid with the grass and mud mixture in a few one-inch thick coats. Let it dry between each coat to avoid cracking. Cover the last coat with leaves while the mixture is still wet, as this aids in camouflage of the cache and adds a little rain protection.

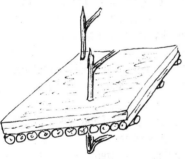

Lid for storage pit

Dried grasses or leaves should be placed in the pit and the food nested within. Adding dried aromatic plants to the pit, like sweet fern or mint, can help mask any lingering food scents. Once food is inside the bin, the top can be laid in place and sealed with more clay or mud for an extended absence, or covered with more leaves if the food will be used every day. Pieces of bark with leaves piled on top can be laid over the lid as added protection against the weather.

TONGS

Tongs are used to pick up hot rocks when you are rock boiling, to pick up coals for coal burning, and to move other hot food items in or out of the fire. To make a pair of tongs:

1. Cut a straight branch twenty inches in length and about one-half inch in diameter.
2. In the middle of your stick, shave a four-inch section on one side, thin enough so that you can bend the stick in half fully without breaking it. The shaved section acts as a spring, holding the tongs in the open position.

To aid in the bending process, submerge the shaved section in hot water or steam, then bend it slowly over a round, one-inch-diameter form or stick.

3. Once the stick is bent, tie one arm to the other while the tongs are opened about three or four inches.

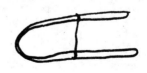

Tongs

Tongs

Variations for Tongs

A "'Y" stick can be used for tongs to provide better stability for lifting rocks or food.

Cut a three-inch-long section of sapling a couple of inches in diameter, and bend the longer "Y" stick around it. The short piece reduces strain on the hinge area and helps the tongs last much longer.

CAMP VISE

A simple locking pair of pliers is great for working on small projects such as projectile heads or bone hooks. To make a camp vise:

1. Cut a one-and-a-half-inch-diameter hardwood branch to a length of six inches.
2. Taper one end and split it in half lengthwise.
3. Pinch a quarter-inch-diameter branch between the two split pieces so that the ends stick out either side at the middle.

Camp vise

Broad scraper

4. Lash the quarter-inch branch in place.
5. Carve a wooden wedge, and you are ready to work.
6. Place your project in the tapered end of the vice and then force the wedge into the other end, pinching and securely holding the work piece.

SCRAPERS

Scrapers for working hides can be tough to make. Discussed here are two types, the broad scraper and the stake scraper.

The Broad Scraper

The goal in making a broad scraper is to create a square edge. This can be done by removing much of one side of a straight leg bone (from a deer or larger animal) and sharpening one edge to at least ninety degrees.

1. Score two parallel lines one inch or more apart for the length of the bone (not including the knobs at each end).
2. With a stone, carefully knock out the bone between the lines. To be precise with your strikes, hold a smaller stone or chisel stone in place with one hand, then strike with a larger stone in your other hand.
3. A little abrading work is required to smooth the edges. This is a rather tedious process but is worth it if you plan on tanning many hides.

The Stake Scraper

The stake scraper is far simpler to make and is well suited to working a hide strung on a rack.

1. Starting with a straight leg bone (from a deer or larger animal), score a diagonal line around one end to form a chisel-like tip.

Stake scraper

2. Break the bone along the score line and abrade it to remove any barbs that might damage the hide (see "Rawhide and Sinew," page 221).

3. Tie a loop of rawhide or cordage to the unworked end so that the loop sits around your wrist and adds support while you are working the hide.

DIGGING STICK

A digging stick is a superb tool for all manner of digging tasks, from digging up edible roots to digging out a food storage pit. Digging sticks are best made from a piece of green hardwood like beech or oak, although softer wood will usually do the trick. The piece of wood should be one and one-quarter inch in diameter and twenty-four inches long. One end can be carved or ground to a round point and the other to a flat, chisel-like point. Fire harden both ends (see "Hunting Tools," page 157) and you are ready to dig.

Digging stick

FIRE PITS

Of the many ways to build a fire pit, the keyhole pit is one of the more versatile pits I have used. Dug in the shape of an old-fashioned keyhole, this pit allows for all kinds of cooking.

The round portion is good for general use, cooking fish and ashcakes, working tools, and providing light and heat.

The box or smaller rectangular section can be used for a variety of tasks. For roasting, use "Y" sticks on either side to hold a spit. A rock can be placed over the top, slowly heated, and used to fry food. Coals can be raked into the box until the rocks are hot and then removed. Meat or veggies put inside are baked in the residual heat from the stones. Rocks for rock boiling are easier to remove from the fire when the area is smaller, because you spend less time hunting around for them. A flat stone leaned against the back of the box can be used for drying mashed berries or other foods (see "Preserving and Storing Food," page 101).

Fire pits lined with rocks will hold heat longer and protect against fire leaving the fire area. When you leave camp for the day, heap the coals together in the box and cover them with ash, where they will last for a day or more. In the case of bonfires, a rainfall wetting the top few inches of ash can seal the coals in, keeping out the drafts and allowing a very slow burning of fuel. In this case, fire can be coaxed from them for days afterward.

It is important to be mindful of the fire danger in your area. Always be on the lookout for overhanging branches and flammable debris nearby. Lining a fire pit with stones, clay, mud, or a mixture of any of these can prevent the fire from traveling along dead roots underground. In most cases, keeping a container of water or soil nearby is handy for dowsing or smothering a runaway fire. Leaving a fire unattended or in a windy area can be risky, so use caution.

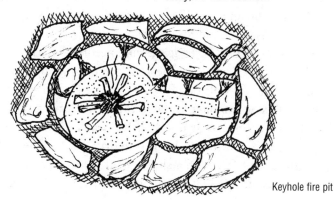

Keyhole fire pit

(continued from page 31)

We chatted and reminisced about days when we had worked together and all the changes in our lives since then. We discussed the goals of our summer and our current status. We each had a different expectation, which is no real surprise. My goal was to "survive," not to work on fine skills, but to have the experience of actual survival for a period long enough that I had to be hunting and harvesting successfully. David wanted to focus his time on practicing a variety of crafts. We did agree to move more slowly into survival; there is so much to do when you plunge into this lifestyle: making shelters, retrieving water, making fires, and gathering food—a lifestyle that involves snares, hunting weapons, containers, and cooking rocks. The list is endless.

Mike left the woods to fetch a bag of granola and returned several hours later. I consented to having two handfuls because I still wasn't feeling a hundred percent. That was all I needed to go from slightly light-headed and groggy to feeling absolutely fine. It felt good to let go of my expectations. We had discussed so little before we came together. What was important was that I was learning.

The storm cleared in the afternoon and we celebrated with a dip in the roaring stream and a much needed wash with soap-wort, which grew in dense quantities in moist lowlands in nearby meadows. By the time we made it back to camp, it was raining again. We worked on the group shelter, moving quickly—too quickly. The shelter collapsed sideways. As the rain increased, we ran for our debris huts.

I lay, buried in sticks, leaves, and needles—warm, comfort-able, and dry. I watched the rain come down in continuous sheets of water outside my awning. The sound of rain on a debris shelter is similar to the sound of rain on a tent. I could-n't help but smile, cozy in my shelter, watching the storm soak the earth around me. As I began to drift off, I suddenly found myself face-to-face with a short-tailed shrew, who ran off into the rain as quickly as it had appeared. I felt very grateful.

opening closed off with pile of leaves

Debris hut

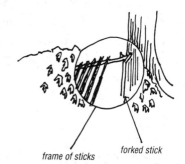

frame of sticks　*forked stick*

Day 6

We all began our day slowly. I made more cordage while huddling close to the small fire, which fought back the chill in the air. It felt like spring rather than summer. We all decided to hunt. Mike went north and David and I went south.

David and I encountered two young deer feeding along a field edge. I followed them a bit, stalking to within about twenty feet. Saplings crisscrossed between us, making a shot with my throwing stick too difficult to risk. But I enjoyed the "chase" tremendously; hunting seems to tingle primitive roots deep within me. Is it odd that through killing animals I hoped to feel closer to earth and natural rhythms? Or is it odder still that I had grown up eating a variety of meats that I didn't kill?

David separated and circled down valley to stalk a few turkeys. As he entered the wood line, he spooked a great horned owl, which flew silently just over my head and across the field to the sanctuary of forest across the stream. I lost track of David among the trees, and I moved on in search of muskrats.

After I felt I'd had enough exploring, I sat along a stream bank and worked on fish line. A tiny shrew—maybe one and a half inches long with an equivalent tail length, visible eyes, massive ears, and a brownish tinge on the head and back—entertained me for a long stretch. Could be a pygmy or cinereus shrew—I've read they can be distinguished only by dental formula. I followed the wee beast along the bank very closely, watching as it explored every nook and root system. It burrowed under leaves and sprinted through forests of towering grass blades. The shrew moved in lightning bursts interspersed with short pauses. Absolutely amazing—the smallest mature mammal I've ever seen!

(continued on page 45)

Meal Preparation and Cooking

Meal preparation is a true delight, especially when you are hungry and have food to work with. Positively identify all plants before you consume them. Use a field guide or ask an herbalist to be sure you are collecting safe plants. Now, let me give you some tips for using wild vegetables and meats, and for preparing food in a cook pit.

VEGETABLES

- Wild carrot or Queen Anne's lace can be eaten raw, added to soup or salad, or roasted.
- Burdock root can be prepared like wild carrot.
- Bulrush seed can be cooked in water as porridge. Add honey and/or berries if attainable. Begin by rock boiling water (see "Rock

Boiling," page 119); add the seeds and stir.

- Wild garlic, leeks, chives, garlic mustard, hog peanut, and Jerusalem artichoke can be added to meals as flavor enhancers, nibbled raw as a snack, or cooked.
- Milkweed pods can be harvested before they open. Put enough water in two containers so that each can easily allow the pods to submerge as well as accommodate the rocks. Rock-boil one container, then add the pods. As the water turns murky, add hot rocks to a second container. Only when this is boiling, move the pods to the clean, hot water. Then, dump the first container and refill it with clean water. Add rocks and boil yet again. Add pods to this third change of hot water, and after three minutes, remove and eat. Note: Do not remove the pods from hot water and place them in cold water, because this can inhibit the leaching out of the sap. Hastily cooked pods will lead to nausea.

MEATS

- Trout up to about eleven inches in length can be stuffed with herbs or herb paste and steamed. (Garlic mustard leaves, mustard seeds, chives, and leeks are a few herbs that can be ground into a paste, either together or separately.) You can also smear lacerations on the outside of the fish with seasoning before wrapping the fish in wild grape leaves. Place the fish in the ashes *near* the coals. White ash, not actual coals, should cover the entire fish. If you don't want to turn the fish to cook both sides, rake the coals into a circle around the ash-covered fish; this will ensure even cooking. An eight-inch trout should take about four to six minutes to cook (overcooking is better than undercooking). Carefully remove the trout. The grape leaves should be dry on the outside and stuck together. Blow off any loose ash and remove the leaves. If the back fin pulls out with ease, the fish is cooked—steamed in its own juices and in those of the herbs.
- Large trout (longer than eleven inches) are better roasted with a stick jammed through the mouth and stuck deep into the tail. Start with the back (spine) down, as this is the thickest part. Then cook either side and finish with a quick heat underneath. Cooking trout on sticks to perfection requires some practice. Cook the fish too long on one side and it will spin on the cooking stick, possibly ending up *in* the fire. If you think a side is done, try to remove a fin. If it pulls out cleanly with the internal bone still attached, that side is done. Once the trout is roasted, lay it on a slab of bark and remove the fins and head (eat the cheeks).

Gently separate the two sides of the fish by cutting the skin along the spine and pulling the head of the spine up and away from the lower side. A stick may be required to help separate the fillet from the ribs and spine. This should give you one boneless fillet. Now simply pull the spine away from the remaining side. Use garlic mustard leaves in lieu of a utensil. Not only does this give you the illusion that your hands will not get greasy, it adds a fantastic flavor to the trout.

- Snapping turtle should *not* be cooked in its own shell. You will only burn it. Instead, cut the meat out and roast or jerk it. Roasting with herbs or jerking suit this meat well. Prepare snapping turtle as you would venison.

- Venison can be prepared in many ways. The longest lasting is to make jerky (see "Preserving and Storing Food," page 101). The easiest and juiciest way to prepare fresh meat is to simply toss a chunk into the fire. The outside will burn and seal in the moisture, allowing the inner meat to steam in its own juices. After it has cooked for a bit (the larger the piece the longer the cooking time—you'll have to experiment), pull it out with some tongs (see "Making Camp," page 32) and break it open. It should be pink, not red. If it is still red, toss it back for a little longer. The

down side to this method is that some meat is lost when the outside burns. Venison fat melts at a very high temperature and therefore does not provide the natural basting action of other meats, such as goose or pork. If you are making venison kabobs or other roasts, cook them to medium rare so that some of the juices are retained.

- Woodchuck is best eaten freshly roasted, as its flesh is marbled; i.e., the fat appears throughout the meat, like bacon. (Woodchucks also have a layer of fat next to the hide.) Because fat will eventually turn rancid and you can't readily cut out every spot of it, woodchuck jerky isn't the best option. However, the fat melts at a lower temperature than venison fat, making this animal great for roasting.

- Geese, ducks, turkeys, and grouse are all fantastic roasting birds. The fat dribbles down the roasting stick into the fire, creating awesome smells and a juicy meal to die for. If you don't like liver as a rule, try roasted goose liver. It can't be topped.

PIT COOKING

The cooking-pit method of preparing food has a number of variations, yet the one described here is my favorite. It is great for cooking large game or big meals. I often cook a

soil
hot rocks
soil
grasses
grid or basket
grasses
large leaves
food
grasses
soil
hot rocks

Pit cook layers

few geese or turkeys, as well as some fish and corn, in one cooking.

How it Works

Rocks are heated in a fire, then moved to the bottom of the cook pit, where they heat the soil and grasses placed above. This creates steam, which surrounds and cooks the food evenly from all directions. Rocks are also placed above the food, radiating heat and ensuring that the top of the bigger food items gets cooked as well. The soil prevents the grasses from burning and thus causing the food to drop directly onto the hot rocks. The basket makes it easier to remove the middle layer of soil without getting your food dirty.

The Pit

The pit should be two or more feet deep and wide enough to accommodate everything you plan on cooking in a single layer without any items touching each other. Keep the soil in a pile close by, and pull out any rocks larger than grapefruit size.

Supplies

1. You will need enough rocks the size of cantaloupes to cover the bottom of the pit two and a half times. Keep in mind that you will need to move these rocks when they are red hot; therefore, only heat rocks you have the means to move.
2. Harvest enough long grasses for two four-inch layers in the pit.
3. Create a safe place for a large fire near the cook pit (ten to fifteen feet away), and gather plenty of wood to keep the fire going for a minimum of two hours.
4. Harvest burdock or other large leaves for covering the meat.
5. Find a forked stick or two long,

stout sticks to transfer hot rocks to the pit.

6. (Optional) Collect some one- to two-inch-diameter saplings and lash them together to make a grid or basket that will just fit inside the pit.

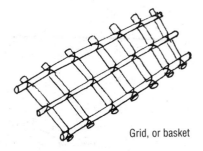
Grid, or basket

Starting the Fire

Once you have your supplies, start the fire. Add the rocks to it and put more wood on top of them before moving well away. I often use rocks directly from streams and have never yet had one explode—and I hope I never do. But to be safe, I move off where I can still keep an eye on the fire to make sure it does not spread, yet not be in harm's way if a rock does explode. (The beauty of the tipi fire is the fact that it does not need to be tinkered with.) After an hour, you can safely approach the fire again.

Packing the Pit

After about two hours, the rocks should be red hot and ready to be moved into the pit.

Moving hot rocks is dangerous. One method is to carry them with a forked stick, and another is to drag them on a piece of bark. Either way, pay attention and watch out for hot pieces of broken rock between the fire and the pit, and wear shoes.

Put one layer of hot rocks in the pit. It is okay if coals or ashes get in there, too.

1. Cover the rocks with about three or four inches of soil.
2. Add a four-inch layer of green grass.
3. Place all items to be cooked on the grasses, being careful that none are touching, as this can hinder the cooking process. The larger the item, the bigger the margin around it needs to be.
4. Cover items with burdock or other large leaves and then with about two inches of grass.
5. Place the basket (optional) on top of the grass and add an additional few inches of grass inside the basket.
6. Add another four-inch layer of soil.
7. Add another layer of rocks.
8. Finally, add another layer of soil.

Be careful not to pack or compress any of the layers in the pit, as this results in poor transmission of heat and circulation of steam.

A fifteen-pound bird takes about two and a half hours to cook, but it does not hurt to let it cook longer ... this is one bird that won't dry out.

Opening the Pit

1. Carefully remove the soil and hot rocks.
2. If you used a grid or basket, it can be removed with any remaining soil. If not, carefully remove as much soil as possible by hand.
3. The grasses are, with luck, very green due to their recent steaming. If not, the food needs to be cooked longer. Remove the hot grasses carefully, exposing the burdock-covered food.
4. Remove the food from the pit with the leaves still on, and place it on whatever your eating surface may be.

A few tips. Do not stand or lie on the filled pit because it will compress the grasses and greatly hinder the transmission of heat and steam, resulting in a greatly underdone meal. This technique requires a good deal of work, and the first few times may take a considerable portion of the day. I like to get the site prepped a day in advance (dig the pit and collect the wood and stones) so that the day I cook, all I need are grass and a fire. I'll usually start the fire around noon or one o'clock, let it burn until two-thirty or three-thirty, then load the pit and let the food cook until five-thirty or six-thirty, depending on how long it takes to get the pit loaded and covered. Note: Smelling cooked grass for the first time may cause you to rethink the pit-cook method, but trust me, the taste of the food will outweigh any reservations you may have.

(continued from page 40)

Poached eggs for dinner. Did I mention that they were water snake eggs? We then followed with the water snake herself. Very tasty. Mike and I felt the eggs tasted best just underdone so they squirt across your mouth when you bite down. While I'd focused on skinning the snake, Mike had handed me eggs cooked for various lengths of time. I didn't realize I was the guinea pig for flavor until after I had given my opinions. He kept assuring me he'd already tried some. Most people would probably be fairly disgusted by water snake, but, as Mike said, "Better than the last snake." We both preferred roasting this snake to boiling the last one.

The days seem profoundly long. We do so much; I accomplish so much. This is one of the benefits of losing an agenda.

Without scheduled events, such as meals, work, meetings, etc., the day is one long flowing free time. I try to remember to eat something and work on a few projects over the day, but that's it.

It's wonderful! If I want to continue doing something I'm enjoying, I do it. If I decide to switch what I'm up to, I do so. So simple, yet immensely rewarding. Even a scheduled meal locks us into blocks of time, stifling our creativity.

I've lost touch with days of the week. They are now numbers in my journal, which allows for greater freedom. I could figure out the day, I suppose, but what would be the point? Just a mental game to keep myself from sinking deeper into life with the woods. For me, this life without schedules—without time, if you will—is allowing for a certain expansion.

Raise glasses for a toast, for I've had my first bowel movement. It was a rather green, large-diameter, bear-scat-looking thing, blunt breaks and all. I didn't linger long or stick my nose in close, but I did notice that the foul stench of modern human feces seemed absent.

Day 7

Last night we decided to journey to town for pizza. David and I were not hungry—at least no growling stomachs or hunger pangs. Mike is always ravenous. It just seemed a good idea to let go of certain restraints we'd placed on ourselves, and a trip out to eat pizza became the physical act to represent that transition. It was late when we made the decision, so we ran for David's car, which he kept nearby for his weekly outings. In we piled, and David whipped along the windy roads. We admired the break in the storm clouds, which allowed for light to create varied hues of gray in the corner of the sky. We finally arrived in a rather dingy town and ordered a large mushroom, eggplant, and onion pizza.

I called my family and my girlfriend Kayla to say I hadn't moldered away in all the storms. At age twenty-three, my sister was going in for a biopsy. Our lifestyles are not healthy these days.

The pizza was delicious. I was almost full after two slices and absolutely bloated after three. Food portions in society are massive and always available. And work for food has become work for cash for food. Therefore, stockpiled cash quickly creates food larders.

Over dinner, we discussed how few real skills were required to attain our pizza—how easy it was to get it. I argued that it took different skills, skills that were easy for us because we had grown up with them. No longer did we need patience, physical prowess, knowledge of ecosystems and wildlife, or knowledge of place and tools and how to use them. Today's jobs required different skills, not necessarily fewer or less important skills. Jobs translate into money, which, in turn and in combination with knowledge of the right question to ask in the right place, results in a mushroom and eggplant pizza.

As we left town behind, it began to pour. I was happy to leave that reality behind and made up my mind that I didn't want to make any additional trips to town this summer. There was also that niggling voice in the back of my head saying I had somehow failed. Apparently the pizza didn't completely agree with Mike, because he threw it up at the base of our hill. Then we ascended to our camp and attempted to fight rain with fire. My debris hut was warm and dry.

I awoke this morning to the call of a hermit thrush. The song resounded clear, almost rebelliously, in our camp dominated by wood thrushes and veeries. Its song seemed the central instrument, supported by a background of chickadees. My dreams had been bizarre. I remembered hunting rabbits near the house of Mike's friends to the north, among other random events.

Last night, in town, we all felt the pull, the ease of that lifestyle. How easy it would be to nip off for pizza often, or to sleep in tents or houses. But we had turned our backs on modern society and headed straight up our hill, deep into the woods. One trip to town had been enough to remind us what we hoped to do this summer—to live from food gathered by our hands, to experience something other than our "normal" lives.

(continued on page 51)

Eat a Balanced Diet in the Woods

A balanced diet is composed of foods that supply enough nutrients to the body for the production of energy and heat, as well as for the growth, healing, and maintenance of cells. Opinions on the particulars of diet and health are many and varied. Given each person's specific constitution, it would be impossible to develop a dietary plan that suited everyone. However, when considering diet in a survival situation, it must be understood that many foods we take for granted in our everyday lives are not local, nor are they always in season locally. Wild strawberries, for example, can be found in abundance in the Northeast during the spring, yet they are readily available in stores year-round.

If you had to go into the wilderness at any given point during the year, what foods could you harvest to sustain life? Now your options are suddenly much smaller. Without fruits or other vegetables being shipped from across the country year-round, and without the aid of refrigeration, acquiring and storing a season's harvest are not only important but somewhat more complicated. According to the USDA, a balanced diet should include:

- 2–4 servings per day of fruits for vitamins A and C
- 3–5 servings per day of vegetables for fiber, vitamins A and C, and minerals
- 2–3 servings per day of meat, poultry, and fish protein for B vitamins, iron, and zinc
- 2–3 servings per day of dairy products for protein, minerals, and vitamins

In the wild, fruits, vegetables, and meat are available, yet milk products are not an option; therefore, these proteins, minerals, and vitamins must be acquired from other sources. Liver is a good source of iron, zinc, and vitamin A. Vitamin D, according to the National Institutes of Health, can be acquired by exposing your skin to ultraviolet rays, because they trigger vitamin D synthesis in the skin.

Carbohydrates are also important in your diet. Sustained activity or a low intake of carbohydrates can cut endurance by half in as little as one day.

Water is also vital. According to the National Ski Patrol, a sedentary person loses 2,300 milliliters (ml) (over half a gallon) of water daily as follows: 1,400 ml (about a third of a gallon) in urine, 800 ml (a little over three cups) through respiration and evaporation from the skin, and 100 ml (less than half a cup) through defecation. In hot weather, water loss jumps to 3,300 ml (three quarters of a gallon), and with sustained physical effort, it can be up to 6,600 ml (one and one-half gallons) per day. Even in cold, wet weather when you may not feel thirsty, you are losing water and need to replenish it on a regular basis.

The best key to your hydration is the color and smell of your urine. It should be clear and odorless. If it is dark and pungent, you need to increase your water intake, not through guzzling one-half gallon at a time, but through regularly taking smaller drinks.

Your body is your most important tool and needs to be properly maintained, like any other tool you wish to use for a long time. Whether you follow the USDA's food pyramid, your family's eating habits, or the advice of a nutritionist or dietician, eating the healthiest foods available will help keep your body in good working order.

In society, we are used to sitting down to a "full" meal, whereas in the wild, snacking on available tidbits is par for the course. In summer, when food is abundant, snacking on berries, roots, and leaves reduces the craving for a meal that will leave you feeling stuffed. Often, the "meal" will be some seasoned meat in between snacks.

It is important, in times of abundance, to collect and preserve as much food as possible for three reasons. First, in the event you are injured, ill, or unsuccessful hunting, having a supply of food can save your life. Second, the winter may be harsh and long, making the harvesting of any root crop impossible. Plants don't have much to offer during this time. Third, sometimes a thaw in the winter will rot meat or a leak will destroy some of your preserved dry foods. Having extra supplies can see you through challenging times.

TIPS FOR A SURVIVAL DIET

Here are a few tips for a survival-mode diet. Because I am not a dietician, I recommend seeking professional guidance in developing your own wild diet. The information below is drawn from personal experience in which health was (apparently) maintained.

• Tea should be a regular thirst quencher. Pine needle and hemlock (from the tree, not from poison hemlock or water hemlock) teas are great sources of vitamin C, an absolute must. Vitamin C prevents scurvy. Mints, young birch leaves, and the inner bark of black birch, pine, and sassafras, are all quite tasty.

To prepare pine needle tea, harvest the needles and dice them. A one-inch diameter bundle makes about two cups. Put the needles into hot water and simmer them until the water takes on a golden color.

To prepare leaf tea, harvest leaves from birch trees when they first come out in the spring. Dry them by placing them briefly in the sun or by hanging a whole branch upside down in a cool, dry place. Mint—either individual leaves or the whole plant—can be harvested in the same way. To make tea, boil water and add leaves. Let them steep for about five minutes before drinking.

To prepare a tasty bark tea, use the inner bark from pine and black birch trees. Strip the bark from a live sapling or branch and add either fresh or dried bark to boiling water. Let it steep for five minutes and drink. Both inner barks, when dry, can be pounded into flour in an emergency.

Sassafras has been used for many years as a seasoning and in teas; it has long been credited with staving off illness. The bark, roots, and leaves are full of flavor and can add to that of any other tea. The root must be boiled in water to really pull out the flavor. The young leaves can be dried, ground into powder, and added to soups.

- Eating some form of carbohydrate daily, whether it be burdock root, wild carrot, leek, Jerusalem artichoke, hog peanut, grass seed, cattail, and, of course, acorn flour helps keep up your energy.
- Consuming meat three times a week is a great source of protein. Meat also provides more energy than plant matter, especially in the colder months when pemmican becomes more of a staple. We had access to fish but also made a point of eating red meat at least twice a week to augment our fish diet.
- Fiber from greens is also worth the effort of harvest. Lambs quarters and lady's thumb are great additions to any stew or salad, and they'll help keep your bowels moving.
- Burdock can be found in disturbed soil, field edges, and stream banks and beds. As a biennial, the energy of the first year goes into the root, which can be eaten raw, boiled, or fried.
- In the fall, any nuts in the Northeast—acorns, hickories, walnuts, butternuts, and beechnuts—are great sources of proteins and oils. Acorns need to be processed prior to use (see "Acorn Flour," page 188).
- During the spring and summer, strawberries, raspberries, blackberries, gooseberries, blueberries, elderberries, serviceberries, grapes, and a host of other fruits are available to provide plenty of vitamins and minerals.
- Meat and animal fat are loaded

with nutrients and are crucial, especially in colder weather. Meat can also be easily preserved (see "Preserving and Storing Food," page 101). Geese, ducks, turkeys, grouse, pheasants, and doves are all fine additions to any diet.

Venison, woodchucks, squirrels, and rabbits are good, tasty sources of red meat, and snapping turtles, fish, snakes, and their eggs add variety to the menu if you're not too squeamish.

(continued from page 47)

As David and I sat about in camp, deer appeared at the edge of our site and began moving slowly toward us. We watched them placidly feed in the drainage dropping off to the north, unaware of our presence. It is not often we are afforded a view of animals as they move within the natural cycle. Tails flicked side to side. We most often see tails straight up in the air—the tail position of deer as they flee.

David gestured that we should hunt them. We began stalking the deer, but their feeding pattern began to pull them away from us at a rate faster than we stalked. We decided to circle downwind and try again. David and I split up, each planning a bisect with imagined patterns of feeding. I moved into my area and was silent. Unfortunately, the deer had already moved through and David had followed in pursuit.

I sat awhile, enjoying an intimate view of a pair of scarlet tanagers. With the sun beaming down through a clearing in the canopy, the male's red was indescribably brilliant. Do they know how beautiful they are?

I decided to explore south along the ridge. I had pine pitch in the back of my mind, because I needed to make a canteen for long walks. The pitch was a necessary ingredient in making natural glue. I hiked to the top of the hill and sat on the edge of a rock face, soaking in the vista. The breeze rode up the ridge and felt cool on my face. I could see hills all the

Scarlet tanager

way to the horizon and a dramatic cloudscape filling the sky. I hoped to return to this spot to watch a storm roll in someday.

I watched a pair of red squirrels wrestle and play, cooing to each other as they chased and rolled. They seemed to be playing "Follow the Leader," where they constantly switched roles as the leader.

An ovenbird came to inspect me. He ruffled his orange mohawk, fluffed his chest, and sang his harsh, rhythmic beats. He was so close, I began to count the spots on his chest: seventeen.

Onward I roamed, collecting little bits of pine pitch along the way, which I piled on a bark slab. I climbed a massive white pine tree to harvest pitch from within holes drilled by pileated woodpeckers and from storm-damaged branches in the crown. High up, I poked and prodded, collecting every bit of pitch available: fresh, sticky ooze and older amber chunks that I pocketed like precious gems. Hugging the tree, tongue out in concentration, I worked and worked; the image of a black bear collecting honey entered my mind. Same diligence and concentration as me. It made me smile.

As I progressed down the ridge, I came across an old logging trail. Suddenly, I knew there was a fawn bedded down just up the road; it was a picture in my mind. It wasn't the kind of knowing you get in your head, but a gut knowing—the knowing that is always right. Downhill was the way back, but I felt drawn to the hunt. Just the day before, I had made conscious my intention to seek out a young deer to hunt, and now I knew where one lay.

Up the road I walked, and within several minutes I saw him, a fawn curled in the vibrant green jewelweed and grass. I couldn't believe he was there; I still struggle with faith in intuition. He was beautiful, with a rusty coat and twitching ears, all accented by sunlight. Then it hit me. I had wanted to hunt this animal, and here he was. Was I really going to do it? I didn't know.

I stalked slowly up to him until a foot lay between him and my feet. I looked down, although not directly at him, because he was ready to bolt. What to do? I was here to live survival. But I needed more time.

I moved quietly past the fawn to a boulder roughly ten feet away and sat down. I watched him, nervous about what I had intended and now felt rather obligated to do. At least I had allowed enough time for the deer to escape. I slowly stood, armed with my throwing stick, and approached the deer. I paused over him—this was what I was here to better understand. I raised my throwing stick over my head, pausing for a brief murmur of thanks.

Then I struck with all my might to the back of his head. Again and again. A red squirrel screamed, chickadees became alarmed, and a ruffed grouse shrieked. It's the only time I've ever heard a grouse sound an alarm. The deer rose up on shaky legs and released a short and mournful bleat. Then he collapsed, his hind legs twitched, and his confused eyes began to glaze. I held him close, hoping to comfort his death. I was anything but proud. I actually cried, while the nearby animals seemed to surround me and voice alarm and protest.

I can count the times I've cried since I was ten on one hand. It was as if I cried for all the times I hadn't—the deaths of my grandmother and grandfather and more. It felt right to cry. I felt I should cry for every life I took. Luckily, there was work to be done: I had to bleed, gut, and carry the animal back to camp. I began the long project that only begins once an animal has been killed. Squirrels and birds continued to sound an alarm until I was finished with gutting and cleaning the deer and had begun to wander back toward camp.

I stopped by a nearby spring—to wash my red hands and stained face, regain composure, and drink. Up the hill I went, finally arriving at camp. Thank goodness the others were there. Mike and David stood and smiled, looking somewhat amazed. I, too, managed to return a smile.

Mike supervised as I skinned and butchered the animal. He grew up fishing and hunting, and his experience far outweighed mine. We then began the long process of preparing meat for jerky, which we could keep indefinitely. We worked until after dark making a stick frame upon which to dry the meat and a fire to coax moisture from flesh. Many people don't realize jerky is dried raw meat—uncooked. Jokes about the size of the deer had started, which kept my spirits light; humor heals much. I insisted that all future retelling of the story substitute the word "buck" for "fawn." "I stalked the bedded buck as the sun lay high in the west...."

(continued on page 60)

Carcass Care

Your hunt was a success! You are standing over a freshly killed mammal. (For the instructions on carcass care, I will use a deer, although other mammals may be mentioned when pertinent.) Now what? Proper care of the carcass is just as important as the hunt. When an animal dies, the bacteria within the gut and intestines continue to live and thrive. The result is ever-expanding gas that will rupture the intestines and foul the meat if the intestines and guts are not removed immediately. Additionally, the removal of the internal organs, intestines, and blood speed the cooling process and thus help delay the early stages of decomposition. The essential steps are:

1. Checking to be sure the animal is dead
2. Bleeding the animal
3. Field dressing or gutting the animal
4. Skinning the animal
5. Cutting or butchering the animal
6. Utilizing the bones

1. CHECKING THE ANIMAL

Approach the animal carefully and look for signs of life, such as movement from breathing or blinking. You can touch the eye with a stick to see if it blinks; if it does, you need to finish off the animal.

2. BLEEDING THE ANIMAL

With animals like deer, cut the throat by driving a knife from the side of the neck just below the lower jaw, through to the other side. Then cut out the front of the neck. This is faster and easier than cutting through the hair, which can dull a knife very quickly. Hair from a wild pig will dull your knife in only a few inches of cutting. Blood clots fast when it is not being moved by the heart. If you complete this process quickly, the blood will gush out readily. Placing the animal with its head downhill can aid in bleeding an animal. In the case of smaller animals like squirrels, the meat can be soaked in cold water and the blood allowed to leach out after the steps below.

3. FIELD DRESSING OR GUTTING

Bucks during the rut have active scent glands on the inside of their hind legs—tufts of hair with a smell you can't miss. These strong-smelling glands can be removed if you don't like the smell or are afraid of the meat becoming contaminated through long hanging in such proximity to the glands. Pull on the long hair to draw the hide away from the leg, then slice through the hide behind and toss the glands away. After dealing with the scent glands, follow the instructions below:

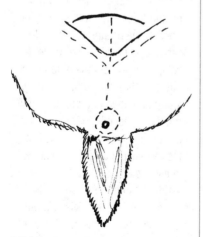

Primary cuts around the anus

• Position the deer on its back, and cut around the anus (and vagina if the deer is a female), to a depth of three inches.

• The urinary tract of male mammals travels from the bladder back through the pelvis next to the small intestine. It then loops back along the belly toward the chest. A buck's penis is located on the belly toward the rear. Make a small cut at the upper base of the penis toward the back while holding the penis up and away from the body. This will allow you to separate the penis from the carcass all the way back to just below the anus. Once the penis has been thus removed, proceed with the next step.

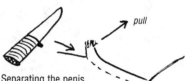

Separating the penis from the belly

• Feel down the sternum (breastbone) until you come to the soft spot at the end (xyphoid process). Pinch a bit of skin—about a half an inch—and pull it up and away from the carcass. Slice through

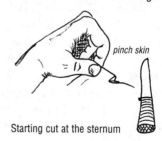

Starting cut at the sternum

the skin and thin layer of muscle, being careful to avoid cutting through the stomach. If you see green matter, you have cut too deeply and will have to deal with the stench as well as wash out the cavity later.

- Once the cut goes all the way through the abdominal wall, slide your index and middle fingers into the abdominal cavity, palm up and facing the rear of the animal. Holding a knife in your right hand, place the blade, cutting edge up, between the two fingers in the abdominal cavity, and slide both blade and fingers to cut the abdominal wall down to the pelvis.

Opening the abdominal cavity

To further protect against cutting the stomach and intestines, you can lift the abdominal wall with the two fingers guiding the knife. I will often continue the cut to the anus, cutting through the muscle between the legs until I hit bone. This allows the legs to spread to either side and gives easier access for cutting any remaining connective tissue still holding the end of the intestines and urinary tract in place. Note that the udders of does can be easily removed prior to this step in the same manner as the scent glands are removed on bucks.

- Above the stomach is the diaphragm, a divider made of muscle tissue that separates the abdominal cavity from the thoracic (chest) cavity. Cut the diaphragm free from the chest wall on both sides, back to the spine.
- Reach up into the chest cavity toward the neck and feel the windpipe, a hard-ribbed tube. Cut this as high up as possible. Gripping the windpipe, pull it back toward you to expose the organs (heart and lungs and, in the intestinal cavity, the liver and kidneys). The connections that have not yet been severed along the spine are weak and can usually be torn by pulling forcefully on the windpipe.
- Harvest the organs you wish to eat, and, if possible, set them in cold water to help the blood leach out. (The heart, liver, and kidneys are great cubed and put in a stew.)
- It is now possible to pull the guts out of the abdominal cavity. Grasp the terminal end of the small intestines and urinary tract from inside the abdominal cavity. Pull them through the pelvis and out the incision along with the rest of the guts and organs.

• Tilt the carcass so that any blood within the cavity can drain out through the pelvis.

4. SKINNING

Some animals part with their hides more easily than others. Deer, for example, can be skinned completely by hand once the primary cuts have been made. Wild hogs and wood-chucks, on the other hand, often need a blade to help separate the hide from the carcass. These primary cuts should be just through the hide and not into the flesh. Skinning, when done well, is a bloodless process.

Primary Cuts

• Cut all the way around each leg at the second joint above the foot.

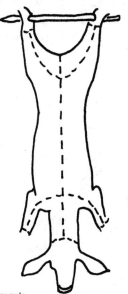

Primary cuts

• Make a cut from the anus along the belly to the lower jaw (usually done during field dressing).
• On the inside of all four limbs, make cuts to connect the ring cuts on the legs to the median cut on the belly and chest.
• Make one ring cut around the neck and you are finished.

With some animals, deer especially, the hide can be pulled away from the carcass with one hand and your free hand can knead down between the two, the hide and the carcass. This is preferable to using a knife, because it avoids scoring or other-wise damaging the hide. Bits of connective tissue, such as little ten-dons connecting the hide to the muscle, allow the animal to shake or shiver portions of its skin to rid itself of flies. These connectors can be broken singly by hand; however, when sliding your hand between the carcass and the hide, you may grab a number of them at once. Pulling hard on these thin, bunched con-nectors can result in a "paper cut."

If you do use a knife or sharp stone as a skinning aid, pull the hide away from the carcass and gently cut the stretched tissue with the cutting edge angled toward the carcass and not the hide. This way, if you overcut, the damage is done to the flesh and not to the hide.

5. BUTCHERING

According to the USDA, food kept at zero degrees Fahrenheit can remain safe indefinitely and at forty degrees for two to three days. I have let carcasses hang for three weeks at temperatures in the thirties with no bad odor or ill effects. Animals taken in the warm summer months are a different matter and should be butchered as soon as possible, because bacteria multiply rapidly in the "danger zone," 40 to 140 degrees Fahrenheit.

Hanging the carcass of an animal serves two purposes. First, it makes the skinning and butchering process much easier. The height can be adjusted and you have access to all parts of the carcass. Second, letting the animal hang lets enzymes within the meat begin to break down the muscle and connective tissue, making it tender and softening the gamey flavor. Hanging is not a necessity but a preference among most hunters. I recommend hanging a carcass for about one week, weather permitting.

A dry crust forms on the exposed meat as moisture evaporates. This crust must be trimmed off before you consume the meat. The longer the meat hangs, the thicker the crust and the greater the loss of meat. Leaving the hide on protects the meat and keeps in the moisture but makes skinning more difficult.

A simple way to get a heavy carcass off the ground is to make a hole through each hind leg at the point that corresponds to the human heel. On most animals it looks more like a backward-bending knee than a heel. Make the cut in the thin part of the leg between the Achilles tendon, coming from the muscle above and at the thighbone. You can use a stick to keep the animal's legs spread apart and to then

Hanging a deer for butchering

lash them together by using the holes you cut. This will allow you to hang the animal from a branch. The easiest method for hanging heavy game is to cut a strong, ten-foot sapling that has a "Y" in the upper portion. Trim off all other branches and lay the sapling over a strong branch of another tree, about five feet off the ground. With the "Y" end of the sapling on the ground near the carcass, lash the spreader stick to the fork in the "Y" and, see-saw-like, pull the raised end downward and tie it to a stake in the ground.

If you have help, you can lift the deer and fasten a piece of cordage to the spreader stick, tying the other end to a sturdy branch.

In temperatures above forty degrees Fahrenheit, all meat *not* to be consumed immediately must be preserved either through freezing or drying (see "Preserving and Storing Food," page 101).

How you cut the meat for storage depends on the way it will be stored.

In warm weather, meat must be dried to be preserved. To preserve meat in freezing temperatures, the carcass can be cut into meal-sized chunks. I remove some of the best cuts first, like the back strap on either side of the spine.

These long muscles are very tender and easy to remove. Start by making cuts down either side of the center ridge of the spine. With your

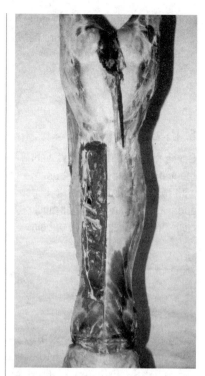

Deer carcass showing one of the two back straps removed (left).

fingers in the cut, slide your hand up and down the incision while pushing them into the carcass. A second skin or membrane covering the back strap should now be evident and can easily be pulled and cut away. Work your fingers into the flesh along the initial incision until you reach bone, then pull the muscle away from the carcass. Carefully tear or cut any flesh still connected to the rib cage.

The legs can be divided easily by cutting at the joints or separating muscle groups. Portions of the carcass with little bits of meat still attached can be cooked and eaten within a few days (temperature permitting) or pulled from the bone, rolled into a ball, and frozen for later use.

6. UTILIZE BONES

Bones for tools (if you don't want the marrow) can be broken open with rocks to allow access to bugs and placed on an anthill for quick cleaning. But their chance of being taken by scavengers is very high. I'll often place bones in trees or hang them with cordage, and within a month they are pretty clean. If I am in a rush to use the bones, I break and boil them to quickly remove the oils and marrow (the broth is highly nutritious). If time is not an issue, leave them out up to a year, as this allows the oils to break down and gives you a solid, white piece of bone (as opposed to an oily translucent one).

(continued from page 54)

We feasted on venison and covered the entire rack with meat. Even hunter Mike was impressed with the amount of meat the little guy yielded. Myself, I was absolutely sapped; taking the life of another can be a draining experience.

Day 8

We hung around camp most of the morning, helping the meat become jerky with a constant bed of coals. I worked on fish and snare line—you can never have too much. I reflected upon the deer, on myself, and on what others would think of my actions. People may wonder why I needed to kill, and they may wonder why I chose a fawn.

I do have my reasons. While walking around this hill, our home, and surrounding woodlands, I have absorbed information on who lives where and how various species are impacting the woods. The more I learn, the more I am able to interpret what I see, and the more I understand the dynamic interrelationships of living creatures.

The woods here tell of large deer populations. Shrubs and trees have stopped regenerating on our hill. Hemlock, oak, striped maple, and white pine are but a few of the decimated saplings in the understory. Life here is out of balance. I'm reminded of Aldo Leopold's famous essay, "Thinking Like a Mountain," in which he recounts a story from his youth when he shoots and then watches a wolf die. He later realized that removing wolves would allow the ungulates to go unchecked, and that they would strip the mountain. Here the deer have done this; they have stripped this hill and surrounding hills.

This is why I hunted a deer. It was my contribution to an unhealthy ecosystem. I hunted a small deer because I was afraid of wasting food. It wasn't without thought or deliberation that I hunted deer; rather, it was with awareness of the consequences. I was standing in for wolf.

Hunting might seem to be the last thing you would do to connect with the natural systems. Yet, my harvesting the fawn showed me how disoriented I've become. If a coyote had come across that fawn, it wouldn't have sat down, contemplated the idea, then taken the fawn's life. Nor would there have been a prayer circle or drum ritual in the taking. No, a coyote would have reacted swiftly and efficiently. A coyote is part of the natural cycle and does not question its role. At the time of the killing, I still believed I was not a full participant in local ecology; I thought I was an outsider. Now I'm certain that no person can truly disconnect from the natural world. In some great feat of mental gymnastics, I'd somehow convinced myself that I could. Why? How? Every person is as much an animal as is the coyote.

Within society, it is easy to ignore natural cycles, because we have constructed buffers with which to protect ourselves. How many people are offended by hunting, yet visit stores and restaurants and order beef, lamb, pork, chicken, turkey, duck, fish, or clams. Those animals were killed, just as are broccoli, beans, and lettuce. Whenever we eat, we are ingesting the remains of animals and plants, yet we no longer acknowledge these deaths; we do not feel we have participated in the killing. These skills of personal deception and avoidance are fruits of the modern world, equally efficient in restaurants and board-rooms, markets, and governmental affairs.

In the afternoon, David and I went off in search of more pine pitch. We moved south along the ridge, through woods and fields. We collected pitch along the way, although we made several more important discoveries.

Along an outcrop on the southern end of our hill stood a massive white pine. Pileated woodpecker holes riddled the trunk, revealing the hidden rotten core. The lowest hole was quite long, about eighteen inches or so, and had healed over to form a narrow slit; the encroaching bark would only allow a few fingers to slip in. David spotted the activity first. The thin entrance was swarming with the buzz and flight of honeybees. We stood mesmerized.

Finding honeybees has given ancient cultures joy as long as history has been recorded. All sorts of extraction methods have been tried, some more painful than others. We craved sweet honey, and we decided we were willing to be stung a few times in order to savor something sweet. I did pause to remind myself that it was a thin line between bravery and stupidity. But honey.... We decided we'd come back another day.

Later we found a flock of wild geese. Their young were mature but still unable to fly. We thought a group hunt would be successful. Last, we scouted out a few smaller ponds for cat-tails, because we had developed a new shelter idea. By this time we had walked many miles and I was tired. We nibbled on sweet daylily flowers as we approached our hill.

In the evening, while I was out for a stroll, a doe approached me to within about thirty feet. She stared at me and I imagined myself as a tree. We remained frozen for a short while, then the deer began to lightly stomp her front right hoof—a steady, rhythmic beat. Deer are renowned for stomping in an attempt to solicit a response from that which they do not recognize, but this was a new approach for me. Her steady rhythm seemed an attempt at hypnotism. And it was working! On and on we stood our ground, eyes locked, her steady beat like ropes holding me tighter and tighter. Birdsong was our background. Time did not exist.

Suddenly, fireworks exploded in the far distance (I think it was the Fourth of July). The doe paused and looked toward the noise. Then she looked back and began the beat again. Too late! I had broken free and my mind was racing again. I suddenly became aware of the countless mosquitoes taking full advantage of my unprotected face. I tried to move slowly, to swat them away, but my movements revealed my true identity. The doe snorted and bounded north. I remained several minutes and listened to her continue to snort from the other side of the knoll before I moved away.

Day 9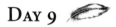

It's the second sunny day in a row. I'm hoping for further sun and dry weather so the stream drops, improving spearfishing. Time will tell. On the other hand, rain keeps greens growing and springs flowing.

It was a slow day overall. Mike visited the beehive and we began to strategize. Mike had opened an abandoned hive several years earlier, and David had read a book on wild bees; both felt they were experts on the subject. I was the only one able to make suggestions with the ease of ignorance. Mike felt that if we entered the hive at night, the bees would not come out. I thought this was hysterical, but he may be right. We'd have to wait and see.

By afternoon, rain clouds had hazed the sun, and by evening, the darkest clouds had reached the hill upon which we camped. We sat in a field at the foot of the hill and rescheduled the beehive raid. It began to rain as night settled in. Mike and I climbed to camp, while insomniac David sought out a dry spot to work on baskets and cordage.

I forgot to mention that I've added a door to my debris hut. I used to rise at first light to the incessant buzz of attacking

The 45° mosquito

mosquitoes; they are a reliable wilderness alarm clock. I haven't discussed them much. The mosquitoes are absolutely horrendous. There are so many varieties and styles: the standard, which is brown to gray, the miniature standard, the black with blue spots on its legs, the zebra striped, and the type that sits at a forty-five-degree angle.

There is not a spot under leaf or needle where you are safe. I seek solace in open places or by huddling near smoky fires.

Anyway, the door stops all this distraction. I'm warmer and with less company. The downside is, I tend to miss the first few hours of light. I may decide to open the door again.

DAY 10

I awoke this morning at first light to a single mosquito—the door had settled and allowed a crack to form. I plugged the hole, killed the intruder, and was at peace again. Two screech owls were holding a conversation near camp and were just audible above the competition between a tanager and a hermit thrush. I listened for some time before I decided to try to find them.

Out I crawled into the drizzle. I paused to wait for an owl call. Setting a bearing, I walked to the east, then to the south, but the owls were silent. Now that I was up and about, I continued on a stroll.

I ended up in a field, sitting on a rock outcrop. A few rash mosquitoes had followed me out of the trees, but I disposed of them quickly. Society was not yet awake. I heard no cars or farm equipment. Lush, rolling hills were all I could see, along with a few freshly mowed hay fields in the distance.

The air was cool and a breeze sent a chill up my body. It was the sort of chill that makes you feel alive. The uniform haze of clouds undulated as they rushed overhead. I love cool air. It reminds me of oceans.

A doe approached the field. She stopped in the tall goldenrods at the edge, looked about, and skipped out to a patch of lush green to feed. A few moments passed before a younger deer approached at the same spot, looked about, and also skipped into the field to feed. The ritual was repeated two more times, for a total of two does and two yearlings. They frolicked about, taking breaks to feed on the greenery. Feeding was done in five- to ten-second increments before they raised their heads to check for danger. Two deer nuzzled a bit, rubbing cheeks together. They all came quite close to me as they circled the field feeding before they moved out of sight over a knoll. When it began to rain, I decided to move on as well.

Recently, I've been tracking the remains of hickory nuts to white-footed mice nests. My first discovery was along a worn trail to the west that was used by many animals, including humans and foxes. I was hiking alone, and there, in the middle of the path, were the remains of four hickory nuts. Each nut had been extracted in the same way. Round or elliptical holes were chewed on both sides of each nut. Edges of holes created by mice are smoother than those made by most species, although sometimes they are a bit rougher than those of southern flying squirrels. The grooves left by the tiny teeth were visible. The midribs of the nuts were left untouched, except for a few nicks from digging incisors. No "carrying notches" or cut slots, created by chipmunks and southern flying squirrels to carry hickories to caches or feeding areas, were present. Over time, I have learned that all of these characteristics are those of hickory nuts opened by white-footed mice.

But why in the middle of the trail? Where did they come from? Mice do not typically feed in the open; they prefer to be under cover, hidden from predators. I looked at them a long time and placed them next to the closest tree on a bed of moss, while I pondered and moved on.

I found the second mouse midden off the trail, just inside the wood line along a field. Again—hickory nuts opened by a

red squirrel

note angle

jagged holes from both sides

*perfect halves:
nut on right partially cut*

*carrying notch
on bottom*

southern flying squirrel
*entered from shoulder;
smooth, round hole*

mice
multiple round holes

*carrying notch
on bottom*

chipmunk
jagged round hole at one end

gray squirrel
pieces

Marks on nutshells provide clues as to what ate them

white-footed mouse. Again—out in the open. This time, however, I also noticed a hole in the base of the tree at ground level. I was beginning to formulate a hypothesis. I peered in to the hole to find a variety of debris and definitive mouse scat. The mice were throwing out the hickories as a sort of "spring cleaning." As I visualized the first tree, I remembered a hole approximately four inches off the ground above a large root, which would be a perfect launching pad for hickory nuts. Since this experience, I have continued to find these holes associated with hickory nut debris. Amazing.

David had recently encountered a mouse in his debris hut. He had crawled in to clean up a bit, and the mouse plunged between his legs to escape unscathed. David, on the other hand, was emotionally distraught about sharing his quarters with a mouse. He immediately began carving a "figure-4" deadfall trap. Mike decided to join the crusade and help David by contributing a "Paiute" deadfall trap, a faster variation of the traditional "figure 4" (see page 14), substituting cordage for the wooden crossbar.

Mike's trap was the first to spring successfully, claiming the life of a white-footed mouse. David's went off the following night, taking the life of what appeared to be a house mouse. The closest house was some distance away, yet this animal had been successfully living high on a ridge in full woods. I didn't expect to see this species up here. David was eventually persuaded to reclaim his sleeping quarters.

DAY 11

The three of us went on a hike into new areas in search of pitch, which we needed for tools and canteens. Following Mike is always an adventure, because he is not allergic to poison ivy. Unfortunately, I am. One particular woodland we passed through was carpeted in poison ivy. It gave me wonderful balance and stalking practice.

Poison ivy appears to do particularly well in disturbed areas. The carpeted woods through which we walked had been heavily and poorly logged time and time again; it was an abused area. I often find poison ivy in places such as this, where heavy human impact has scarred the landscape. I wonder if the appearance of this plant is a statement by, or evolutionary defense mechanism of, the land. No words, clear message.

We collected loads of pitch as well as bark, which we formed into sun visors and containers. We ate berries. We always eat berries. As we separated on personal adventures, we scheduled a group hunt for geese in the evening.

(continued on page 70)

Working with Pitch

Conifer pitch is a tremendous asset when you are living out in the woods, and I collect it whenever the opportunity arises. It can be used for all manner of things from ornaments to glue. In the applications covered here, it is used with a hardening agent, either white wood ash or ground charcoal. A high density of these agents hardens the pitch to a brittle state, and a lower density keeps the glue softer and more flexible.

COLLECTING PITCH

When I'm on a pitch-collecting mission, my tools of choice are a container and a stick sharpened to a point at one end and a flat screwdriver-like point at the other. As I walk through the conifers, I look for old branch breaks and, with my stick, prod the areas that are healing over. It is important to note that pitch is often dirty, hard, and clumpy. It can later be softened and purified (described below). Looking up in trees for woodpecker holes, broken branches, and other wounds is a good way to locate a pitch cache. Creating a wound to provide sap is another option, though often unnecessary, as so much is available from old wounds.

Often pitch has impurities in it, such as tiny pieces of bark. Some of this should be removed while you are cooking it, although a *low* density of fine impurities does not seem to have a negative effect on the pitch when it is used as glue. Too high a concentration of fine impurities will result in weak and more brittle glue.

The best way to work with pitch is to heat it slowly in a stone or pottery bowl until it has gently boiled. Have your projects—such as canteens, knives, spears, or arrows—ready to go. Add white ash to the pitch in small measured amounts (5 percent by volume), keeping in mind that even with heavy amounts of ash (up to 50 percent), the pitch will still be very workable when hot. Yet, when heat is removed, pitch will harden very quickly.

Depending on your intention, you may need the pitch to maintain some flexibility. Case in point is the canteen. In my first attempt, I used about a 50:50 pitch-ash mix, which became so brittle that gently squeezing my canteen caused the pitch to flake and chip off. Spears and arrows need to have stone or bone heads firmly affixed (see

"Hunting Tools," page 157), yet brittle pitch will often shatter when the spear or arrow impacts anything hard, such as the ground or a tree.

PREPARING PITCH FOR USE

- Heat a stone bowl (see "Stone Pecking," page 126) slowly to avoid cracking.
- Add the pitch. Remember, pitch is flammable, so keep some dirt or a lid handy to smother flare-ups.
- When the pitch is simmering, add some ash in small quantities. Mix it well.
- Test the hardness by smearing some hot pitch onto a piece of cloth, leather, or flexible green twig. Let the pitch cool, then bend the cloth or twig and see if the pitch flakes off at the slightest bend. If it does, you likely have too much ash. If you can bend the cloth or twig over on itself, there is not enough ash.

Keep in mind that if you are working with a smooth gluing surface, you may need to score it prior to applying the pitch.

USES FOR PITCH

- Fixing (hafting) stone or bone spearheads and arrowheads to their shafts (see "Hunting Tools," page 157).
- Waterproofing seams on canteens or canoes (see "Canteens," page 88).

- Making engraved bone ornaments. These look great when charcoal or colored stone dust is mixed with pitch and smeared into the engraving; this can be a brittle mix.
- Making temporary tattoos by drawing a design on your skin with small amounts of sun-warmed pine pitch and dusting it with charcoal or colored stone dust.
- Securing knots or lashings that will not need to be untied.
- Making buttons with pitch is simply a matter of tying a knot in a piece of cordage and dipping it in a pitch mix with a lot of ash. Build up to the desired shape by adding daubs of pitch with a stick. While still warm, the pitch can be patted into the desired shape with a flat stick.
- Coating knife handles, wrapped in cordage, with pitch containing a high ash content.

As with many things, your imagination is your only limitation.

Note that pitched products that will have a lot of contact with hands or clothing need to be well coated with ash. If they are not, when they warm up from the sun, your hands, or the fire, they will become sticky and might weaken. As a general rule, keep pitch products away from the fire or other heat sources.

I recommend experimenting with plenty of caution. Hot pitch is like natural napalm. If it touches you, it will stick and it will burn! Create your own recipe. Start with a 20:1 pitch-to-ash ratio and see if it is too soft or too hard. Play with it.

(continued from page 67)

As the sun sank and approached the hill to our west, Mike and I approached the steep climb to camp. We heard a raucous mass of birds to our left. Robins and wood thrushes had congregated to make a fuss about someone. The birds tell us so much about everything, if we only stop to listen and learn a bit of their language. Jon Young, a birder and naturalist, has helped me realize that with practice and experience we can interpret alarm calls. What a beautiful lesson was unfolding. Robins and wood thrushes do not sit at ground level like towhees, nor in the high canopy with the tanagers, which continued to sing without worry. We knew our predator was in mid-canopy, and after listening a bit, we knew this predator was not moving. It had to be an owl.

Armed with our deductions, we slowly approached the alarming mass of birds. I saw the robins and thrushes first, flitting about branches roughly fifteen feet off the ground, circling an area of dense, young hemlocks. Closer and closer I stalked, scrutinizing the hemlock stand. The predator saw me first and swiveled its head to study me. The screech owl sat comfortably against the trunk of a small tree. I crept closer still. Finally disturbed, the owl flew silently over my head and into another hemlock stand twenty-five feet away.

Mike and I had a second look before climbing our ridge. Remarkable. We had learned something about alarms this evening. Imagine how much information is floating about on air, and all we have to do is learn to listen.

Mike and I returned to camp but David was not there. We waited and waited, watching the sun drop and slip behind the western hill—still no David. Well after dark, he appeared at the edge of the firelight, gosling in hand. His competitiveness had driven him out alone. He had wanted to make a solo kill.

David told us he had also been picked up by the local police for trespassing. He had hunted in daylight on someone else's property. Not only had he jeopardized himself, but all of us as well. Luckily, he had been without throwing sticks or the goose, and the cop let him off with a warning. Nonetheless, I was angry. I said things that I thought at the time needed to be said, but in a tone I regret.

As we pondered all the potential consequences of being caught doing what we as a group do each day, we were reminded how illegal these skills are and how the general public might view our adventures.

I'm not the psycho survival sort, or a bloodthirsty hunter. I'm not one who wishes to abuse our natural resources. Quite the contrary, survival skills immerse us in the wonder of nature and help us consciously interact with natural cycles.

Yet modern laws prohibit us from caring for ourselves. We are made dependent on society for food, shelter, and warmth, which of course means playing by the rules. It's interesting to look back. Our country prides itself on its frontiersman start—the hardships of living in a harsh land, of ingenuity and personal freedoms. How times have changed.

I find this to be a strange contradiction. Obviously, if everyone alive today walked off trails and hunted and gathered year-round, our remaining wild places would be decimated quickly; we'd create greater impact than the deer. Yet, these skills connect us with our environments and ourselves so directly. I'd be willing to bet that if everyone were conscious enough to hunt with throwing sticks, we would not be teetering on the edge of environmental catastrophe.

DAY 12

Goose for brunch. I finished my fishing line and bone hook and was itching to give them a go. Mike and I wandered off to try our luck. As Mike and I were crossing a road, he recognized a friend whiz by on a motorcycle. The friend circled back to say hello. After the teasing about our basket of blackberries subsided, he informed us we weren't "missing anything." I thought he meant that the social scene in the area was slow, but he went on to explain that there were no "major wars, government scandals, etc."

(continued on page 75)

Bone Hooks

To catch a fish with modern tackle is not very difficult and even less so if you care nothing about the particular species. A line, a hook, and a worm will almost always guarantee a bite from a sunfish, a bony yet delicious fish. However, in the wild, fine-pointed metal hooks are not available and other options must be explored.

It is worth noting that some bodies of water have more fish than others and thus give you a greater chance of success with *any* hook. If you want to improve your ability as a fisherman, regardless of your current level of skill, then it is important to ask yourself:

- Why would a fish bite my hook?
- Where is food more abundant?
- Where does nutrient-rich water flow into this lake or that pond?
- When are fish feeding?
- Is fishing better in the rain or in the sun; the early morning or the evening?

- What do fish really like to eat?
- Do bass like mice better than frogs?

Asking questions teaches you to be more aware as you seek out the answers. You might notice something others may not. Perhaps fish really like a particular type of caterpillar that you saw fall into the creek and be devoured by a trout.

The basic principle behind hooking a fish is lodging something attached to a string in the fish's mouth or stomach. Fish as a general rule do not chew their food;

therefore, if the object is appealing enough, they will simply swallow it. Consequently, a simple pointed piece of bone with a string tied to the middle sometimes does the trick.

MAKING THE HOOK

The toe bones of a deer are the right shape for making a conventional hook. A slice out of the center of the bone works well. The edge pieces of the same bone need more work but are stronger.

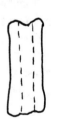

Deer toe bone
(side view)

Follow these steps:

1. Draw two parallel score lines around the bone, then score deeply along the lines with a knife or other sharp object.

Deer toe bone
with scoring
(front view)

2. Split the bone along the score lines and carefully carve or abrade away unneeded bone.

Shading indicates
the area of the
toebone that is
removed when
carving the hook

3. Do not make an eye for the fishing line. Instead, thin the shaft below the top end, leaving a wider portion or button at the top to keep the line from slipping off.
4. Once the line is tied, dab pine pitch over the knot and sprinkle it with ash.
5. Slide a squirrel femur with both ends removed down the line to the hook. This protects the line from sharp teeth and barbs in the fish's mouth.

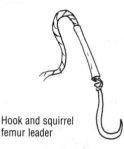

Hook and squirrel
femur leader

Another good hook is a wishbone from the breast of a bird, with one end broken and abraded to a fine point at about midshaft.

Wishbone hook

BAIT

Attach a fifteen-foot length of strong cordage, dogbane, or yucca to the hook. Live bait, while often very effective, can be hard to find and tough for some people to use. Some excellent live baits are frogs hooked through the upper hind leg, small fish hooked through the mouth, crayfish hooked through the tail, and mice hooked through the hide. Other baits include anything that will draw fish, such as bread, dead worms found in puddles after a rain, and pieces of meat, feathers, or reflective objects such as pieces of shell.

CASTING

These directions assume a right-handed individual is casting; reverse the procedure if you're a lefty.

1. Coil the cordage loosely on your left hand, leaving about two feet of slack on the end with the hook.
2. With your right hand, spin the baited hook around in a clock-wise circle so that your target area is at nine o'clock, the ground is at six o'clock, and the area behind you is at three o'clock.
3. Release on the upswing. The line should uncoil off your left hand (hold onto the end) and land your hook about fifteen feet out.

FISHING

There are many different ways to fish, and which one works best depends on the sort of fish you are targeting. Do you jerk the bait on the surface or let it sit on the bottom? Generally, I let live bait stay on or near the surface with little movement from me. Crayfish and minnows tend to do better deeper down, and dead bait seems to work well on top as well as down below. Experiment and see what works for you in your area. Have fun, and remember, fishing is an art.

SETTING YOUR BAIT AT A SPECIFIC DEPTH

To set your bait at a specific depth, say for example three feet, tie a rock one foot from the hook and a wooden bobber (big enough to hold the weight of the rock) three feet above the stone. If your hook tangles with the rest of the gear, you can tie a stick to the line between

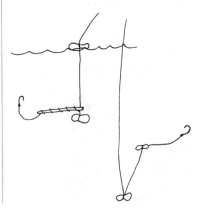

the stone and the hook, with the line wrapped around the stick.

Another option for placing your bait a given distance off the bottom, say two feet, is to tie on a weight and then a small bobber two feet from the weight; your hook line is then attached to the bobber. The bobber will float up as far as is possible, keeping your baited hook just about where you want it.

LANDING THE FISH

Once a fish has hit your hook, keep *constant pressure* on your line by

backing up until the fish is well on shore. A stick or stone can be used to finish off the fish, or you can break its neck by bending the head back until the nose touches the spine.

DRESSING THE FISH

With a sharp rock or knife, cut from the rectum along the belly to just below the gills. Remove the guts and rinse out the cavity. Bon appetite! (See recipes at the end of "Trout Hunting," page 77.)

(continued from page 72)

It seemed an odd statement for our conversation in the middle of a country road, without traffic, surrounded by lush green hills. We hadn't asked about the current affairs of the nation, and quite honestly, I didn't care. I appreciated the break from constant bad news. Even when I am immersed in modern society, I filter out most of the current events. I find it too depressing to intake negative media coverage from around the globe all day, every day. And I'll not allow myself to be bombarded into submission by a government that so consciously chooses what it wants me to hear and think about the world.

Yet I remain active in government processes. For years, I dreamed of disappearing into the woods without a trace. But I could no longer watch decisions about wild places and wild creatures being made, knowing that I had not contributed my opinion. So, I vote and write to politicians, hoping to remove cattle from public lands, stop tree harvesting our remaining roadless areas, be more aggressive about the removal of logging roads in ecosystem restoration, promote more respectful foreign policy, and a host of other issues.

I don't remember who told me that for each letter the government receives, it is considered the view of five thousand people. This is due to the fact that so few people write to their representatives. I really don't know whether the source was sound, but it's great incentive. In this time and age, warriors must wield the pen more often than the sword. Perhaps its time to step down off my soapbox.

So, why am I here in the woods? What started years ago as a fantasy of the ultimate rebellion—leaving society completely behind—has instead become a search for self. Tracking and survival skills provide the mirror and opportunity for me to see myself and the effects of my behaviors. If we were able to practice only that which we needed to survive this summer and allow everything else to fall away, I think we might glimpse or comprehend something of real *humanness*.

We continued upstream, poking and exploring along the way. Walking in streams is such an exhilarating experience. There are so few activities that can quickly transform adults into children again. I found myself prodding in and around rocks and logs, laughing and smiling at darting trout and crayfish. The water current and stony bottom challenged our balance, and the diversity of color and texture within the stream pushed our imaginations.

One pool in particular held several large trout. Against the far bank, tucked under a jungle of wild grapes, lay a massive log. The trout retreated to hide under this log when we approached. It was here that Mike demonstrated hand fishing. Within fifteen minutes, he had pulled a twelve-inch trout out onto the bank, using its gills as a handle. Talk about impressive!

I had to give it a go. What a fantastic location. You could look over the log into the water and see the fish, as well as the tips of your fingers. My first few attempts did nothing but scare the fish. I moved too fast, my mind raced, and my hands were too eager.

I stepped back and took a deep breath. Hand fishing was yet another lesson in slowing down. I slid my hands under the log and watched from above. I touched the trout and began to

(continued on page 84)

Trout Hunting

Wading upstream in a long, shallow pool, I continue to probe under the banks with my hands. The water is like ice, and it doesn't help that I'm in the shadow of the streamside trees, sheltered from the warm touch of the sun. At one point, I force my goose-bump-covered body beneath the surface to reach farther back under the bank. Aha! The unmistakable smooth side of a fish brushes my fingertips and moves even farther back beneath the bank. I am no longer cold—the fish has my attention—and I consciously calm the excitement within me; it is as if the water embraces me.

Lying in a shallow pool, my nose, one eye, and a quarter of my mouth are all that are exposed to air. My fingers, swaying like grass in the current, slowly move upstream, searching. There! A trout, and a big one, too! I've found the alpha trout of this pool, hiding about three feet back under the bank. I can't see it, but I can taste it. I dance my fingers gently along its lower side, envisioning how the fish is sitting in its hiding place.

I'm going to need two hands! My right hand locates the gills, thumb gently caressing one side and middle finger stroking the other, while my left hand cups underneath, about six inches from the trout's tail. I am relaxed and do not rush. Then, I jam my thumb and middle finger together through the gills, and at the same time, I clamp the tail. I've got the fish! Slowly, I emerge from beneath the bank and marvel at this magnificent trout measuring eighteen inches in length. If it were not for my hunger, I would surely return this beautiful creature to its waters.

As it was, he cooked up quite nicely. I am still grateful.

People are infatuated with food, and even though it is number five on the list of priorities in a survival situation, it still claims a lot of head time (at least initially). Over our summer, the meals that stood out above all others were trout, for which we hand fished and spearfished in nearby streams.

FINDING THE TROUT

Before jumping into technique, you must find the trout. The features of streams and rivers are widely diverse, but allow me to present several features that have afforded me great success. I do very well fishing in shallow streams and rivers that have pools of varying size, depth, and flow. Even ankle-deep streams with intermittent pools can hold massive trout. I recommend moving upstream for two reasons. First, any sediment you stir up will not cloud your fishing area, and second, trout tend to face into the current—they are hard enough to stalk without moving directly in their field of vision.

In Moving Water

Moving water includes shallow to chest-deep rapids and waterfalls. As water moves over the riverbed, areas of both swift and still water are created. Even within whitewater rapids there are pockets of still water. It is in these pockets, usually underneath or on the downstream side of rocks or other objects, that trout seem to wait for food to swirl in on the current. Many times I have given a quick jab with my hand into an *unlikely* spot, only to have a trout go streaking off to who knows where. *Move your hands with the same characteristics of the water in which they are immersed.* Just because the surface may be roiling whitewater does not mean that the conditions a foot below are the same. Check under and around rocks that might hide a trout. Even at the base of waterfalls, big or small, you will often find calm water; check these areas for trout. Feel with your hands along the edges of rapids, because it is not

always apparent where or how far the river has cut into the bank.

In Still Water

Still water includes any still-water pools from ankle depth or deeper. In long, still, shallow pools, make sure to check under large rocks, under banks, and in sedge clumps, using your hands to "look" for holes leading into cavities that may house trout.

The foundations of bridges are often scoured out, creating perfect trout traps. Floods also create ideal trout-hunting grounds—some better for the hunter, and some better for the trout. The root systems of downed trees, trees along banks, and trees transported by floods create a myriad of hiding spots, some of which may be inaccessible to the hunter. Certain situations require exploring hideouts and catching trout while you are completely submerged, which isn't as tough as it sounds once you get some practice. In my experience, the biggest trout in a given pool use two hiding spots. They are also the most relaxed of all the fish in the pool, because they are at the top of the pecking order. Thus, the larger the trout, often the easier they are to catch. They are used to smaller fish wriggling up against them in tight quarters. I found a hole in a shale riverbank, which led to a small cavern about two feet long and one foot wide. There were so many trout in there they left no room for the water! So, spook the trout and see the available sizes and where they are hiding.

Be persistent. I remember a pool with a five-foot, submerged rock face. After several frustrating visits to the pool, where the fish just disappeared, I finally found a small hole that led into a cavity. It was jammed with fish and made for easy fishing! Explore every possibility and refuse to become trapped into thinking you know where trout will and will not be. I am continually surprised.

It is important to learn about the various hazards in your hunting area, such as pollution, snakes, and snapping turtles (I've grabbed many northern snappers by the head under water with no ill effects, but the alligators and alligator snappers of the South are another story entirely). In pools four feet and deeper, keep a wary eye out for beavers. They do not seem to mind underwater visitors as long as you do not corner them or appear threatening.

TECHNIQUE

Over the years, I have found only literary tidbits on hand fishing. Some writers tell about slowly mesmerizing the fish by stroking its belly. Others suggest placing your hands below a trout and quickly flipping it onto shore. One source even suggests using your hands to make a false cave entrance to lure the trout. Once it's in your hands, they say to simply grab the trout. Maybe these techniques really work, although I've yet to be able to catch a trout with them. What follows are some of the trout-hunting techniques Mark and I have used and taught with great success in streams and shallow rivers.

Spearfishing or Hand Fishing?

The flow and characteristics of the water are what dictate whether you should hunt with a spear or with your hands. In pools that have little or no cover for fish, a spear is preferable, whereas in moving water and in pools that have cover (overhanging banks, big rocks, clumps of grass, root systems), hand fishing may work the best. Trying to dislodge your spear from a tangle of roots while trout are nibbling your toes is a humbling experience not easily forgotten.

I really enjoy both hand fishing and spearfishing in pools, where the varying challenges are consistently rewarding. Pools without vegetation or hiding spots tend to house skittish trout. Without vegetation, fish do not become accustomed to being touched, and without hiding spots, they will swim laps around you. Use a spear! It's almost impossible to hunt with hands in these situations. Or, you can create hiding spots, then use your hands. Stack rocks to form niches or add logs and brush where the fish will feel safe. Then, check these spots in about a week.

Spearfishing

Making the Spear
Spears are simple to make and easy to use.

The following design is for pinning, not puncturing, the fish.

1. Find a somewhat straight sapling about eight to twelve feet long and no thicker than one and one-half inch at the base.
2. Sharpen the thick end to a point after cutting off all the limbs.

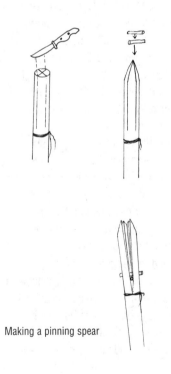

Making a pinning spear

Leaving the bark on is a good idea and aids in camouflaging the spear.
3. About nine inches down the shaft from the point, tightly wrap some artificial sinew, wet rawhide, or other string, and tie it off).
4. With a sturdy knife, create a split from the tip to the tied-off string. The string will keep the split from running too far down the shaft; therefore, it must always be left in place.
5. Now, make a second split perpendicular to the first one. This gives you four sections at the tip of your spear; sharpen each one.
6. Jam a twig into each of the two splits, splaying the tips apart. These twigs can be tied in place or held in by friction. I use the friction method, because it allows for a quick change of twig; i.e., if the twigs are too big for the fish I am hunting, I can put smaller ones in, thus reducing the splay of the prongs. Another option is to put a larger twig in one slot and a smaller one in the other, providing you with two size options.

Fishing with the Spear
When you spot a fish along the bottom, bring the spear directly over it (vertical is nice but not imperative) so that two of the four points straddle the "neck" just behind the gills. Approach from the back to avoid spooking the trout. The other two

points of the spear lie farther back. The splay of the points should be such that when the spear is jabbed downward, the body of the fish forces the points farther apart. At this point, you can reach down and recover the trout, or, with a sharp, quick twist of the spear, you can break the trout's spine.

Using the spear is rather self-explanatory, although there are some definite no-nos. The tip of the spear must be practically touching the fish if you hope to be success-ful, so don't strike prematurely from too far away. The most common mistake occurs is the "windup." When you are in position and ready for the final jab, do not pull the spear away from the fish. The fish is *not* behind you. The only move-ment your spear should make is *toward* the fish. Mark and I found out that if we leaned forward and started to tip, we could effectively use our weight to add force and speed to the thrust. Because the spear tip is already in the water, refraction is not an issue—you can clearly see the spear tip in relation to the fish.

If you are shooting fish with a bow and arrow, however, you will need to aim low to account for refraction. How low depends upon the lateral distance from you to the fish; the greater the distance the lower the aiming point.

Sharp spears for puncturing fish work well in situations that allow for side shots for a few reasons: (1) the side of a fish presents a larger tar-get; (2) it is also far softer than the dorsal portion of the fish; and (3) a missed strike is less likely to break or dull stone, bone, or wood tips.

The spear is adaptable, so use your intelligence and apply it as needed. For example, Mark and I came across a hole in a stream bank a few feet above the water. I crawled in and found a glasslike pool. It was connected to the river below the water line, diffusing and giving a bluish cast to the light. Suspended in the water hung two beautiful trout. We tried unsuccess-fully for a while to catch one. I used my hands from inside the cave, and Mark used a spear from the outside. We switched back and forth, getting hungrier and colder with each attempt, both wanting to be the one to catch supper and neither wanting to be the one to call it quits. The problem in the cave was that the trout were too skittish and the area too confined. Outside the cave, we only got occasional glimpses of the trout before they moved too far back in the cave for us to see.

In the end, Mark stood in the river outside the cave with the spear tip just inside the cave by way of the underwater entry, while I lay in the cave giving him instructions on what direction and how far to move the spear. When he had the spear positioned near the trout, I gave him the word. The water clouded with his lunge, and I couldn't see a thing. Slowly and carefully, I moved my hand through the water, found the spear shaft, and moved down it to the tip. Gravel!?! Mark had jabbed so hard he'd sunk that trout a couple of inches into the gravel. I managed to dig it up and grab it, and together we shared dinner. The lesson? Be flexible.

Hand Fishing

Probably 85 percent of the time, you will not be able to see the trout you are trying to catch. This means that your fingers must become your eyes under the water. When you reach under a riverbank "looking" for trout, keep your fingers limp like seaweed. Let them flow as if with the current, exploring every possible hiding spot. *Most* trout are used to having bits of grass and other debris touch them as it floats past. They are not, however, used to being goosed.

I once reached under a bank for a trout only to find a twelve-pound snapping turtle; it was quite tasty. I've found snakes that way, too— kind of chewy and tasteless, although Mark and I both found their eggs to be delicious when poached. Once you've felt a trout, you'll never mistake anything else for one. Be careful and count all your fingers after each trip.

Let's stick with trout. Once you come in contact with a fish, STAY RELAXED! Slowly and gently feel along its body to locate its head and determine its size. Don't take anything too small, although too small depends directly on how hungry you are. Small fry are not bad when toasted, and you can eat them, heads and all.

If the fish is fourteen inches or bigger, use two hands when fishing. Cup both hands under the fish, keeping one hand near the little fins just in front of the tail. Use the thumb and middle finger of your other hand to locate the gills. Do not apply pressure yet. But when you do, you must be fast and severe. Drive your thumb and middle finger into each other *through* the gills while gripping the tail with your other hand. If the fish is in a cavity, you can pin the trout against the wall or roof without touching the gills. Do this if you do not have access to the gills or mouth. Once you have grabbed the fish in this manner, it will struggle once and then relax. At this point, you can also relax, but only slightly. Once again, the fish will struggle, after which you can pull it out with minimal fuss. Make sure you have a good hold on the trout before you remove it from the water.

If you pursue this skill, you will inevitably find yourself in varying situations. For example, some places where trout hide will not allow you access to both gills. This being the case, you may have to adapt using one gill and the mouth instead. Be careful, though, because large trout have teeth that can puncture a callused hand. The pain is really not that bad—just a pin prick—but if you cannot handle that, you don't deserve the trout.

If You Do Not Want to Harm the Fish

Some of these maneuvers can be done without harming the fish. If you want to return the fish to the water and *have not squeezed it too hard or put your fingers in its gills*, then hold it in your hands and gently set it back in the stream. Hold it at its normal attitude (facing into the current, belly to the bottom and back to the sky) until it regains its equilibrium and swims off on its own. Please keep in mind that *touching the gills damages them,* and putting the fish back in the water will only result in a snake or raccoon eating trout for dinner. The trout will not survive even if it swims off apparently fine. Here is another way to catch fish without causing any immediate harm.

Place your hand under the fish as usual, except this time, have the fish lie diagonally across your palm so that its head comes between your middle and index fingers and the tail just touches your wrist. By squeezing your fingers together and simultaneously making a fist, you can effectively immobilize the fish. Experiment!

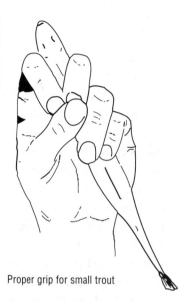

Proper grip for small trout

PRIMITIVE COOKING

Trout hunting is tremendous fun and very rewarding. It's a great way to see familiar land from a new perspective and provides you with a fantastic meal using simple tools. Remember, though, that you are taking a life. It is important to give thanks and maintain proper respect. Check with your local Department of Fish and Game regarding the legality of this activity in your area, and avoid overfishing areas—we all want to continue fishing trout well into the future.

(continued from page 76)

stroke its underbelly. Its beautiful body was adorned with colorful freckles and striped fins. A caddis fly larva struggled along the stream bottom below the trout, carrying its wooden house. I was petting and stroking a fish! It even nuzzled closer as I tickled its belly. Its body would occasionally go limp in my hands, its fins loose in the current.

I attempted to catch several trout a few times, but to no avail, as they were remarkably slippery. So, I kept stroking and touching their soft bodies. I stopped when I could no longer control the shivers and the "pinch" between my thumb and pointer finger moved in slow motion. Add to this the fact that I was turning blue. I sat on the bank, and Mike demonstrated on the dead fish he'd caught where you need to grab to bring the fish to shore. I had been aiming too low. Next time.

I warmed up over the next hour as we hiked back to camp. The cold was a small price to pay for such an experience—touching wild creatures in a clear, clean stream and hovering above rocks that provided a beautiful mosaic of colors in the background. The stream gurgled, yellow throats sang, and the electric blue of bluebirds streaked overhead.

DAY 13

Mike and I were alone in camp, because David had left yesterday to visit home. As we walked for water in the morning, I scouted for potential spears for fishing. I was eager to spearfish. We separated after filling our containers. I had planned to pick up clay for pottery but was distracted by the possibility of finding decent tracks. I had discovered a farm road filled with holes, and it provided a wonderful, muddy medium for tracks. Here, tracks were often absolutely perfect, and absolutely irresistible.

I explored the mud holes slowly, taking note of which animals had been moving in the area. I stared at a set of woodchuck tracks. I lay on my elbows, exploring the ridges of each

front   rear

Woodchuck tracks

palm pad with my fingers while engaging my imagination in the recreation of the animal.

After staring at the details of the tracks and absorbing what I could only sense, I was able to pick out the more difficult tracks, which lay beyond the perfect mud. The woodchuck was walking in one of two common woodchuck gaits. I then knew where to look for the next track, and my imagination was able to add the flowing movements of woodchucks I had watched in fields so many times before.

I also spent time staring at cottontail rabbit tracks. I don't look at tracks while I'm standing up unless I'm quickly follow-ing a trail. I prefer to be right up close. I could see all the lines made by the fur that covers its feet, the asymmetry of the track, and the claws that registered so prominently. Even the rudimentary fifth toe made an appearance. Again, I felt the track and used my imagination to visu-alize the whole animal. When tracking, I engage as many senses as possible.

Today, I realized a great benefit of tracking. Tracking immerses you in nature. You must get down close to look at the intricate details.

As I stared at the cottontail tracks, I noticed that a possum had also walked by. The mud had been drier and harder and the tracks more subtle. Numerous bird tracks appeared next, then those of rodents and insects. I was breaking through different levels of awareness. The longer I looked, the more I noticed.

The road was also dotted with house-cat tracks. They, too, are beautiful, with asymmetry and perfect toe registration. Cats flex their paws and roll their feet, molding to the landscape. House-cat tracks may look like bobcat tracks in one step, and like domestic kitten tracks in the next. One moment they are large, the next moment tiny.

Finding cat tracks in nature always strikes an odd chord inside me. Feral and domestic cats are responsible for the deaths of millions of rodents and birds annually. They are an enormous impact on our native fauna, our country, and world. Yet, people complain when a fisher, bobcat, coyote, or great horned owl kills a cat. I say, "Go fisher! Go owl! Go coyote!" Cats breed like rabbits. If folks don't want their cats to participate in natural cycles, then they should keep them indoors.

Harvesting a serviceberry, I created a spear and went fishing in the afternoon.

Downstream proved quite difficult, as two streams joined to become one larger and deeper stream. Chest-deep water levels made it challenging to spear fish; I was often swept up on the current. It also began to rain, and the ripples created by the raindrops, although beautiful, made rocks and trout look similar.

I met Mike on the way back to camp. He held aloft a woodchuck, dispatched by a throwing stick. I held up my empty hands and waved. We collected water, wild garlic, and garlic mustard for our

Eight-foot pinning spear

feast. I found woodchuck to be similar in flavor to the other meats we have eaten. Possibly varying the cooking style would alter the flavors. Mike, on the other hand, felt that the flavor of woodchuck was inferior to all the foods we've collected thus far.

Each night as I lay in my debris hut, I reflect on the day and acknowledge all the lives that were sacrificed so that I might live. I also contemplate the beauty I witnessed. Maintaining a ritual of appreciation was an important reason why I decided to take this adventure this summer. Not in the sense of asking for anything or reciting complicated verses. Rather, I simply acknowledge and speak my appreciation for what I experience and what I harvest. I don't drink from the spring without first giving thanks, and the three of us give thanks for our food each evening. I pause at beauty in nature. These expressions are neither complicated nor long. They feel natural.

Some might call this prayer, yet out here, surrounded in woods and wild creatures, prayer and religion seem complicated and potentially unnecessary affairs. Rituals, religious guilt, and structure fall away in the simplicity of things. Contemplating the ways of wild coyotes and of wild people has helped me challenge certain cultural foundations.

Day 14

We awoke to drizzle. I walked about and sought a short reprieve in mosquito-free fields. I sat very close to a song sparrow's nest, which sent the pair into quite a chatter. They paid less attention to me as time passed and I gazed across the foggy valley. In open spaces I feel more expansive and free. Breezes carry my thoughts to distant hills, far away from me.

Morning progressed, and the three of us met under a shelter up valley. David had a fire waiting when I arrived. We worked on skills and chatted; it was a peaceful time. Mike and I had decided previously that this day would be devoted to making new bark canteens.

(continued on page 90)

Canteens

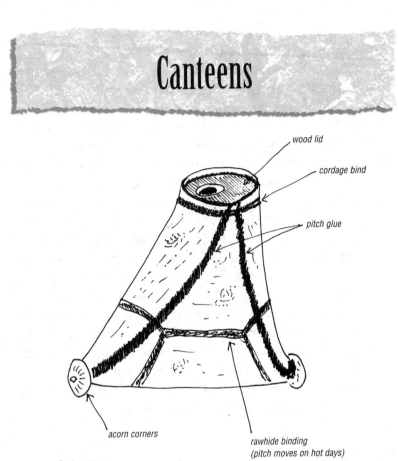

wood lid

cordage bind

pitch glue

acorn corners

rawhide binding
(pitch moves on hot days)

Bark canteen

I used to walk all over the land near my childhood home, drinking from streams whenever I was thirsty. I was never made ill by these waters. However, with the prevalence of pollution today, water must often be boiled in order to purify it for drinking. This means that any hunting trip or hike is limited by your ability to go without, acquire, or carry drinking water with you. To carry purified water from camp, pine bark canteens can be made.

1. Strip an eight-by-sixteen-inch piece of smooth bark from a live white pine with the grain running the long way (see "Cooking Containers," page 111). Be sure to utilize all bark from the limb or tree you fell, or take a piece that doesn't reach all the way around the tree.
2. Trim the bark as indicated in the next illustration.
3. Gently fold, without creasing, as indicated.

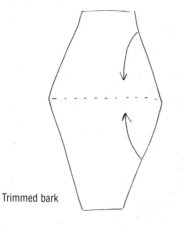

Trimmed bark

4. Carefully curl one side within the other.

Canteen mouth (overlap detail)

5. Make a cork or stopper and place it in the opening.
6. Lash with some remaining bark and let it sit a day or two. This

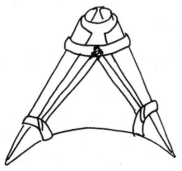

Canteen lashed for drying

allows the bark to dry out a bit and "remember" the shape desired. Be sure to leave it where it will get copious amounts of smoke to discourage bark-dwelling parasites, which may drill holes in your unfinished canteen. Many are often in the bark already but can be killed with a careful application of heat and smoke.

7. Once the canteen has dried a day or two, remove the lashing and score, scratch, or otherwise roughen the areas that overlap, as well as those areas adjacent to the seams when closed.

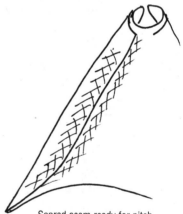

Scored seam ready for pitch

The score lines will help the pine pitch and ash mixture adhere (see "Working with Pitch," page 68).

8. Apply pitch.
9. Attach a bit of cordage just as you applied the lashings previously. This time, leave enough for a strap.

Finished canteen with carry strap

10. Acorn caps or hickory nut halves are a nice touch and add further protection to the corners.

To ensure the durability of your canteen, do not let the canteen get too warm, as the pitch may become too soft, allowing the seams to split. No hot beverages! Holes from insects can be plugged with a bit of pitch with very little ash mixed in. Periodically allow the canteen to dry out, put some coarse sand inside, and gently shake to scour it out.

(continued from page 87)

The rain was daunting, but off we went in search of a decent white pine from which we could harvest bark. Rains no longer stopped us from going about our business.

We decided to visit the spring we use for water and discovered that an obstacle had cropped up in our path—a camp had been set up that morning. Tents were spread about and tarps hung from trees. It was like a small circus in the woods. Mike had heard there was to be a two-week kids' program in the area at some time. We took the long way around, pausing to peek at the invaders and the setup. Life would be different now. We'd have to be far more aware.

We finally selected a tree down valley for our bark harvesting. For me, trees and animals are the hardest to kill. Trees are remarkable. They stand tall, rooted, and completely grounded. Yet, they are flexible when necessary. They silently witness so much, offer countless resources, and provide beautiful diversity in form. Silent they stand, but I feel their singing.

We managed a complicated felling, including one snag, which Mike climbed to dislodge. We thanked our white pine by making quality containers, honoring the tree with functional skills. We returned to the shelter soaked to the bone, although we made impromptu burdock-leaf hats to divert the relentless rains from our heads. One great leaf formed a large visor and another kept our necks dry.

From our shelter, we were gifted with interesting views of short-tailed shrews. A pair continuously worked the area around us, moving with amazing speed and energy. A network of tunnels just under the debris surrounded a nearby brush pile. However, the shrews spent as much time on top of the debris as they did underneath it.

There were constant, long chase scenes. When the chaser caught the leader, they would tumble, grappling and chirping, then begin chasing one another all over again. The speed of these animals took our breath away. They would zip from one spot to another, a nonstop metabolic energy burn. They ran up woodpiles, fell off woodpiles, zipped over roots and under leaves. I was exhausted just watching them.

We pulled back a section of leaf litter where a shrew had been tunneling, and found the remains of earthworms, the abandoned portions writhing, unable to escape. We also watched one shrew chase a frog that narrowly escaped and bounded away. The shrew held close pursuit for about four bounds.

What a wonderful experience. I had worked on projects for awhile, then switched to shrew TV, which had delivered nonstop action.

Day 15

Today is Mike's birthday. He awoke pining for Belgian waffles, topped with fruit and maple syrup. Instead, we spent the morning harvesting a basswood that was growing across the stream. The lower leader had died in the water, and the remaining upper leader was destined to the same fate. I stripped the branches for cordage materials. It was like skinning an animal, because the entire bark, leaves and all, would come off together—a hollow replica of the branches.

We weighted down the logs in the stream to *ret*, which means to rot. As the cambium begins to break down, the fibers with which we make cordage become more pliable and easier to separate from the inner wood. The wood itself is great for carving, coal burning, and fire making. We'll see.

In the afternoon, we visited a place far upstream, miles from camp. A sacred place to be sure, where water, shale, and the passage of time have created an intricate sculpture and waterfall. The layers of shale were smoothed by water flow, and the remaining lines looked like waves within rock. Moss, ferns, and lichens held to steep faces, and water dropped ten feet into a small pool, surrounded by shale walls.

Above the pool, I stood in a moment of apprehension. I knew the water would be frigid, and I didn't really know how deep the pool was. I waited for the sun to reappear from behind the clouds, then I jumped, commitment made, mind unsettled. I watched shale whiz by, and my body tensed in apprehension of cold and impact. Wooh! It was cold! I swam against the current just below the waterfall. The walls made me feel like I was in a well, with the water pounding down next to me. What force, what noise, what energy! Bubbles and froth massaged my body and clear waters swiftly flowed away. I felt so alive! I yelled, I smiled, I laughed out loud. This was living!

Wow. Those moments of indescribable living—feeling sensations pulse and flow through you, so full of joy you can't help but smile widely. We can't let these moments slip away. We must seek them out!

Day 16

We awoke to rain. My canteens had become leaky, so I went to drink from the spring. As I came close to the new camp on the hill, I approached from below. An outhouse was being finalized, adjacent to our pristine water source. Typical, they hadn't seemed to have noticed the spring. Avoiding detection, I made the final approach on hands and knees, crawling slowly. I kept a watchful eye on a woman as she worked.

I came up to the water, gave thanks, and lowered my head. I laid flat, drinking slowly. I took frequent breaks to make sure I hadn't been discovered. Then it struck me—I had become *animal*, flat out on the ground, drinking nervously. My head constantly jerked up to check in with my surroundings. Having their head down is a vulnerable position for animals. Here, amidst modern humans, I was prey. Would they understand my intentions in the woods? I didn't know, and today I wasn't willing to find out.

The rains have been intense and are beginning to impact the surrounding landscape in dramatic ways. Autumn nuts and fruits are falling off trees, undeveloped and immature. I examined a handful of hickory nuts, still in their green sheaths. I cut them open. The outer shells had not hardened at all, and the nut meats were absent.

For the first ten days of our experience, I was unable to live in the moment. I was here, in beautiful woods, practicing ancient skills and fulfilling a summer I had long anticipated. Yet, I often thought about what I was missing. I was eager to practice American Sign Language and to revisit the tracking projects I was working on. I also wanted to start new projects. I was already planning the skills I would focus on at home and the trips I would like to take soon. Future, future, future.

With time, distractions have faded. I'm finally here soaking up woods, feeling breezes across my face, and listening to the wind in the canopy. I'm no longer tainted by planning, goal setting, and mental gibberish.

My pace has slowed down; I'm no longer in a rush. I am seeing smaller things. Previously, I had often lost the experience at hand because I was busy planning the next one. Now I know that vacations shorter than ten days are useless. Less than ten days, my mind does not rest. Instead, it moves like the shrew that often eats three times its body weight in a day to feed a lightning metabolism. After ten days, both my body and mind were relaxed, allowing for glimpses of a different me. Perhaps the true me?

In the afternoon, the three of us roamed to the west to explore a wetland and gather cattails for a new group shelter. The sun emerged from behind the clouds and the wind picked up. The purple seed heads of grasses blew in the fields, creating waves of lavender dotted with the yellow flowers of cinquefoil and "butter-and-eggs." It was a stunning sight.

As we entered a hidden meadow, we noticed a woodchuck feeding away from cover out in the green. Mike had his throwing stick; David and I picked up stones. The wind was in our favor. Mike and I moved together in front. David formed the triangle a few steps behind.

The woodchuck fed on clover, pausing only occasionally to look about. Oblivious to our presence, she moved toward us on a feeding run. Closer and closer we approached each other. The woodchuck was massive and her guard hairs glistened in the sun. Her coat was thick and healthy.

The gap between us shrank, until the woodchuck was just two feet from me and a bit more from Mike. It stopped gorging on greens and looked up. Mike lunged with his stick, and the woodchuck ran. The throwing stick and stones followed. I hit the woodchuck square on the back, and she flipped over, switching from flight to fight in an instant. Mike tried to trap it with his foot, while I looked for his throwing stick. He had the animal pinned, or … did the woodchuck have him? Her teeth tore into the sole and side of his shoe! Lucky for him he was wearing thick leather booties.

We used the stick to pin down the woodchuck. A quick stab to the throat and the struggle was over. Our first group kill. I looked away for the stab, not yet comfortable with all the killing necessary to survive. I guess I can still convince myself I'm somehow disconnected, that I'm not really an animal. We gutted and covered the woodchuck for our return.

(continued on page 100)

Stalking and Hunting

Hunting as a survival tool is critical. It is through hunting that you provide yourself with many of the tools you need to remain in the wild and the sustenance to survive in the short term. For instance:

- Hides give you leather for clothing, rawhide for lashings, snowshoes, hard protective cases, cordage, hide glue, bags, and more.
- Meat and fat provide immediate and long-term sustenance, whether they are fresh, jerked, or made into pemmican.
- Sinew is great for sewing, lashing, making bow strings, backing bows (a technique used to add strength to a bow), making snare lines, and more.
- Bones can be made into fishing hooks, knives, awls, needles, buttons, and decorative ornaments. Teeth and jawbones can be used for abrading or cutting (wood or grasses).
- Guts can be used for pouches, water bags, sausage casing, and lashing.

Clearly the value of good hunting skills can make the difference between life and death.

MOVEMENT AND BALANCE

The way in which modern people move is more like a controlled fall. It is as if people have a string attached to their chests or foreheads and are being pulled along. This causes them to walk with their body at a slant, with their head out in front, completely out of balance. This incorrect way of walking also causes people to look at the ground; consequently, they see little of their surroundings. For a hunter, balance is paramount. A hunter may need to stop on a moment's notice and remain motionless, sometimes with only one foot on the ground.

Stumbling through the woods in this fashion is not likely to yield a successful hunt. It is crucial to slow down and raise your head. Start out by standing squarely on your feet. With your eyes gazing out levelly, stretch both hands out directly in front of you, touching each other at eye level. Now, while wiggling your fingers, move your hands simultaneously apart, maintaining both your forward gaze and visual contact with both hands. Bring your hands as far back as possible until you can just catch the movement of your wiggling fingers. You should feel a shift in your vision as you do this exercise. The effect is similar to looking out through a picture window while standing at the back of a room, rather than looking through the same window with your nose to the glass.

This peripheral, full-view, or splatter vision is used so seldom that your impulse will be to quickly shift back to a specific point in view. Keep practicing until you can shift into full-view vision without any effort. Athletes in basketball, soccer, and other big team sports use this way of seeing to visually cover a larger portion of the court or field while paying specific attention to a particular player.

You will notice that full-view or peripheral vision gives you far more sensitivity to movement and light. Pinpoint vision (looking from point to point to make up a whole picture) is time consuming and gives you weak details pertaining to the overall view. Taking one glance in full-view allows you to clearly see the whole picture. For example, leaves moved out of place by a passing deer lay differently on the

ground than those that have not been disturbed. Full-view vision makes the trail stand out, whereas pinpoint vision does not.

Once you are able to easily shift into full-view vision, you are ready to move. While balancing on one leg, lift the other foot and slowly move it forward such a distance that you are able to place it flatly on the ground while applying no pressure or weight to it. Remember to bend your knees as you move. Do not lock them during periods of waiting, because this can result in a sudden lurch when you begin stalking again.

If you are in full-view vision, your feet can to some extent become your eyes on the ground. Before putting weight on your forward foot, gently touch the ground with the inside ball of that foot (the "ball" is between the toes and the arch). Slowly roll the foot to the outside so that the entire ball of the foot is in contact with the ground. Then let your heel and toes settle to the ground as well. Be aware of sharp objects or sticks that may break under your weight

If your foot is well placed, slowly shift your weight from the back foot forward to the newly placed foot, and repeat the process. When you are hunting animals, taking one step per minute (or moving even more slowly) will enable you to at least move, even when the animals are looking at you. With a lot of slow practice, you can learn to move at a brisk walk and eventually at a similar run.

HUNTING

The principles of hunting wild game are universal regardless of the weapon used or the game hunted. First, you must locate your quarry, and second, you must get within an effective range of the animal for the weapon you are using. Locating your prey without modern-day technological tools requires that you learn about the animals' habits. You can accomplish this goal by tracking animals, reading available literature on them, and actually observing them when the opportunity arises. The more you learn, the easier it will be to predict where and when a given animal will be. If time is short, a regularly used trail often offers good opportunities for finding animals. You may, however, have to wait a day or more for them to appear. Randomly walking through the woods, hoping to stumble upon game, can be time consuming and requires great proficiency in stalking.

The effective range of a weapon is the distance at which the hunter can deliver a strike with deadly precision and force on a regular basis. One person's effective range with a spear may be fifteen feet, whereas someone else's range may extend to twenty feet. Most primitive weapons require the hunter to be within close proximity of the animal.

Another variable is the force required to kill an animal. For example, rabbits typically are more fragile than woodchucks, allowing a hunter to throw a rabbit stick from farther away when hunting rabbits than if one were hunting woodchucks. To prepare for a hunt, you must become proficient with your weapon of choice and familiar with your hunting areas. While walking your hunting grounds ask yourself these questions:

- From what direction does the wind normally come? This will help predict how your scent will be carried.
- What do the prey animals in the area eat? Knowing what they eat will help you locate them.
- What is the best direction to approach prey from in a given area? This can help you decide if stalking the prey once you see it is better than sitting and waiting for the prey to come to you.
- Will my body be silhouetted against the sky? If it will, then perhaps a belly crawl will get you close enough, or you can look for other approaches or perhaps investigate camouflaging yourself into the area prior to the regular arrival of your quarry.
- What time of day will the sun aid me by being at my back? If the sun is low and at your back, it is

also in the eyes of your prey whenever it looks your way.

- What type of substrate will I be stalking on or through? Some substrates may be so thick and noisy that you are better off finding a way around them.

These are standard questions, and you will undoubtedly add to them as you practice stalking prey.

Though it is not always possible, try to select a specific individual to hunt. Watch it and learn its strengths and weaknesses. When is it alert? If it's a burrow-dwelling animal such as a woodchuck, does it wander farther from its hole than others in the area? How can you use its weaknesses to help you make it your meal? Deer, for example, fall easily into many patterns, and often will not stop to assess potential dangers before entering a familiar meadow to graze. You need to take the time to observe the local population.

Once you have chosen your quarry and you know when you will hunt it, you must prepare. What you do spiritually to make peace with the animal that you will hunt and then kill is up to you. Here is a good way to physically prepare for the hunt. Three to four days prior to the hunt, eat bland food to help reduce body odor. It also helps to wash in the stream using soapwort (see essay on Hygiene, page 208) or other natural locally present scent,

or nonscented soap. Using a sweat lodge is another good way to help remove human scent.

Leave your clothes out in the woods away from camp in a rainstorm, or wash them in the creek and hang them to dry. In a pinch, you can stand in the smoke of a wood fire to cover your scent. Because it is natural, smoke does not seem to startle animals unless it is accompanied by heat and flames. Carve and handle your rabbit stick or weapon of choice (see "Hunting Tools," page 157) with clean hands, and either stain it with smoke or rub it lightly with charcoal to hide any bright white carving marks.

It is time to start. There are many animals whose meat can make a nice addition to a wild food diet, and there are many hunting tools with which to take them. This example will describe a hunt using a rabbit stick, and the quarry will be a woodchuck.

Approach your hunting area carefully. Pay attention to the wind, the sun, and anything else that might give away your location. When you spot the woodchuck, watch it for a moment before you begin stalking it. Do not look directly at the animal. Watch it only in full-view vision, because an animal's sensitivity is acute; the hunt could be over before it starts. As you stalk, note whether the animal is wary or if it is feeding contentedly. Take note of the direction it is moving, and then try to predict where it may be in twenty minutes. If you make a noise, you may have to remain motionless for a time until the animal settles and resumes its normal activity.

As you approach, bring your rabbit stick to the ready so that once the animal is in range, you have only to release the weapon without having to cock it back. Once you throw the rabbit stick and hit the animal, move to it quickly and quietly. Be ready to give a killing blow if necessary. If your initial strike only wounds your prey, you must keep the woodchuck from escaping to its hole, where it may die a longer and more painful death, leaving you hungry and feeling terrible.

A mortally wounded animal may sprint off into cover, exhibiting no signs of serious injury, only to collapse shortly after reaching "safety." If your quarry successfully reaches cover and you believe you had a solid strike, stay put. An injured animal will often lay up in a thicket to recover or rest, and you may startle it into flight and be unable to follow and catch it. After waiting for about twenty to thirty minutes, slowly stalk toward the place you initially struck the animal and check for visible tracks or a blood trail. Follow the trail as best you can, weapon at the ready, and scan the area. If you get a second shot, make it count.

The best advice is to practice, practice, and practice some more!

Injuring an animal is worse than killing it. If it is dead, you can make sure that its body is appreciated and fully utilized. Every time you use a tool that incorporates some of that animal's body, you can't help but give thanks. However, an animal's injury without death takes an unknown toll not only on the animal but also on you as you wonder what is to become of it. Good can come in the form of valuable lessons in a botched hunt. When you injure an animal, you note the mistakes you made and vow, for the injured animal's sake, to never repeat them.

There is no substitute for practice. Every landscape is unique in some way or another, and the only way to find out the best way to hunt a given area is to stalk and hunt there.

Practice hard, hunt well, and give thanks.

For proper care of the carcass, see "Carcass Care"(page 54). And be sure to check local hunting regulations for learning acceptable methods of taking game and how you can obtain a hunting license.

(continued from page 95)

Woodchucks are remarkably tough creatures. This one was not about to roll over and die for us. Her hide was thick, her disposition sharp. Quite an animal.

On we continued, noticing accumulations of pine pitch in holes created by pileated woodpeckers feeding on carpenter ants. We crossed a highway and entered a swamp with meandering creeks and waterways. Muskrat sign was plentiful. Deer and other animals left sign as well.

We stumbled upon a pair of jumping mice that gracefully leaped ahead of us in a high-arcing trajectory. As we followed, we watched them plunge into a waterway. They swam with such ease, rapidly propelling themselves across open waters. Their beautiful two-toned coats barely entered water, as they swam so high out of the stream. A wonderful encounter! Although a fairly common track, I've only seen jumping mice a few times in the wild.

As we looped back to camp, we grazed on raspberries and selected deer bones from a skeleton we found for various projects. We also collected cattails and hauled them in bundles on our heads, gathering pitch and cached woodchuck along the way. A woodchuck meal and beautiful sunset followed. As the blood red sun disappeared behind the western hill, the bottoms of the clouds turned hot pink with accents of orange. A breeze blew our smoke northeast. We hoped it would not bring rain.

As night moved in around us, I laid back to relax and watch treetops sway. The silhouette of a flying squirrel soared above us from tree to tree. Flickering firelight caught its white undersides. I find hickories and acorns opened by these squirrels frequently, so I'd say there are many on this hill.

Day 17

We made an early morning cattail run. Our shelter is coming along—maybe one more cattail run to finish it. The wind is whipping through our camp, the trees bending and swaying. Wind cleans areas, bringing new energy while moving out the old. I feel so refreshed, so invigorated, sitting in wind.

I discovered a wild pear tree to the northeast. The small fruits are not quite ready, but I'll be visiting again when they are. As I explored, I visited a massive raspberry patch. First I gorged to fill my belly, then gathered extra berries to experiment with drying the fruit for future use.

(continued on page 105)

Preserving and Storing Food

Hunting and food gathering are necessary components of natural living but should not consume all of your time. As seasons change, various edibles come and go, and with this in mind, we gathered beyond one meal's worth of food when opportunities presented themselves.

PRESERVING BERRIES

Here in the northeast corner of the United States, summertime is filled with an abundance of berries—more than Mark and I could possibly eat, and not for lack of trying. (Any trackers on our trail would have thought there were a couple of huge raccoons in the area if they were to come across any of our scat!) In order to capitalize on the abundance of raspberries near our camp before they passed their

prime, we harvested many baskets and brought them to camp to dry them. We crushed our berries into a jamlike consistency on our frying rock (see "Making Camp," page 32), then spread the berry paste evenly over it. The rock was then propped at a steep angle facing a bed of coals in the fire pit.

It is important that you not cook or burn the mush, only dry it. A good gauge is to watch the drippings; if they start smoking, pull the rock back carefully. Keep monitoring the berry mush until the steam coming off it is greatly reduced. Then set the rock aside to cool. It will take some trial and error until you get it just right.

If you leave the mashed berries near the heat for a shorter period of time, you will end up with sticky fruit leather, whereas longer exposure will result in fruit chips (easily reconstituted with water). The chips will last indefinitely *if* they are kept dry—a tall order in humid conditions. A good idea is to store them in a well-dried-out pine bark box in the rafters of your shelter or in a protected location where the heat of your fire will regularly dry the air around them.

PRESERVING MEAT BY DRYING

The meat we eat nowadays is so full of spices, preservatives, and foreign flavors that few people can really differentiate between venison and beef. This is not to suggest that all meat prepared in the wild must be eaten with no spices, but merely that the true flavor should not be drowned out, only enhanced. Contrary to popular belief, all meat does not taste like chicken, and each has its own unique qualities and flavors.

Why Dry Meat?

Without the aid of cold weather to preserve meat, utilizing an entire deer carcass before it begins to rot requires a great many mouths, a large appetite, or another way of preserving it, such as drying. Survival has traditionally been a group effort, with each person specializing in a few skill areas. This made for easier utilization of a large animal carcass and therefore was not as daunting a task as it was for an individual.

Drying the meat of an entire deer carcass is not difficult, but it is time consuming, and in warm weather you must tend the meat and fire continually. The first time I dried the meat of a deer, it took two and a half days. My weather-forecasting skills, or lack thereof, detected rain only once it started falling; thus, a big, sustained fire was needed to keep the meat from spoiling.

There are a few important points to keep in mind when drying meat. One: The goal is to *dry* the meat in a number of hours, not cook it. Cooked meat will spoil and bad meat will make you sick. Two: Flies must be kept away from the meat, and the meat must be kept clean prior to drying. A fresh piece of meat dropped on the ground will have all manner of things stuck to it, both visible and microscopic. I use the animal's hide as a work surface for the meat as I prepare it for the rack. Three: Wide crossbars on the rack will prevent speedy drying of the meat that is in contact with the wood and will require regular shifting to expose its entirety to warm, dry air.

There are three major steps to follow to preserve meat by drying: prepare a drying rack, prepare the meat, and tend to the fire.

PREPARE A DRYING RACK

Do this before you even begin to hunt. Drying racks are simple affairs.

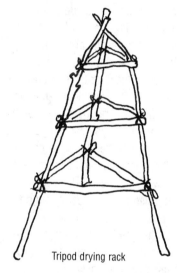

Tripod drying rack

Larger constructions have a main skeleton of heavier sticks (one to two inches in diameter) for support and thinner cross-sticks on which to hang the meat. Smaller racks can be built entirely out of thin (one-half inch in diameter) sticks. Make your rack free-standing and sturdy enough to be moved when loaded with meat. Note: Large animals may require more than one rack.

PREPARE THE MEAT

For gutting and skinning the animal, see "Carcass Care," page 54. Here I will deal with a skinned and gutted carcass either hanging from a tree or laying on the green hide. It is a good idea to have a fire next to your work area to help keep flies away.

1. Remove the fat and separate the muscle groups (meat is muscle and is divided into easily definable pieces separated by a thin membrane) in the hindquarters.
2. Work your way up the carcass toward the head. Some parts, like the ribs, may be put directly on the fire for immediate consumption.
3. Set aside a choice bit like the tenderloins or a piece of the back strap; the rest is for jerky.
4. Looking at the meat, you will notice that it has a "grain" formed of parallel muscle strands.

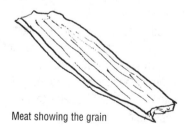

Meat showing the grain

Tough jerky is cut along the grain (the same direction as the muscle fiber), and soft jerky is cut across the grain. I like it either way. A piece of pine bark, inner side up, works well as a cutting board (see "Bark Containers," page 111). The meat is sliced into one-eighth-inch-thick pieces and as long and wide as is manageable.

5. If you've harvested some spices, now is a good time to rub them into the meat. Garlic mustard, wild leeks, wild garlic, chives, and other mustards are some of my favorites. Look in a field guide to find out what is in season, and make sure you are 100 percent positive of the plant's identity and edibility.

6. Place the pieces of meat on the rack close together but not touching.

TEND TO THE FIRE

Tending the fire is important, as is the meat's proximity to the fire. For small quantities of meat, I'll place the rack on the leeward side of the fire so that the breeze blows warm, dry air over it. If it is windy, you can create a windbreak with stacked wood, hide/cloth, or stone. Better yet, you can find a more sheltered area in which to work. At no time should the meat be hot to the touch. You should be able to place your hand anywhere over the rack and keep it there indefinitely, but you should also be able to feel the constant warmth of the fire. Once the drying process starts, you need to keep at it until the meat is dry. The jerky should be dry enough to crack when bent but not brittle. Nor should it be greasy or shiny. Shininess often reveals fat in the meat, which must be removed in order to prevent the meat from becoming rancid.

PEMMICAN

Pemmican is a mixture of rendered fat, jerky, and dried berries. Because fat is flammable, a great way to render it in a primitive situation is to rock-boil water and add chunks of fat to it. It takes a lot of hot rocks, but the end results are great. When the fat chunks have been greatly reduced or have disappeared altogether, any chunks floating on top should be removed along with any impurities you can see. Let the water cool. When the fat is cool, it will congeal, and you can lift it off the water. You can grind up jerky and dried fruit between two stones or pulverize them with a stick, then add them to the fat. Stuff the mixture into rawhide containers (see "Rawhide and Sinew," page 221) for storage. As long as it is kept dry, pemmican will last indefinitely.

(continued from page 101)

The constant breeze has allowed for an experience I haven't had since winter. I sat in field and forest without the buzzing and biting of gnats and mosquitoes. What a huge relief. Without distraction, I sat like a stump, silent and still, absorbing the natural cycles around me.

David returned to camp as the sun became red, carrying three sunfish. He was ecstatic. Cordage and bone hooks had worked, and we all reaped the benefits.

Day 18

David and I woke early to try our luck with bone hooks in a small pond on the next hill, where Mike had seen the shadows of large bass in the cattails the day before. The fields were carpeted in white as the seed heads of grass held the morning dew; it could have been the first frost of late fall. Our bare feet were soaked within steps.

The pond was small and still, a hollow between two hills. Murky waters reflected the massive hickories to our east, and cattails lined the far bank. We cast and cast, each of our hooks baited with crayfish. Both of us had nibbles, nothing more.

We met Mike on our return, who had been hunting. We peered into another pond bathed in morning sun. In the shallows were masses of tiny blood-red worms, filter feeding like the feathery appendages of barnacles. When we touched or poked them, they would quickly withdraw into tiny holes in the mud, but would reappear to feed moments later.

We made another cattail run as a group, and were thrilled to discover a small patch of ground-

Bone hook

nut. We collected the bulbous roots for dinner, which are cooked and taste like potatoes. Hauling massive bundles of cattails was draining. Our camp was atop a steep ridge that required sections of crawling: visitor unfriendly. My legs burned with each step.

David was heading home again. He's clear how this is not his time for survival. He prefers to spend time trying new skills and worrying less about food. Mike and I were off to try new fish spears upriver. We've been without rain for a bit except for a quick shower last evening.

The first pool we encountered provided habitat for a school of suckers and a few trout. I began stalking deeper into cold water. Frigid stream crept up my inner thigh, and I paused just before the cold water reached that crucial part of a man's anatomy. I took a deep breath and was up to my waist. Standing still with spear poised, like a great blue heron, I began to separate sucker from trout. The mottled skin of trout blends so well with stony streams. As I continued to stare, I was suddenly able to discern trout shapes among rocks in the current. Brook trout also have white edges along their fins, which helped to further differentiate fish from stone and trout from sucker.

I selected a trout and began to stalk forward. Mike, on the shore closest to the trout, offered his opinion on the distance between spear and fish. I closed in, leaned forward, quickly prayed I'd catch the fish, and lunged. A cloud of silt whirled up about the spear. I held firm, spear embedded in the stream floor. I felt a wiggle—I had him! Not quite, actually. In chest-deep water, it was difficult to submerge and still keep the fish pinned. Mike came to the rescue and held the spear down from land. I submerged and found the gills, which I used as a handle. I reemerged, trout held high, and let loose an exuberant yell. A twelve-inch trout, a beautiful beast! The high lasted some time before I realized how cold I was—chest-deep in cool water in the shade. Spearfishing is yet another skill that completely immerses you in nature.

I speared two more trout further upstream and caught my first fish by hand. Mike also caught two by hand. We feasted on six trout seasoned with wild garlic and pennycress, which we call

Self portrait; pinning a fish for Mike

"jimmies," because they look like the chocolate sprinkles that cover ice cream cones. We wrapped chunks of cooked, boneless trout in garlic mustard leaves and popped them into our mouths. What a day; what a meal! I closed my eyes, and the flavor seemed appropriate for the finest New York City restaurants. Today we were not "surviving," we were living like yuppies.

Food seems to be coming in fairly regularly, but we all still tease each other with fantasies of sweets and modern meals. The toughest part is not filling the gaping hole in your stomach but ignoring the mental desires for a more varied diet. Of course, if I knew more plants and more about wilderness cooking, I'd be able to further diversify my diet.

The dried raspberry experiment worked well—a fruit leather with magnificent flavor.

DAY 19

Last evening, I began to feel a bit headachy. I passed it off as a lack of water, but it persisted. We lounged about, then decided to hunt and explore down valley. I stalked several woodchucks but was unsuccessful. I watched one animal strip the leaves of goldenrods for food. I never knew they ate goldenrod. Watching animals yields so much. Even a glimpse teaches you immeasurable amounts about movement and behavior.

Last night, I watched the sun set over the western hill and continued to sit as dusk settled. A changing of the guard occurred all about me. Flying barn swallows and catbirds were joined by chimney swifts and waves of bats. The bats displayed such prowess of flight, looping, diving, and spinning to catch insects.

I slept poorly last night. I awoke feeling very hot and my mouth, lips, and tongue were dry. It was still dark outside. The birds had not yet begun to sing. I pushed holes in the door and stretched for fresh air. A cool breeze trickled in, refreshing me. Mosquitoes began to fly about my head. I managed catnaps for the remainder of the night.

As dawn approached, the first bird to sing was the peewee. It sang single solemn notes with great silent lengths in between each note. It never completed its songs. After some time, the tanager joined in, and eventually a veery, a hermit thrush, then others.

With predawn light, I pushed through the door and lay outside. I was groggy, cotton-mouthed, overheated, and feeling a bit like I had the flu. I decided to wear shoes and socks, because I didn't have the energy to concentrate on walking right away—a strange contradiction, because I was off to hunt.

I headed straight for drinkable water and refueled. I felt exhausted and ill. I had to hunt, though. I wandered fields looking for woodchucks and was surprised to see absolutely none at this hour. I saw only a few deer, and that was about it.

I paused often to regain energy. I stared at the dewdrops on red clover to distract my mind from my body. The flowers looked frosted; they were covered in tiny droplets—their hairy stalks illuminated by water. I don't know if I'd consciously recognized their hairy stalks before. They were beautiful.

I took another long break next to a pond. Steam crossed the pond and swirled upward into the air in two places. All the steam on the left side of the pond swirled up in one spot, and all the steam on the right accumulated in another spot. Why two spots? I wondered. I closed my eyes momentarily, and when I opened them, the right spot had disappeared. All the steam rolled along the surface and swirled upward in the place on the left side, venturing high above the trees before dissipating.

I lounged on a flat rock in a field, hoping to feel better. But I did not improve, so I headed for more water and then back to camp. I met Mike along the way, who had discovered on a hill to the south a small stream that had recently dried up. He had found and gathered fifty to sixty tiny bass flipping about in the mud.

We roasted them on sharp sticks. Mike absolutely loved them. He claimed he was eating gourmet. I tolerated them, preferring the flavor of woodchuck jerky.

I was still feeling woozy and not up to par. I worked on the group shelter a bit—it would be nice when finished. I thought I'd take the day easy, performing tasks that could be done sitting, and see what happened.

The cicadas were singing today. Either this was the first day or I've been oblivious thus far. Cicadas have a fascinating life cycle. Females cut slits in tree branches, where they lay their eggs. The nymphs hatch and drop to the ground, where they burrow into the ground and feed on root systems for four to twenty years before climbing a tree and emerging as an adult. Nature never ceases to amaze me.

I accompanied Mike on a hike. My body was so hot I just wore shorts, exchanging cooler temperatures for mosquito bites. I dipped in the stream to lower my body temperature, and this was effective for a short while. Maybe I'm cleansing, trying to burn something up in my body. I forgot to mention that I started the day with two cases of diarrhea. Something's not right.

I napped in the afternoon in the debris hut to escape mosquitoes. There is a brown cricketlike species that lives in the wall near my head. I'd thought the noises I'd heard during the night were some sort of chewing, but in the light, I saw the two spines that projected from its abdomen rub together to create the sounds.

I hadn't been up long when David returned from town with the good news that David's girlfriend, Leah, and Kayla would visit in about a week. We then discussed diet and lethargy, and he agreed a lack of carbohydrates might be the cause of my illness.

So we set out to dig roots, to see if they would help. We harvested burdock and wild leeks along the stream near a popular hiking trail leading to a pond. While we dug about in the earth, shin-deep in leeks and Virginia creepers, a family hiked by carrying swimming and picnic gear. We sat twenty feet from the trail in plain view, yet only the youngest, about five years old, looked in our direction. It seemed as if some part of her was aware of our presence, but not consciously. Modern education had perhaps beaten intuition and vigilant attention out of her elder companions. Luckily, they can be revitalized with coaxing and practice.

DAY 20

I awoke fairly early, again uncomfortably hot—unhealthily so. Luckily, there was water in camp, which I poured down my throat. I sat next to the fire pit, cooling slowly, adding leaf litter to the remaining coals to keep the merciless mosquitoes at bay. I slept on and off another hour before the others joined me.

We spent the morning making new cooking containers, because bark containers wear out with use. We're hoping to fire some pots soon, for longer-lasting cookware. As the morning progressed, I began to feel better. We all agreed to convene at the most recently felled pine when the sun was directly above to go "crayfishing" for dinner.

Arriving first, I sat down at the steam edge to await the others. A kingfisher landed just across the stream, and shortly

(continued on page 114)

Cooking Containers

Myths are plentiful about possible cooking containers if metal ones are not available. When you are in the outdoors, four materials are available for making cooking containers.

1. *Hide:* Unfortunately, hide is not durable enough for cooking containers (it will work for only five to eight meals). It requires a successful hunt and seems like a waste. Hides are not easy to come by.
2. *Stone:* Stone containers are time-consuming to make and hard to lug around. Your best stone option is a pothole in a stone riverbank. These are usually found where water has cut through rock for thousands of years and formed rounded holes of varying size and depth. Even then, it needs to be cleaned, and during the cooking process the surrounding rock will absorb plenty of heat.
3. *Clay:* This is a good option but also requires a lot of work and extensive processing. Plus, the results are not guaranteed. It is, however, an excellent choice for a long-term stay.
4. *Bark or wood:* Of the options listed, bark and wood are often the most accessible and are definitely the fastest choice. They are discussed below in more detail.

BARK CONTAINERS

Of all the barks I have tried, that of the eastern white pine has proven to be the best. Other good barks come from birch, tulip poplar, cedar (eastern and western), and elm, but you should experiment with others. Historically, birch bark was used because it could be harvested and dried in flat sheets. When needed, it was merely heated to regain its pliability. Birch bark also has a natural preservative.

A suitable tree or branch for harvest is one that has smooth bark and can provide enough material in one piece for your project. Bark can be harvested from a live tree with little chance of killing it as long as you do not remove so much that you girdle the tree. Harvesting a whole tree and making many containers is also an option.

When you look for a tree to harvest, seek out one that makes ecological sense to remove. This would mean a tree that is either going to die in the next few years or one that is crowding out more desired plant species. A tree that is going to die could be one that will clearly be crowded out in the next few years or perhaps one that has begun to fall, toppled by heavy winds or stream-bank erosion. Whatever the case, survey the surrounding area and think about how the removal of the tree will affect the area over the next few years. When its removal lets more light in for other plants, how will they respond? What would happen if the tree were left standing? Would it survive? The goal in tree selection is to be as sure as you can that the tree's removal is more beneficial to the area than if it were left standing.

Some barks, such as cedar and elm, take more care to bend. These must be scored along the fold or bend lines. Whether you score the inside or the outside of the bark is up to you, although scoring the outside has a couple of benefits. First, the outside bark is often less flexible and is liable to break or peel away from the inner layer, weakening it. This can lead to leaks. Second, the flexible fibers are on the inside of the bark, not the rough outer portion, and scoring on the inside cuts some of them and reduces the number of effective fibers.

Apparently, scoring on the inside is more common today, the idea being that the tough outer bark will protect the fold lines. But of all the books I've read mentioning bark

containers, only one speaks of scoring the outside, and this was only in reference to an undated museum piece. Both ways seem to work well, so see which suits your needs.

1. Fell the branch or tree.
2. Make cuts all the way through the bark.

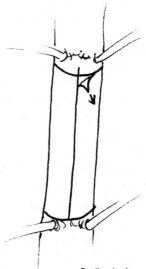

Peeling bark

3. Gently peel up one corner of the piece of bark with a knife or your fingertip. Then, with your fingers sliding up and down the straight cut, separate the bark from the log. If you remove the bark from a fresh-cut tree or limb, it will come off easily and have the pliability of green hide.
4. Small strips of the inner bark of a pine tree work well for tying and stitching. Care must be taken when making holes for stitching.

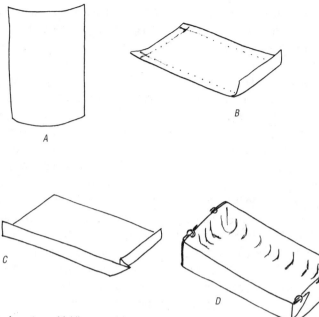

The four steps of folding a container

Due to the straight grain of the bark, ripping is a threat. Use a small, blunt twig as an awl, twisting as you push it *gently* through the bark. When stitching and tying, do not cinch down too tightly, as tearing can result.

Any container that can be folded from paper can be made with pine bark.

The container will stiffen within a few days and can be used regularly for both cooking (rock boiling) and eating. It is possible to cook directly on the coals one or two times. The bark will burn to the water line and the outer bark will also burn off, leaving a very thin, fragile layer.

WOOD CONTAINERS

Finding a piece of wood suitable for making a bowl is a trick in itself. In the absence of a saw or an ax, large pieces of wood can be found and burned down to a workable size. This is done by slowly burning away unwanted material, frequently removing it from the fire and scraping away the charcoal to help prevent your piece from cracking. If the process is rushed, large cracks can appear and ruin the project. Cracks are not always bad, however; sometimes you can exploit them by driving a wedge of stone or hardwood into them, splitting the log in half and saving yourself time.

Once a manageable piece is secured, you can hollow it into a bowl by placing a small heap of hardwood coals on the area you wish to hollow out. By blowing softly on the heap either with your mouth or through a hollow tube, the coals will burn into the wood. Blowing on the coals is optional when you are working with a small pile of them; however, if a breeze is blowing, make sure to turn your bowl now and then to avoid burning out one side. Periodically remove the coals and scrape out the charcoal. Add more coals and continue. If an area is becoming too thin, place sand, stone, or mud over it to prevent further burning. If you see flames, dump the coals in the firepit and scrape the bowl. Flames indicate too much heat and are a sure sign that cracks will soon appear if you don't act quickly.

Spoons can be made in the same manner. Carve out a spoon blank (a piece of wood made to look roughly like a spoon), and use a single coal held in place with a stick. Blow with long, slow breaths on the coal, dump it in the fire pit, and scrape out the charcoal. Use a blunt stick as a scraper to avoid scoring the inside of the project. A little sand placed in the bowl and rubbed around works well as sandpaper. Once you're satisfied with the "bowl," finish carving the spoon to your liking.

(continued from page 110)

afterwards Mike approached and sat down. No words were spoken, and we both watched the nearby bird. Kingfishers are remarkably hard to approach and extremely skittish. The beautiful bird sat motionless, her blue headdress in perfect form. The red belt under her blue collar, which is absent in males, was stunning and accentuated by her white chest. As the bird switched

views on the surrounding pools, she would simultaneously flick her head and tail upward. The bird's amazing beak was longer than her head.

We watched and watched, enthralled by such distinctive features. With a rattle call, her mate approached and landed a few feet from us. Two stunning birds fishing under a hazy sun. Suddenly, the male dropped into a pool and was off downstream, prize in beak, female in pursuit. David had not appeared, so Mike and I moved on.

Crayfishing lasted maybe twenty minutes before it became an expedition focused on hand fishing for trout. I was the first to become distracted when I discovered a sizable fish under a rock I had checked for crayfish. There was no other exit for this fish, so I reached in, cornered it, found a handle, and pulled it out—the first trout catch we deemed opportunistic living. We still planned to gather crayfish.

Then we heard children's voices. Mike and I slipped up the bank and they clambered into view upstream. The group hiked toward us in the stream, armored with rubber soles and swimsuits. The counselor stopped at the pool just below us and said, "Look at the fish." They all filed up, half looking, half joking with each other. One girl asked if they would bite her.

Mike and I lay several feet above their heads, but they never looked up. They were too concerned with where their feet would land in the stream. A second counselor announced, "Well, we'll stay here and wash our hair." We silently crept off to collect our dinner elsewhere.

Just a bit upstream, Mike glimpsed a massive trout as it sought refuge in a hole under the bank. He had to have it. He submerged his body and reached under as far as his body allowed. His faced was etched with determination and contorted as he tried to gain a few more inches. Eventually, he pulled forth about a seventeen-and-a-half-inch trout (Mike's hand has a spread of nine inches, or so he says). Wow, what a fish for this stream. It was enormous.

I caught one next, then Mike caught one, then I got one again. The feel of trout on your fingertips is incredible. You "tickle" them and they press into you. Beautiful fish. David joined us and wanted to catch one so badly, he stayed until he had caught two.

Dinner in hand, we turned to collecting bulrush seeds to make a carb-loaded gruel that would help us gain energy and balance. Roots had definitely helped, and we hoped a gruel would complete the healing.

Hand drill

So what's a meal like up here anyway? Meals are quite an affair indeed. Tonight, I built the tipi of small twigs and prepared a tinder bundle, while David created a coal from friction and abrasion between two pieces of black birch. The coal was cradled in tinder and blown into flame. The flame ignited the tipi, cooking rocks were added, and the fire was built up around them.

(continued on page 118)

Tipi Fires

How do you build a fire that can be lit with only one match or a coal in any weather? Use the form of a tipi. A well-built tipi fire can burn with no attention for extended periods of time, because as the wood burns, it collapses inward, thus feeding itself. Also, as heat rises, it passes around the wood. This means that, in wet weather, the wood in the tipi fire begins drying the moment the tinder is ignited. Finally, the outer firewood protects the flame from severe weather, be it snow, rain, or wind.

TIPI FIRE COMPONENTS

Tinder
True tinder consists of any dry, thin, flammable material that, when nested around a coal, can be blown into a flame. The following are all good for your tinder bundle: the outer bark of red cedar; the inner bark of any dead poplar, basswood, or maple tree; dry grasses; cattail down; cottonwood cotton; and milkweed fibers and down. The downy materials are good additives but do not make very good tinder on their own. Buff or briskly rub the other tinder between your hands to separate the fibers. This promotes brisk burning when the tinder is ignited.

Fine Kindling
This kindling can be lit with a small flame from a match or a tinder bundle. Kindling that can be lit with a flame includes pine needles (which

can also be used with a coal in a pinch), birch bark, freshly dried strips of pine bark cambium, the smallest of branches, and other woody materials. Dead hemlock branch ends are also superb, as is dried flood debris from along streams.

Rough Kindling

Thin, dry branches and plant stalks up to the thickness of a pencil make great rough kindling to get the fire going.

First Wood

The first wood that you add to your fire should be the thickness of a pencil to that of your wrist. This wood helps ignite the actual firewood.

Firewood

Firewood should be the thickness of your wrist or larger. It is used to keep a fire burning for extended periods of time.

COLLECTING WOOD

Dry wood burns far better than wet or green wood and is *necessary* for starting fires. Because wood on the ground tends to absorb moisture, try to use *dead* branches from trees that are either alive or dead and that are still standing. Check with local authorities about regulations regarding the harvesting of wood. Even during wet weather, branches on trees are surrounded by air and dried by the wind. Even if a branch is wet on the outside, the inside is usually dry. If you have any doubts, break a piece of wood. If it snaps in two without much bending, it should be good to use.

A broken branch can be held against your upper lip, which is highly sensitive to moisture, as another "dry test."

When you are collecting firewood, keep in mind that it is not necessary to break all of it into eighteen-inch lengths. Let the fire work for you and burn longer logs into shorter logs Caution: Be knowledgeable about fire danger in your area, and always keep the fire contained within your fire pit. See "Making Camp" [page 32] for more on fire pits.

BUILDING YOUR TIPI FIRE

1. Take a handful of twelve-inch fine kindling and rough kindling in both hands, thumbs down, and bend or break it in the middle (they need not separate).
2. Place the kindling in your fire pit and form it into a rough tipi or triangular shape. Use your thumbs to ensure that you have a doorway and an open area inside for the tinder. Face the opening to the wind to help spread the fire into the tipi.
3. Lay on more kindling and first wood, starting with smaller

pieces and building up until your tipi is big enough for the job.

4. Practice making fires of different sizes in a safe location, such as a riverbed (if flash floods are not a threat), to determine what size is adequate for various needs.

5. Set aside wood of all sizes to cover your tipi door once the tinder is lit and placed inside. If you are using a coal to start your fire, either ignite your tinder and place it in the tipi, or place the smoking tinder bundle into the tipi just prior to ignition. Give it a final breath of air once it is in place. Then just cover the door and sit back. The fire should need no tinkering for some time.

(continued from page 117)

Mike held cooking containers made from white pine bark that were folded and sewn so they could hold water. He stuffed them with greens and roots to prepare for the addition of cooking rocks. He had piled various seasonings for the fish along bark strips, which we used as plates. He lined up the fish, calculated even amounts, and found skewers for roasting. We had tried baking trout in grape leaves and cooking them on rocks, but we preferred roasting trout until we heard the sounds of skin bubbling and juice dripped into the flames.

We always started with the smallest fish and worked our way up. We had discovered that with trout—which isn't true for all foods—the larger the fish, the more tender, the more flavorful, and the more juicy. By the time we ate the first few fish, the rocks were ready. We boiled our veggie stew and served it with the remaining fish. I ate the two together—layers of cooked greens and trout. Mike and David alternated between them.

Overall, our meal was superb. The large trout had pink meat, like salmon. It also remained pink when cooked, unlike the smaller fish, which turned white. We then lounged around the fire. We often joked about desserts. Mike smoked a cigarette, leaning against an oak, then said he'd quit soon. David returned to a project—he never sits still. I usually lean back and watch for the silhouettes of southern flying squirrels in the last remnants of evening light, enjoying the productivity of being nonproductive.

(continued on page 120)

Rock Boiling

Rock boiling is a technique whereby rocks heated in a fire are used to cook or purify liquids such as soup or water. You will need the following items:

- A waterproof container (stone, bark, or other)
- Eight egg-sized stones (per half gallon of soup)
- A pair of tongs (see "Making Camp," page 32)
- A good fire

Follow these steps:

1. Collect your rocks. If you gathered them in a water-rich area such as a creek bed or lakeshore, heat them slowly and/or keep out of the fire area to avoid injury due to exploding rocks. (Some rocks have small cracks that are invisible to the human eye. Over time, these cracks allow water to enter. When the rock is heated, the water in the stone turns to steam and leaves through the crack by which it entered, or expands faster than the crack can accommodate, and breaks the rock. Often, the rock simply falls apart because there is not enough room within the stone to allow pressure to build up. However, sometimes there is room and the pressure builds to such a level that the rock explodes with potentially deadly force. Quartz rocks are known for exploding because of the many cavities found within them where steam pressure can build.)

2. Place the rocks in a hardwood fire, leaving a few inches between each rock to allow for better heating.

3. Fill the container (see "Cooking Containers," page 111) one half full of water or soup and wait for the rocks to heat (it will take about forty-five minutes) until they are glowing hot.

4. Remove rocks from the fire with tongs, and carefully blow the ash from both. Slowly lower the rocks into the liquid, and keep adding rocks until a boil is achieved (a half gallon of water requires three to five egg-sized rocks and about thirty seconds; eight rocks were suggested to account for some breakage and/or to maintain a boil for a few minutes). To maintain a boil, periodically remove stones and add more hot rocks.

(continued from page 118)

There were no wrappers to throw away, no wasted containers or plastics. All refuse was burned or left away from camp for others to eat. Even our bark containers will eventually return to the earth. When we tear out the fire pit and sprinkle debris across the area, only skilled trackers will know we had ever been here.

DAY 21

I had another hot night, but I'm feeling better. The weather the last few days has been extremely hot and muggy. Mike and I started the day with a good bowl of gruel. We worked on new ideas for canteens, then hiked to look for more bulrush seeds and berries. Low-bush blueberries were ripe in places.

We discovered the nest of a warbling vireo, a bird you usually hear rather than see. It made quite a fuss, calling continuously, while coming down to our level. Round and round the vireo circled, calling, calling, calling. A female redstart came to see what all the fuss was about and silently moved on.

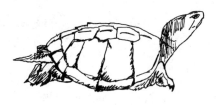

We all collected crayfish during the afternoon, and we caught a small snapper. We studied its feet for a while and finally let it go in a nice plot of mud for tracks. Mike and I had recently been discussing snapping turtle tracks, so it was a wonderful opportunity to watch them being made. The snapper also left us a scat to marvel over, an interesting crescent-shaped deposit reminiscent of toad scat.

DAY 22

I awoke hot, of course. As I lay in my shelter, I listened to David approach. He knelt outside my debris hut and began gulping water. I listened as he gulped and gulped and gulped. It was community water, but the night before I had asked the two of them if I might put it outside my hut, explaining how I had been waking so hot. No one minded. There was enough for all of us to start the day. But, as I listened to David's endless gulping, I began to worry.

I pushed at my door and watched David walk away. He didn't turn to say "good morning" or acknowledge me in any way. I reached for the container and discovered he had left nothing but a debris-ridden corner of swill. I was most perturbed. David had been angry with me the day before, because I'd told him he was too competitive, and I felt this was his passive-aggressive way of pushing me.

It must be noted how short my patience had become in the last few days. I wiggled out of my debris hut and grabbed the container. On my way to the fire circle, I decided not to con-

(continued on page 125)

Liquids, Water Gathering, and Purification

If you were thirsty while out in the wild, where would you find a drink?

I grew up drinking from streams and lakes and never suffered any illness because of it. However, I can recall a time when a fellow drank from the same spot I did and became ill by the end of the day. It is a risk to drink from any untested body of water. If you are in doubt, purify water by boiling or filtration. Obtaining a drink from other sources is also an option.

SAP

Tree Sap

In the spring, during cycles when the temperature drops below freezing at night and warms up during the day, sap will run in the trees. Fresh sap from some trees is delicious and safe to drink. Maple, walnut, and black birch trees can be tapped in the following manner:

1. On the side of the tree that is exposed to the sun, carve, chop, or abrade a vertical channel through the bark and into the green wood.
2. At the bottom of this channel, bore a hole with a knife tip or sharp stone, and hammer in a pointy, fire-hardened twig or stick in such a way that it slopes gently downward.
3. Add channels radiating out from the center channel at an upward angle.

4. Place a container at the base of the tree, under the lower end of the protruding twig or stick, to catch the sap.
5. As the sap moves in the tree, it will flow from the grooves into the central channel, and from there it will move to the twig, drip off the end, and collect in the container.
6. Boiling the sap down will give you ever thicker and sweeter syrup as the water evaporates, leaving behind the sugars and other flavors. The pure sap, however, is delicious and safe to drink. Forty gallons of sugar maple sap will provide one gallon of syrup. Twice that amount is required for birch.

Grapevine Sap

Grapevines can be cut and the sap collected in the spring and fall by the following method:

1. Cut a grapevine three to five feet above the ground.
2. Bend the vine over and, if need be, tie it so that the fast-dripping sap falls into a container.
3. Re-cut the vine end every day or so to maintain a flow; otherwise, the plant will heal enough to stop the flow altogether.

SURFACE WATER

Surface water from streams, ponds, and the like may require some sort of purification prior to consumption. Filters to remove sediment and other larger debris can be made with clothing or layers of grass, charcoal, and sand, but it is boiling that ensures a safe drink. According to the National Ski Patrol, bringing water just to a boil will kill almost all harmful viruses, protozoa, and bacteria. The Centers for Disease Control and Prevention (CDC) advises bringing water at elevations from sea level to sixty-five hundred feet to a rolling boil for one minute, then allowing it to cool to an ambient temperature. Above sixty-five hundred feet, CDC suggests maintaining a rolling boil for three minutes. (For more on boiling, see "Rock Boiling" on page 119.) If you choose to drink from a stream, do so from an area that has a good, steady flow, such as from near the bottom of rapids or riffles.

Other Ways to Gather Surface Water

- Clothing can be used to soak up dew by dragging it or brushing it over grasses and then wringing the moisture out into a container. Let the water stand, skim off anything floating on the surface, and carefully pour off the water into a clean container without disturbing any sediment on the bottom.
- Catchments can be made from bark or clothing to collect rainwater.
- Springs come in many forms. In

the Northeast, seeps are the most common, often appearing as small, moist areas of earth. They can be dug out into shallow depressions and allowed to fill. Once the sediment has settled, water can be drawn off the top. Springs vary in form from area to area and from one season to another, and seeps are by no means the only form a spring will take. In the Southeast, I have found hillsides where holes the size of quarters spout clean water in wet times and seep in dry times. In the West, I have seen some extreme springs where holes I could fit in gushed water at such a rate it was almost impossible to force my body down against the current.

SUBSURFACE WATER

Digging is sometimes the best way to secure water. In a number of situations, digging a hole (seep hole) and allowing it to fill with water is the easiest option.

You should not dig a hole in any random spot and expect to find water. The best option is to look for water indicators. Dry creek beds are good places to dig, because often the water is still flowing fairly close to the surface. Wetland trees (willows, basswoods, cottonwoods, and sycamores, to name a few) require a fair amount of water and are usually good indicators of water near

the surface. I have never had to dig more than three feet using such indicators and have often found water seeping in in less than two.

Other good places to dig are near swamps, lakes, or moving water. In these situations, digging a seep hole will provide somewhat filtered water, as opposed to collecting water directly from the source.

Along the coast, where saltwater is abundant and freshwater harder to find, animals like coyotes dig down at the lowest points of dunes, where wind has carved out swales. Mark Elbroch found a number of such "wells" and noted that deer, crows, and other animals were able to capitalize on the coyotes' work. So can you.

SOLAR STILL

The purpose of a solar still is to promote evaporation of moisture from plant matter or other moisture-containing objects, provide a surface on which the water vapor can condense, and give you a means of collecting the drinkable end product.

Quick Still

The quick still requires one plastic bag, a pebble, and a few inches of cordage. Place the bag over the end of a branch and put a pebble in one corner to create a low spot. Tie the bag shut, blocking any flow of air in or out of the bag.

If the branch has green leaves, water will evaporate from them, condense on the inner walls of the bag, and run down to the low spot. To improve this slightly, drape more green matter (strips of inner bark, leaves, grass, etc.) over the branch prior to covering it with the bag. To collect the water, untie the bag and tilt the low spot with the pebble upward, allowing the water to run out of the bag and into a water container.

Clear plastic is more effective in making stills than black plastic. I believe this is a result of the sun being able to pass through the clear plastic and heat the leaves or other moist material directly—something that is not possible with black plastic. Keep in mind that a number of such stills are required to provide an individual with an adequate water supply.

Water is a valuable resource that must not be squandered or taken for granted, and it is always good to know where the nearest supply can be found. Take note of various indicators as you move through the landscape, and take them into account when thinking of a shelter location.

(continued from page 121)

front David just then and continued to what we called the "Geronimo Trail," which is steep enough to require climbing gear. I began to slide down, heading for potable water.

About a third of the way down, I paused to reflect on my lack of patience. I had lost tolerance for smaller issues over the past few days. It appeared the others had as well. Was it diet, or long days, or heat? Who knows. People's eccentricities, and experiences such as the constant presence of mosquitoes, were beginning to annoy me. I breathed deeply and reminded myself to let it go.

Noise to my right brought me back to reality. The animal was large, whatever it was, and by the way it moved, I knew it wasn't human. The beautiful head of a coyote came around the corner. The splendid mix of rust, black, gray, and white of its coat gleamed without sun. The animal trotted, cutting across the steep hillside, displaying the typical cruising, traveling gait of a canine. The animal crossed the Geronimo Trail about twenty feet below me, and in an attempt to prolong the encounter, I produced a few chirps. The coyote paused, locking eyes with mine. Its eyes were deep and dark. The moment of the coyote's recognition was clear, and it turned, bounding away at an angle down the hill. Staring at this animal, I could see why coyotes were called "brush wolves" in colonial times.

If David had left enough water at camp, I would have risen more slowly, lounged a bit, and missed the coyote altogether. Synchronicity? Pure magic.

I found a suitable pecking stone along the stream, a porous rock soft enough and large enough to be shaped into a bowl. I had suggested to Mike that he use his stone bowl for heating pitch, and it worked like a charm. So, I'm hoping to add a second to our camp over time—a long time based on my progress thus far.

(continued on page 129)

Stone Pecking

Simple yet very useful stone tools can be made with little skill and a lot of patience. Pecking is simply hitting a softer rock with another, somewhat harder rock. Tiny fragments of the softer stone break off and eventually, a groove for holding a handle or a bowl can be formed. This method is not quick but is well suited for rainy days around camp.

Walking any streambed will illustrate how many kinds of rock are available for use in a given area. Some are very hard and work well for smashing bone to get the marrow or making shards that can be made into spears or arrowheads. Some are soft like sandstone, which can be used to smooth handles or other articles. Some of the best rocks to use for bowls are soft stones like soapstone and alabaster, although I prefer the medium-grain sanding stones such as basalt, found in riverbeds and elsewhere all over the country. Not to be confused with sandstone, medium-grain sanding stones are hard enough to use as a bone-hammering stone, yet soft enough to be worked.

When selecting a stone for a hammerhead or a bowl, look for rounded stones that have a slightly coarse feel to them. Look them over carefully for any variation in their appearance. They should be uniform, with no lines or cracks, as these will likely be breaking points.

White quartz rock is hard enough to use as a hammer stone for working the rocks mentioned above. It is also easy to find a piece that fits comfortably in your hand and has a fine enough tip to allow precise strikes. With such a hammer stone, tap on the rock you have selected and there should be a little mark where each strike occurred.

If you are making a bowl, start pecking (tapping) away. Always work on a soft surface like your lap, your hand, or in sand. Otherwise, you will likely crack your piece. I love pecking. I find a comfortable position, leaning against a tree in the sun or lounging in the foyer of my shelter while the rain pours down, and I'll work for hours at a time. Tapping on my project becomes a meditation of sorts. My rhythm, matching that of my heart, is somehow soothing. Two or more

The harder rock on the left has been used to peck a groove into the rock on the right

people working projects at the same time will, in short order, all be pecking the same rhythm.

Wetting the stone seems to make the work progress faster. Striking hard will, in all likelihood, break your stone project. Thin-walled bowls are very tricky, not so much in the making, but in the keeping— they break easily. One to one and one-half inches thick is pretty good. Just remember to heat the bowl slowly and evenly or it will crack.

For a stone hammerhead, a groove can be pecked around the center of the stone. The groove is to receive a bent, wooden handle made in the same fashion as in tongs (see "Making Camp," page 32). Additionally, a one-inch diameter branch or sapling, sixteen inches long, can be split all the way down its length, and the split sides of one end can be shaved down. These can then be placed in the grooves on

Split-wood handle for hammer

either side of the hammerhead with at least three inches extending above the hammerhead. The split sticks are then bound above and below the hammerhead with wet rawhide (see "Rawhide and Sinew," page 221).

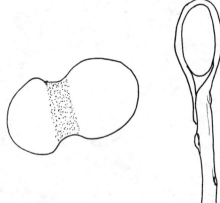

Bent-wood handle

With your quartz hammer stone, tap other stones and listen to the sound. Dull sound comes from softer rocks. Higher pitch is an indicator of a harder rock. Try chipping pieces off various rocks. The flakes may be sharp enough to use for small tasks. I'll often use such flakes for gutting fish.

(continued from page 126)

Pecking, which is essentially tapping two rocks together, is such timeless, meditative work. I could go on forever, the rhythm driving thoughts away and carrying me deeper and deeper into the stone. I feel so primitive tapping stones. The birds do not send out alarms over the noise, and the animals go about their business. It's as if hearing these sounds was part of their evolutionary process. Just a primitive man, working along a rolling stream as the sun hits the valley floor.

We had a brief shower.

Day 23

The three of us slept by the fire for various lengths of the night. The air was a pleasant temperature, which means we would broil in our heat-conserving shelters. Sleep consumed me between mosquito attacks on the head; their assaults on the rest of my body didn't seem to wake me.

I spent the morning cleaning a woodchuck skull in the stream. Flesh had rotted away to reveal bone and teeth, and the skull had fallen to pieces; it was a puzzle of plates and teeth.

I had kept an eye on the decomposition process. Flies were the first to discover the animal, two days after I had set it out in the branches of a hawthorn bush. Fresh kills are too easily discovered on the ground by those that would carry them off. More often, flies find dead flesh much faster, but the two days of continuous rain must have lowered fly activity or somehow masked the scent of death. They did find the woodchuck on the first day of sun and laid eggs in the mouth and nose.

A few days later, maggots hard at work were competing with carrion beetles. Only the red species of beetle were present—no yellow ones this time. I lowered the specimen to the ground to keep the teeth from scattering too far. Another few days passed, and I found sign that a burying beetle was at work. The head of the woodchuck had fallen into a hole, having been excavated from below. The beetle had laid eggs along the floor of the hole, and the woodchuck's rotting flesh would provide food for the next generation. Earwig-shaped creatures had joined the host of others at this point, along with tiny insects of various forms.

On my final visit, a flap of skin remained. A lone carrion beetle hid underneath it. A few tiny insects were about, but the feast was over. All that remained was bone and teeth. I've found pillbugs, or sowbugs, sometimes appear at this stage, but not here, not today.

I've begun a practice to help me see more details, to notice the smaller things in life. I choose a tiny bit of woods, maybe an eight-inch square, and won't allow myself to move until I find several strands of animal hair. This is not an exercise I undertake standing or sitting. To look small, I lie flat and stare at the mosaic of litter, twigs, hemlock needles, and varied debris. Depending on my mindset, it may take a minute or ten minutes. If I find one too fast, I find another.

For me, the goal is to stare continuously to the point where I've just about convinced myself I've discovered the first patch of woods without animal hair. At this moment, I'm ready to leave, to move on to something more interesting, but it is this moment that is the start of training. Just beyond, I find my first hair.

Today, I found a red fox hair in a myriad of hemlock needles every tone of brown imaginable. My second woods plot took some time, and I grew impatient. I had discovered the perfectly shed exoskeleton of a tiny insect with every leg intact, mouse-opened seeds, and tiny sprigs of moss, but it was some time before I pulled out my first red squirrel hair. The second was easy.

I caught a woodchuck away from its burrow. In an attempt to escape, he climbed a white pine. The tree was too large a diameter for easy climbing, and the woodchuck clung to the trunk eyeing me suspiciously. I decided to try to harvest it for dinner. We hadn't had fresh woodchuck in some time.

I picked up a large tree branch and walked about, deciding on the best approach—one that would end the ordeal in one blow. I was somewhat squeamish. I was fine throwing the stick after a stalk, but this seemed a bit odd. Well, the woodchuck must have seen my apprehension and decided to take a chance at running. Off it went, me in close pursuit, stick too large to throw. The woodchuck made it into a raspberry patch and was gone. I'm no great hunter, yet.

All day I listened to thunder rolling toward us from the west. In the afternoon, the storm arrived: dark clouds, intense winds, and claps of thunder. This was a big one. I made straight for camp, arriving just before David. We worked quickly on another layer of "thatch" for the group shelter, which may now be the longest project known to humankind. Mike arrived about the time the first raindrops began to fall.

We huddled in our incomplete shelter as the torrents of rain commenced. We watched the exposed supports and the unfinished bits catch rain. The water ran down the wood and dripped onto our heads and bodies. We decided to run for an alternative makeshift shelter down the hill to the south.

We all arrived soaked. We sat watching the storm dump water on the area. The clouds swirled and the air seemed alive with color. A green hue hung in the air, thick enough to touch. As dusk approached, the deluge passed. We returned to camp and coaxed forth a fire. Mostly dry, I retired to my debris hut, a completely dry shelter of leaf and stick. Amazing.

I also learned an important lesson this evening: Don't hunt in shorts and a T-shirt unless you have mastered your body's unconscious responses to physical distractions. There I was,

(continued on page 139)

Fire Making with the Bow and Drill

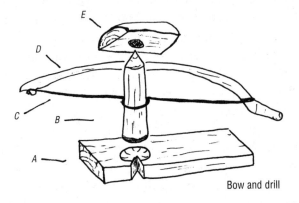

Bow and drill

I have been told that trees consist of stored sunshine. I believe that natural fire making is a way of asking the sunshine to release itself, and that asking in a humble manner is the only way you will achieve the desired results. Here you will be given the technical directions for this fire-making ceremony; the humility must come from you.

The bow-and-drill apparatus is made up of five components: the fireboard (A), the spindle (B), the cordage (C), the bow (D), and the handhold (E).

OVERVIEW ON HOW THE BOW AND DRILL WORKS

With the fireboard placed on the ground, the spindle wound once in the cordage, and the ends placed in the sockets of the fireboard and the handhold, the bow is moved back and forth parallel to the ground. The bow strokes rotate the spindle in the sockets via the cordage.

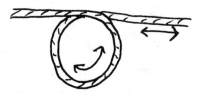

Simultaneously, you apply downward pressure on the handhold, creating friction on both ends of the spindle. Conifer pitch or needles placed in the handhold socket minimize friction at the top, which also results in a greater amount of heat-generating friction in the fireboard socket.

As the spindle moves within the fireboard socket, small particles of wood wear off both fireboard and spindle and fill the notch with a fine dark brown or black powder (fire powder). Because of the intense heat, the fire powder melds together and forms a coal. You remove the coal from the notch and place it in a tinder bundle (see "Tipi Fires," page 116), then blow the bundle into a flame and put it into a prebuilt tipi fire.

HOW TO BUILD A BOW-AND-DRILL FIRE

The specifications given here for making a bow-and-drill fire are those I have found to be the most effective. This is not to say that other ways will not work as well. Try them all!

Selecting the Wood

It is possible to make a bow-and-drill fire with any nonresinous wood. Working with hardwoods such as oak, ironwood, and others is a fun challenge, though not desirable in a survival situation for the following reasons: First, hardwood takes more time and energy to fashion into a bow-and-drill set. Second, the endurance required to make a coal with hardwood will use up your valuable energy. And third, making cordage that can withstand such continuous use required for an oak bow-and-drill fire is difficult.

Woods such as white cedar, juniper cedar, cottonwood, aspen, sycamore, maple, birch, and basswood work beautifully for the bow and drill; aside from the first two these are the softer deciduous trees.

Each tree is unique, and the hardness of wood will vary from branch to branch. An aspen growing with one side to a cliff and one side in the open will give you very hard wood on the cliff side and much softer wood on the exposed side. It is best to experiment on your own with various woods.

When you harvest wood for a bow and drill, try to find a dead branch that is still on the tree. A branch on the ground can feel dry yet be moist inside due to absorption of moisture from the ground. A branch in a tree is surrounded by air, and the wind helps to evaporate moisture quickly even after a good rain.

Making the Spindle

Spindles that are nine inches in length and the diameter of a quarter are preferable, although in damp weather you may want to use a wider spindle that will create greater friction between the fireboard and the spindle. This helps to dry the wood and thus the fibers that fall into the notch. The spindle can be taken from a dead branch with the desired diameter or split from a log and carved round. Both ends should be shallowly tapered.

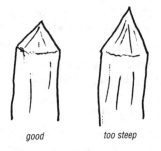

good   too steep

The spindle tip should be shallow

Make the spindle from the same wood as the fireboard or from wood of a similar hardness. This apparatus can be made from pocket size to something requiring four people to operate. Materials used are key, so note your observations as you practice. The description below uses a size I have found to be easiest.

Making the Fireboard

Length here is not as important as the width. A piece of wood that is nine inches by three or four inches will work well. Make the thickness of the board about one inch, but no more.

As with the spindle, split the wood from a log or take it from a dead tree branch. A fireboard from a dead branch will likely be narrower than three inches in diameter and should therefore be split lengthwise to create a flat bottom for the fireboard.

If you are using rocks to make your apparatus, you will need to crush the branch with a larger stone

and use the sharp edge of a rock to abrade your notch when ready.

Making the Handhold

The handhold should be comfortable in your left hand if you are right-handed (in your right hand if you are left-handed), and the hole for the spindle should be directly below the center of your palm. CAUTION: If the circumference of the handhold is too small, your fingers may touch the spindle and suffer burns.

The key feature of a handhold is that the socket is deep enough to hold the spindle well, yet not so deep as to create more friction when the spindle sides contact the socket wall.

Making the Bow

The bow should be about waist height with a very slight curve. A bow with some flexibility is preferable but not necessary. Keep the bow light, because a heavy bow will require more energy to move back and forth. A diameter of the size between a nickel and a quarter works well. One end should fit comfortably in your dominant hand. Notch the bow ends to help hold the cordage in place.

Making the String or Cordage

See "Cordage" for instructions (page 198). Tie the cordage to both ends of the bow, being careful not to make it tight. Exactly how much

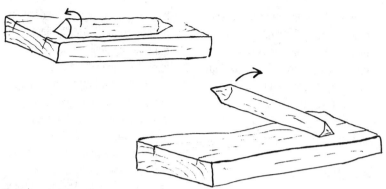

Finding and making the socket location

slack is required will depend upon the diameter of the spindle.

HOW TO USE A BOW AND DRILL

Marking the Socket Location in the Fireboard and Handhold

1. Place the spindle on top of the fireboard flush with either long edge.
2. Roll the spindle toward the center of the fireboard a quarter inch and stand it up on point.
3. With your hand, twist the spindle back and forth, creating a small dent in the fireboard.

4. With the handhold end of the spindle, make a small dent in the middle of the handhold as described above.

Stringing the Spindle

1. Place one end of the bow under your right armpit, with the rest of the bow out in front of you.
2. With the spindle in your right hand, place it across the cordage (Figure A).
3. Using both hands, swoop under and around the cordage with the end of the spindle (Figure B).
4. Force the spindle to a perpendicular position with the cordage

A

B

C

Stringing the spindle

(Figure C). Hold the cordage and spindle firmly, because the spindle is held under tension and could fly out. Note: If the cordage is too tight (you can't complete Figure C) or too loose after you complete Figure C, then adjust the cordage and try again.

Burning In

1. Place the fireboard on the ground, keeping the small hole that you started on the right end.
2. With the ball of your left foot resting on the fireboard to the left of the hole, drop down to your right knee and place the spindle tip into the hole in the fireboard.
3. While you continue to hold the spindle to prevent it from being flung out by the cordage, place the handhold on the top so that the point of the spindle rests in the handhold starter hole. At this time, you should be resting your chest on your left knee while you bring your left wrist against your shin and exert downward pressure on the handhold.
4. Grasp the end of the bow in your right hand and begin moving it back and forth so that the spindle rotates.

   In all likelihood, the spindle will pop out with annoying frequency and the cordage will ride up and down the spindle and come off. This is due to a lack of form and occurs when the spindle is not kept perpendicular to the cordage or the handhold. Really "lock your hand in" by pulling your wrist joint back against your shin so that both your hand and arm are stabilized. This will keep the spindle perpendicular to the fireboard and handhold.

Giving even, level bow strokes will keep the cordage in the center of the spindle. There is a trick for helping with this process: On the back stroke, when your bow hand is passing your right knee, try to drive the back end of the bow into the ground a foot or so behind your knee. Pay attention to the effect this has on your bow wrist. Do the *opposite* on the forestroke. By using full bow strokes (i.e., all the string, not six-inch strokes) and by adding more or less downward pressure in the handhold, you will produce enough friction to cause the sockets to smoke. As you play with the speed of the strokes, more or less smoke will be generated. This "burning in" process is generally done until the sockets have the same diameter as the spindle.

Note: Carving a cordage groove in the midpoint of the spindle will not aid your efforts; in fact, it will hamper them greatly.

Lubricating the Handhold

The handhold socket is now ready

for some lubricant. Conifer needles work beautifully, as does conifer sap. You can also use animal fat.

1. Put a few pine needles or animal fat in the socket and forcefully twist the spindle end in the socket, smashing and smearing the needles or other material around.
2. Once you have lubricated the handhold, mark your spindle so that you can tell which end goes in the handhold. If the lubricated end is used in the fireboard, it may be difficult to start a fire.

Other Types of Handholds

A handhold made of pine often does not need to be lubricated, because it has residual pitch still in the wood. In areas that have no conifers, a bone or stone handhold works well, although it may take more preparation if you cannot find one with a pocket for the spindle end.

Carving the Notch

To carve your notch in the fireboard, look at the burned-in socket and imagine it as a whole pie. Your notch should be no greater than one eighth of the pie. It is important

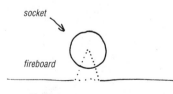

Notch (as viewed from above)

that it be wedge shaped and clean on the sides. It should go into but not include the center of the socket.

Making a Coal

Now you are ready to create a coal. Tinder (see "Tipi Fires," page 116) can be placed either under the fireboard and notch or set aside, and a wood chip or leaf can be placed under the notch to catch the coal.

1. Begin with smooth, even strokes and watch the dust build up in the notch. Light brown or white dust means that you are not using enough speed. Coarse brown dust means that you need to use less handhold pressure. No dust at all and loud squeaking indicate a crack in your spindle tip and/or fire hardening, a process that polishes the spindle tip and fireboard socket to a mirror shine. If this happens, you need to greatly increase your speed and pressure in order to burn through the shiny layer, or you need to rough up the affected surfaces. Your goal is to create fine dark brown or black dust.
2. When the notch is full and a lot of smoke is coming from the fireboard, add ten good strokes to "pack" the coal. These packing strokes ensure that the coal has enough material to feed on as it grows.
3. Stop your bow strokes and gently remove the spindle from the fire-

Removing the coal from the fireboard

board. A wisp of smoke should be rising from the dust in the wedge.

4. Place a twig or the back of your knife blade gently on the dust, and hold it there.

5. Roll the fireboard away from the dust, leaving the coal in the open. If the smoke is weak, leave it alone for a minute or so, because the coal may grow.

From Coal To Fire

1. Gently deposit the coal into your prepared tinder bundle, and fold the tinder over it. It is a good idea to let the coal heat up the tinder a little before you give a few long, soft breaths into the bundle. Holding the tinder up to the sky is another good idea. Not only is it a great way to give thanks, but it also prevents the coal from burning a hole out of the back of your bundle and dropping to the ground, and it keeps the smoke out of your face.

2. When the smoke builds to a good billowing cloud, you can put it in your tipi fire and blow it into flame then, or you can do so in your hand and quickly transfer it to the fire.

3. Once the bundle is in place, you may need to give it a few breaths to really get it going.

Work through the frustrations. Sometimes it is a good idea to take a break and set the bow and drill aside for a few days before going at it again. Good luck.

(continued from page 131)

frozen in midstep, about twenty feet from a suspicious cottontail. The animal had stopped feeding, and was sitting up and waiting. If I moved, potential dinner would bound off at incredible speed and I'd begin the process again somewhere else.

I could feel the bite of the mosquitoes—not one insect, but probably ten biting at a time. As they pulled blood, there was a subtle burn that lasted and lasted. Having my throwing stick cocked to fire allowed me an easy view of my forearm, where I watched the mosquitoes jerk their heads and pull out. They would lumber off slowly, leaving a drop of blood on the skin as a marker of where they had been. I still couldn't decide what was the greater distraction—the physical burn of the bite, which wasn't really so bad, or the mental torture that I was contributing blood to females for reproduction. I was aiding in continuing the enormous mosquito population on this hill!

Now couple the mosquitoes with gnats. The burn of mosquitoes was tolerable—the mental torture a challenge—but the gnats were my nemesis. Twenty to thirty gnats surrounded my head, taking turns on kamikaze flights into my eyes and ears. On a few occasions they switched to flying up my nose, but the trends were short-lived.

So there I was, in the field, mosquitoes biting, gnats dive bombing, cottontail watching. The first time I lost concentration, a gnat flew with such precision, it struck my inner ear without having to crawl. Squinting protected my eyes a bit, but the gnats soon learned they could land on my cheeks, crawl up, and find entry. A few gnats in the eyes and my defensive movements sent the cottontail fleeing.

The second stalk was better, or worse, since it was longer. I completed a full-body itch before beginning my second stalk. I held both rabbit sticks up this time, one on either side of my head in an attempt to deflect any direct inner-ear penetration. Slowly, I moved forward, squinting for eye protection. Progressing, progressing, almost to firing range.... My legs were burning from hordes of biting and bloodsucking insects. Oops, gnat in the eye. I was off-balance. The cottontail never looked back.

DAY 24

Last night the temperature really dropped, and I had the best sleep I've experience in a while. I slept longer than usual; I needed it. It seemed I'd been becoming a bit more tired each day. It's important to sleep well. For me, cool nights are the prescription.

I believe I've decided to take a solo—a vision quest, if you will. So much of this experience so far has been physical. So many skills and projects needed to be done to reach the place where we are now. Of course, there are many more I'd like to do. But I'd prefer to spend more time gaining a deeper understanding of my connection to this place.

My body seems to have achieved some sort of balance. I'm never starving anymore except for an occasional growl. Small amounts of food are sustaining. I can operate all day on a small meal and trailside graze. What a contrast to what I pack away in society.

I am also feeling a greater sense of food security. As a group, Mike, David, and I know many plants, and there are always a few handfuls of berries to be found. The bulrush seeds are filling and we have gathered a large quantity. Fishing also seems to be a fairly sure thing. We continue to hunt so that we can learn and diversify our diet. Do we still crave pizza, vegetable lasagna, spanikopita, chocolate chip cookies, Ben and Jerry's ice cream, and so forth? Of course we do.

Whenever I go without food for a short time or go with less food diversity, I dream of a meal prepared by Sonny Noto's, a restaurant in East Boston. I crave a massive portion of their chicken ziti broccoli served with a doorstep of bread and butter. I doubt I could finish a plate now, but I'd like to try.

I realize there is a great deal about this experience that I don't write down; I leave so much out. The animal tracks and signs, the birdsongs, the sunsets, the cloud formations, and the wildflowers are all constantly overloading my senses. The list is endless.

Just this morning, and on countless mornings before, a red-tailed hawk circled over our camp. Just skimming the treetops, she caught the updraft, circling higher and higher. Today, with the sun directly above, light filtered through her rusty tail and illuminated her creamy chest. The light emphasized the dark band of feathers across her chest, which birders use to identify red-tails at a distance. She was absolutely beautiful.

I'm reminded of an earlier hunt. We were exploring to the north of camp, setting snares. Mike carried his newly made bow and arrow, but I had opted to leave my throwing sticks behind and instead carried cordage to set new snares.

While I identified cottontail and woodchuck runs through a hedgerow, Mike moved up the drainage to a small pond. He yelled to gain my attention and gestured to come quickly. He then yelled for me to grab a few throwing sticks. Unfortunately, I was in a hedgerow between two fields. One massive hickory tree lay between Mike and me. I grabbed the only two pieces of wood not entangled in poison ivy and ran toward Mike. They were gnarly, light, stubby things, which I only hoped would do the job.

As I approached Mike, he made the signs for BIRD and MANY. Then he pointed to the pond, and I knew they were geese. Mike circled to the right, and I knew I was to circle to the left. When you move slowly, really aware of your environment, with another person, a silent communication develops. Just as I crawled to the rise, I watched Mike flush the geese on the far side of the pond. The birds fled and took off, flying low over the pond in my direction. I stood up as the birds flew past.

Later Mike told me he wasn't exactly sure where I was at that moment, and that I appeared like an apparition from primitive days, throwing sticks cocked in the midday sun. The hunt, without maintaining visual contact, had been executed absolutely perfectly.

Of course, the hunt was perfect until at point-blank range I released my throwing sticks and somehow missed every goose.

I hunted in the afternoon. I watched a doe feed to the north. Her elegant neck alternated between periods of grazing and periods of looking for predators. Deer spend as much time assessing the area for potential danger as they do eating. The life of the hunted is so different from that of the hunter. Yet, the lives of the hunted and the hunter are intrinsically connected. In terms of evolution, prey are shaped by the predator, and vice versa. Hunters and hunted evolve together. This beautiful doe is the result of pursuit by our human ancestors, cougars, and wolves. The form of our human bodies is a result of our hunting hoofed animals for generations too many to count. It is amazing to ponder such a relationship and to track our very form to the animals we hunted through the millennia.

Modern people have lost the edge kept by deer and other prey animals. We have eradicated all potential threats to ourselves, except in a few remote areas where people rarely visit or do so only from within the protection of their cars. We have become the top of the food chain and can now wander about without worrying about what's around the next corner. Subsequently, our intuitions and instincts have faded away.

Myself, I have never felt more alive than when I am walking in grizzly country or after hearing the scream of a nearby mountain lion. Every sound becomes distinct and crisp, every color sharp—an adrenaline rush of sorts. I suppose that's why extreme sports are so popular. They are an outlet for the displaced, intuitive warrior that evolved over thousands of years; we can't rid ourselves completely of our accumulated knowledge in a few centuries of agriculture and technology.

In woods where large predators roam, you develop a certain awareness. You turn at every cracking twig and feel around every corner with gut intuition. I remember my feelings when I was twenty-three yards from a grizzly bear in Glacier National Park. I was part of a team completing the bear sign survey for the National Park Service. We worked in groups of four, because four people together have never been mauled by a grizzly (as of yet).

We were just getting started after a long lunch break when a grizzly stepped onto the trail. I had never been this close to a grizzly. The bear was massive—larger than life. I found myself moving slowly backward without thinking about it and feeling my heart pound at the base of my throat.

I studied his bristling guard hairs, which gleamed as they danced in the breeze. His eyes held a certain self-assuredness present only in animals of immense power. His muscles were bulging, visible under his thick coat. His claws were so long they were clearly visible from our distance. He stared at us a long time. Who knows what went through his mind, but he decided to run. Off he went, with shocking speed, crashing through the brushy understory.

We soon discovered he had just killed a black bear and cached it immediately below the trail. He had ripped the back of the bear completely off. The organs hadn't been finished yet, the kill was so fresh. We all stared at each other, knowing that bear would be back to reclaim his food cache. I photographed the scene and we quickly evacuated the area.

The adrenaline produced by such encounters is impossible to describe. We all shivered and mumbled excitedly for hours. We smiled for days. Woods where large predators roam should be cherished, not feared. Environments in which you wonder what's around the next bend bring us closer to true living than in tamed woods. You live in the moment, aware of the surrounding details and the messages and signs left all over the landscape.

Here, in our tame woods, with no poisonous snakes or mountain lions, we are able to crash about without any worries at all. And we miss so much along our journey.

A few black bears dared to wander into this valley. The state quickly returned them to where they were "supposed to be." I suppose for now that the fewer people/bear interactions that occur, the better, because these encounters only result in dead bears. We adapt our environment to fit our desires, regardless of the larger picture.

This reminds me once again of my work in Montana. Our group met with a representative of the Blackfoot nation, whose land borders the eastern side of Glacier National Park. He told us how conservationist Doug Peacock and others had asked to buy Blackfoot land to help protect the bears. The Blackfoot people said "no," and that they had given enough land away.

This representative of the Blackfoot people, however, had an interesting suggestion to help protect the bears. He said we should support Blackfoot children being taught in their native tongue. He told us there was no word for "bear" in Blackfoot; it was the same word as "brother." In the Blackfoot language, bears were considered family and thus could not be hunted or pushed to extinction by creating small islands of suitable habitat. Rather, bears were embraced and supported as brethren. As this man left to go, he mentioned that if we were to get the chance to look into the eyes of a bear, we'd understand why bears were considered as brothers.

Several years later, I found myself sharing time with black bears in New York's Adirondacks, and the experience I had in Montana finally felt complete.

Several weeks before I arrived here, I attended an American Sign Language immersion program in New York. One evening, a staff member tore around the corner to tell us about a pair of bears out front. The entire class went out to see wild bears.

A pair grazed in a small clearing next to the front parking lot. As people encroached, the bears began to fade into dark spruce woods. Losing the opportunity to photograph further, people began to trickle away. The staff show was starting shortly. I, on the other hand, decided to follow the bears.

I was amazed how silently the pair moved. Their thick hair absorbed the sounds of rubbing branches, and their padded, hairy feet rolled over the landscape, conforming to rises and ridges. Even though I chose my steps carefully, I made far more noise than they did as I attempted to catch up. They knew I was following and would stop occasionally to peer back at me. They pulled jack-in-the-pulpits, rolled about in the ferns, and scraped the ground in areas to remove rootlets.

One bear alternated between rolling in ferns and watching me for quite some time.

The bears disappeared into a wetland via a fallen log, where cattails arched from either side to form a natural entrance. The water level was so low that it was not visible, but I chose to follow on the log to decrease the noise I was making. The male grazed on cattails in the middle of the wetland. He crunched and crunched, like dogs eat crabgrass. I moved closer and closer until about thirty feet of young cattails divided us. I had studied bears for a long time and had experienced numerous encounters in the wild. I had learned to expect certain responses as I approached....

Suddenly, the female stood up to my left, about fifteen feet away. She stood at my height, the cattails just mature enough so that our heads cleared their leaves. Two heads floating in a sea of green: one bear, one human. The bear and I locked eyes. I thought to myself, "Remember this forever"—her beautiful, broad, black head, her chocolate snout. A light breeze swayed her fur and she wiggled one ear. Her dark, ink black eyes mesmerized me. They had great depth; they were big black wells swallowing me.... Her eyes told only of remarkable intelligence and gentleness. It was magic, a perfect experience, every naturalist's dream.

It seemed like forever that we looked into each other's eyes before the male woofed and charged. I watched rustling cattails approach. It all happened so fast, I didn't have time to be afraid. It was a false charge, of course; he veered around me. Both bears "woofed" and started walking to the far side of the wetland. I had encroached enough and walked back to camp absolutely exhilarated by the experience.

I should mention that it is not advisable to lock eyes with any wild animal. This is often interpreted as an act of aggression. I can only say that, in that moment, it was a decision of heart, not of mind.

I stalked three deer in another area. I caught Mike stalking in from the other direction, and so did the deer. They didn't know what or who he was. The young buck, spikes in velvet, began a series of snorts, violent bursts of air that flared his nostrils. Small stamps with the forelegs were added. Mike did not respond, and the deer returned to grazing. They kept tabs on him, though, which allowed me to creep closer. Eventually they could stand the mysterious presence no longer and decided to move on. The buck walked up to the cattle fence and bounded over it with an ease and fluidity only possible in an elegant, long-legged ungulate. Slowly, they moved away.

Tonight we decided to try for the honey again using a new, more technological approach. We'd had a long discussion about the realities of honey extraction. With what we had in camp, we could get the honey. Mike and I had knives sturdy enough to be used as chisels. We could also take the tree down with fire and stone tools. However, taking a beautiful and very large tree was a complicated and energy-expensive endeavor, and then there was the fact that the tree stood on someone's private property. We abandoned these ideas quickly.

Personally, I felt too much energy would be wasted in extraction. But Mike had made up his mind. Rather than beat up our knives, he suggested retrieving a chisel and mallet from the outside world. I added that if he really wanted to bring in a chisel and mallet, then he'd be stupid not to grab some protective gear as well.

And that's what we did. We all went down to an open field one night, and Mike and David crept off to borrow the necessary tools. I fell asleep watching stars and woke up when they returned. I wasn't comfortable wandering streets at night; I preferred not to return to town, and no doubt someone would think we were stalkers if they spotted us.

We had learned on previous visits to the hive that honeybees do not take to flight easily at night. We held a torch to find the entrance completely hidden by a writhing mass of honeybees crawling around and over each other. They buzzed their wings constantly, which we hypothesized would keep the hive warm. On many nights, we stood watching the wriggling mass ebb and flow, listening to the hum of thousands of wings working as one. We also learned that when we smoked the writhing mass with burning birch bark, the bees would retreat inward, leaving the entrance completely unprotected. It was at this stage we were able to apply a "patch" of carved wood, which acted like a cork to keep the bees inside the hive.

Patch in place, Mike used a chisel and mallet to create a hand-sized hole in the back of the tree. The process took some time, but he broke through eventually. We were ready, with smoky birch bark blazing to protect us. Mike reached in and liberated a few handfuls of comb. Then we sat back to watch the bees' response.

I cannot explain the flavor of wild raw honey after a period of hunting and gathering. Most of the plants we eat have a bitter flavor; sweetness is absent. This honeycomb, oozing with raw honey, was incredibly sweet and rich in flavor. Also, whatever flowers the bees had used to create this honey had endowed the honey's delicious flavor with an additional fruitiness. We sat, leaning against hemlocks in the pitch black along some rocky ridge south of camp, tasting wild honey. It didn't get much better than this.

We were exhausted and decided to investigate the bees' reaction to the new hole the next day. Would the bees abandon the hive or patch the hole? Only time would tell. We tripped and stumbled our way back to camp, too tired to walk in any balanced manner.

DAY 25

A pile of shit lay next to our spring this morning, just above our drinking hole. My choice of vocabulary reflects the true profanity of this act. I love that spring—dropping to hands and knees, looking at my reflection, pausing for thanksgiving, then drawing the cool, fresh water into my mouth. I drink like a mountain lion, pausing to look around, muscles tensed in case I need to flee.

No more, though—at least not there. Stained toilet paper

blew along the banks of the tiny spring. The worst part was that a pit toilet stood within sight. I suppose some city camper could not stand the company of spiders.

The main entrance to the beehive did not display the usual daylight bustle of activity. The new hole in the back side, however, was a different story. The entire area was carpeted in bees. We took turns peering into the hole. They appeared to be moving honey, patching comb, and doing other chores. Bees don't sit back and complain about work to be done. They just get to it.

We smoked the bees a bit to see their response and to gain a better understanding of what they were working on. They appeared to eat as they retreated. David later read that beekeepers believe smoke brings about a state where bees prepare to flee by gorging on honey. Smoke also makes them more docile. We liberated a few more pieces of comb and took turns watching the bees while standing on the log we had leaned against the tree.

Inside the hole, a funnel of bees and bits of comb had formed. All of the bees were moving, which created psychedelic patterns of writhing comb. The buzz of the creatures was continuous. I could feel the energy of the hive and a physical warmth around the hole. The comb itself, freshly excavated from the mighty pine, was warm to the touch. A winter wren alighted in the area and sang its exuberant, long-winded song over and over again.

The comb itself was equally fantastic—hexagons of dark wax, sealed at the top. When squeezed, honey gushed out onto our fingers. I now know why cultures around the world, since the beginning of time, have gone to any length to obtain this wonderful flavor. Wild honey is such a treat.

The bees had obviously not abandoned their home. We decided to clean out what we could reach, then patch the hole. If the bees wanted to stay, why should they leave? We could carve a piece of wood to fit the hole and they could wax the seams for a perfect fit. It sounded like a plan. We'd see how it actually worked.

David left this morning after we inspected the bees and should be back tomorrow evening. Mike and I were hungry and decided to fish to ensure a large meal. We had a wonderful afternoon hand fishing and spearfishing.

There was a particular pool that will forever stand out from the rest. The trout hid under a massive root system. They were too far back to spear and too deep to reach with our hands. The root system was that of a multi-stemmed basswood tree. The bank seemed to have given way, and the root system had collapsed downward, lying perpendicular to water. However, we noticed a hole at one end of the root system, an entrance to the cave formed by bank and tree. Wiggling in, we encountered one of those rare, absolutely astounding scenes of nature.

The walls of the cave did not allow in light from above, plus my body plugged the entry. Thus, the only source of illumination filtered in through the waters of the stream itself, which formed a serene pool that covered the expanse of the cave floor. Ten trout sat motionless in the pool, their bodies bathed in light as if they were in an aquarium. Their orange and brown spots were accented against mottled silver and brown bodies. They occasionally flicked fins to hold position, and their mouths opened and closed to individual rhythms. The water was so clear, so light. There were no ripples; the pool was smooth as glass. The fish looked fake, gliding about. Of course, they were real. It is just so rare to glimpse wild creatures this clearly—perfect creations in their own environment.

I hoped to hand fish the largest of the crowd, although this was a bit tricky. In hand fishing you need something to push and pin the fish against—a rock or tree trunk. Not here—just fish in a clear pool with a sandy bottom. The fish also had a clear view of my looming body and lengthy arms attached to the tickling hands that touched them. Over and over I tickled the fish, the gills just out of reach, my body inching deeper into the chilly pool. It wasn't long before most of my body was under water. I missed the first time, but the fish eventually meandered into arm's reach again.

On the second try, I drove my fingers into the body—somehow punching through the flesh without the aid of the gills. Outside, Mike heard a muffled "Wahoo!" Then a wriggling fourteen-inch trout appeared from the hole, followed by my smiling face. What a feeling! To catch such a splendid creature and feel its slick body wriggling in your hands cannot be fully expressed in words.

Each time I catch a trout, I find myself apologizing and hoping the fish will understand that I am learning. On one level I'm happy to do this, but when will I shed the mental gymnastics? When will I accept the facts that I am an animal and that hunting is natural? Do I need to feel guilty participating in natural cycles? I think not; I simply need to be respectful.

Each time I hold a trout, I also try to memorize every detail of its coloring and shape. A trout has seven fins. The two that run along the back, as well as on the upper half of the tail, are spotted like its body. The lower fins have leading edges that are a brilliant white color. The upper body varies in color but is often a glossy golden or brown. The coloration varies with tiger striping of darker or lighter skin, which helps the fish blend even more with the rocky streams. A trout's sides are often yellow to off-white, and underneath it is snow white. A mixture of large and small red to orange dots is splattered across its sides. Some brook trout are more speckled than others. Their gills are a deep blood red color. Their teeth line hardened lips and tongue, all aiming backward. Their eyes are dark round circles surrounded by off-white. And when you're fishing, looking down through water, they appear brown, yellow, striped, or even blue. They are the work of an artist.

We were thrilled to secure our meal.

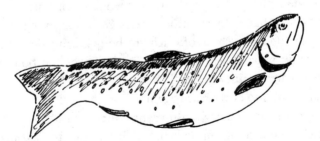

Day 26

I spent a peaceful morning working on skills. Kayla visits this evening. I was told by David, our "real-world" connection, to meet her on Monday at 6:00 P.M. Hmm, a bit of a challenge. He helped me with the Monday part, but the 6:00 P.M. still posed a problem. I estimated the level of sun and hoped.

Kayla and I met when we were teaching wilderness skills to youths and adults at the same program where I met Mike and David. Side by side we worked together, and for three and a half years we shared a house. I thought I'd marry her for sure, yet recent decisions we'd made seemed to be leading us apart.

Mike and I explored a ridge to the north in late morning. He wanted to show me what he thought was an old cottontail nest, where the young had been kept. Off we hiked, crossing roads, walking deer trails, and wandering through fields. Along the way, I caught a glimpse of a mud patch way off-trail. I knew in my gut that we'd find red fox tracks there. We meandered over, and sure enough, we saw the most beautiful fox tracks of the summer so far. Every hair had registered, and the "bar," or strip of heel pad without hair, registered perfectly. We followed the fox, discovering older trails along the way. When I slow down and listen to myself, I'm often able to pick up things just beyond the physical senses. Is this an inkling of what is possible, a glimpse of our human potential?

We finally found the cottontail nest, an excavated area at the base of a tussock along the edge of a field. It was clearly a nest, where the scentless young had remained protected under a mat of grasses and fur. The chamber was very small, about the size of my hand, held as if I were gripping a ball. The entire nest was lined with cottontail fur, which I've read the mother pulls from her belly. It was a wonderful find. We studied it for some time, then meandered off to explore further.

We peered into an old well that appeared to be about sixteen feet deep. The well was constructed beautifully—a perfect circle of slate slabs just wide enough to climb straight into the earth. The remains of an unlucky opossum floated below. We imagined how many perfect skeletons must have been at the bottom of the well. We contemplated pumping or hauling water out to discover and collect skeletal treasures. We'll see. Right now, our energy is needed elsewhere.

We discovered the remains of a foundation and an apple orchard beyond. The apple orchard, abandoned and unkempt, was competing—and losing—to native species; the orchard no longer produced fruit. The trail we hiked had been an old carriage road. How land changes. The surrounding woods were young and thick, but reforestation had reclaimed, and continues to reclaim, much of this land. Our camp, tucked among hemlocks and chestnut oaks high on a ridge, was sheep pasture a generation ago. The Northeast forests are nearly all young. How rare old-growth trees are across the country. Soon, remaining pockets will become too small to use as a reference for how mature woods function.

The trees surrounding me were the same species as would have been here 400 years ago, but the current trees are genetically different from their towering ancestors. The newer trees will never grow as tall or live as long. Our "harvest the best and biggest" mentality over many years is evident in the remaining genetic stock that surround us now: shorter and shorter-lived trees.

We had a powerful storm in the afternoon. Mike and I sat in camp and thunder exploded just overhead. We looked at each other wide-eyed and laughed nervously. Kayla arrived safely, having traveled directly from Yosemite National Park. She told stories of bears and raging streams of melted snow. She said I'd lost weight. It was good to see her.

Day 27

I spent my morning rebuilding the woodchuck skull I had cleaned. I became absolutely engrossed by the three-dimensional puzzle. When it was complete, we compared it with muskrat, cottontail, and squirrel skulls we had collected.

Our camp was discovered by an adventurous group of hikers armed with day packs and a desire to hike the steepest ridges. Our ridge, which we thought would be our greatest protection, attracted these extreme hikers. We heard them coming long before their arrival. I diverted them around our camp, but they could see our group shelter as they passed. The discovery worried us somewhat, and we've begun to talk about moving.

Leah, David's girlfriend, arrived in the evening to visit. Kayla too was still with us, so it was a full camp for an evening.

A gourmet cook, Leah felt she had to bring food when visiting another "household." She had brought bread, a Mexican dish, and cake. She told us how long she had been cooking, and without any real twisting of our arms.... We couldn't resist.

We began with bread topped with veggies, like a salsa. I was then passed a scoop of the main dish. It was a Mexican mix, topped with a cornbread-like crust. It was a sort of veggie shepherd's pie. Wow, the flavor! My serving seemed normal, by society's standards, but I began to fill quickly. I plugged on, though, knowing my next such meal wouldn't be for some time.

Then the food felt like lead in my stomach. I went from full to completely, uncomfortably stuffed. I sunk lower and lower against my wooden backrest, feeling worse and worse. People continued to eat, helping after helping, while I fought a torturous stomach and urge to vomit.

I laid flat on the ground, unable to speak or think clearly. Conversations about intuitive successes, northern lights, and luminescent plankton floated about. Homemade bread and chocolate cake were eaten. Can you imagine what everyone would have thought if I'd been sick on the fire? Not much of a thank-you to our guests.

I was unable to participate. All of my energy had turned to digesting this lump of Mexican food I'd deposited of my own accord. The flavor was delicious, and how I wanted to taste homemade bread with butter, and chocolate cake, which were passed over and about me. The uncomfortable stomachache and looming threat of purging kept me from both. When I awoke the next morning, feeling the food had at least partially digested, the camp was still, and I'd missed my chance. Leah had left.

Day 28

We explored for new campsites and discussed options for a more invisible lifestyle. The group that had found us still weighed heavily on our minds. We didn't really have the drive to set up an entirely new camp. At least, I know I didn't.

We decided to keep using our debris huts. We would take down the group shelter and move our firepit and belongings away from camp. It should appear we had stopped using the area and just left our debris huts.

With nightfall, we returned to extract honey from the hive. The bees were setting up to protect the hive from the cool night. Single strands of bees—chains of their bodies—spanned the length of the hole. These strands were the start of a bee plug, which would seal the new hole with their bodies. Bees are remarkable. I look forward to researching them more when our summer experience is over.

The honey extraction didn't take long. The bees were smoked with birch bark, and Mike enlarged the hole and began to pull comb from the hive. It was an amazing picture. The night was dark and moonless. A circle of light was given off by a small fire at the base of a large pine on a ridge in the woods. The needles of hemlocks swayed and glimmered in the firelight. Mike stood on a fallen log, propped against the tree, up to his armpit in beehive; great chunks of comb were held to the torch for inspection. From our distance, we would occasionally see honey drip from the comb, glistening in firelight. Unbelievable. We were gathering honey—*wild* honey.

Many bees died as we reached into the hive and tore out chunks of comb; our hands crushed their bodies. Guard bees caught their stingers in our clothing and in our hair and died after their stingers detached. Yet, we escaped with about thirty pounds of comb and hadn't been stung once. The hive had given so much. We wondered if the bees would move. If so, we would investigate the hive completely. If not, we would install a wood patch for them to begin reconstruction.

Kayla was still with us and split her time between wandering on her own and participating in our adventures. Seeing her cringe each time an animal died at our hands has made me think. Survival involves taking the lives of others every day. Killing. There are no buffers like those set up in society. And participating in natural cycles brings about reflection. How do we as humans fit into ecology? What's our role in natural systems? And how do we hold these roles in modern America?

Not all of living and wandering in nature is blossoms and honey. Death is as natural a part of the life cycle as birth. "Kill sites," places where animals, birds, fish, or insects have been eaten by others, are as numerous as any other animal sign in the forest. I remember spending considerable time one day marveling at a beautiful blue and green iridescent dragonfly with coal black wings. It ate several equally stunning butterflies, and their wings floated down from the dragonfly's perch and were taken by the swirling rapids of the stream. Wings in kaleidoscopic color and pattern, wings you'd be afraid to touch in case you disturbed their beauty, surfed the currents until they were lost around a bend in the creek.

There have been times this summer when raw nature has made me cringe. David and I were exploring when I spotted a house cat playing with a meadow vole. I ran to intervene but arrived too late. The cat had just delivered a crippling blow. The vole limped, dragging its hind legs as it wiggled under a few blades of grass in a meager attempt to hide. The kindest thing I could do was let the cat finish the job it had started. David said his cats break the legs of small mammals and then sit around and play with them—many times every day. How many cats are loose around our country? Millions.

Once, while Mike and I were hiking, we discovered a young robin on the ground. As we approached, it opened its mouth wide in anticipation of food we did not have. Something was very wrong. I peered down at the almost fully grown bird and was startled to see it had no tail. Rather, a mass of wriggling maggots was slowly eating the bird alive from behind. Maggots kill and consume many young animals every year. Mike killed the bird quickly while its mother sounded an alarm just overhead. The maggots would continue to feed.

As we become more aware of the natural cycles this summer, I have realized how every part of our existence involves sacrificing the lives of others. In society, we are protected from this knowledge. And ignorance is bliss. David, Mike, and I kill trees for containers, food, and shelters. We harvest plants constantly, and we fish and hunt to feed ourselves. We tread on insects and swat mosquitoes and deerflies. Moths kamikaze into our fire every night. One night a frog leaped into the flames and was cooked before we could save it.

I've read about one ancient culture that survived without hunting, but they were very rare among a global history of hunting and gathering societies, and lived in a particularly lush environment. When I look in the pond when there is no wind, I see the characteristics of an omnivore reflected back at me. My eyes point straight forward, like the bobcat and coyote, providing the depth of field that is essential for hunting. Prey animals, such as deer and cottontails, have eyes pointing to either side, which allows them to better catch any movement and thus any potential threat. Human beings also have well-developed canines, teeth that are able to rip and tear flesh, as well as molars for grinding meat and seeds.

In my early twenties, I worked hard for animal-rights campaigns. And for long periods, I was completely vegetarian. To this day, I still refuse commercial red meat, although my reasons for doing so have changed. The politics of the beef industry sicken me. Cows feed on our public lands, displacing native species, and are protected with public money through the U.S. Department of Agriculture's Animal Damage Control program. Millions of predators are killed every year to protect cows and sheep pumped full of steroids and hormones. Millions of dollars subsidize the greatest destroyer of wilderness in the world.

Some people feel it's better to eat plants than animals. I attended university with a woman who refuses to eat "anything with a face." Personally, my perspectives have shifted. Now, I believe that planting vegetables in tight rows, harvesting them in the prime of their lives, and cooking them is equally as brutal as harvesting woodchucks or cows. Both are killed for our benefit. Yet neither killing plants nor animals is truly brutal, but necessary. The brutality comes about in the method and attitude of the person or organization doing the harvesting.

Without the sacrifices of trees, fish, plants, and other diverse animals, we would not be able to live. They have all given generously this summer, and I have needed support from all of them to survive in these woods. Other than gratitude, what can I offer in return? Is reciprocity a component to healthy ecology?

(continued on page 165)

Hunting Tools

Many tools have been used for securing game over the past ten thousand years, but a few of the handheld weapons that we successfully put to use include the rabbit stick, the thrusting spear, the throwing spear, and bolas.

THE "RABBIT STICK"

The "rabbit stick," quite simply, is a club specifically for throwing. It is the easiest of hunting tools to acquire and can be very effective with a bit of practice. Any solid stick of a weight that can be easily

Weighted rabbit stick

thrown and that measures from your armpit to your wrist will suffice. This measurement is a general rule. You must take into consideration that the shorter the stick, the faster you can throw it, but the more accurate you must be. A larger stick is more forgiving of poor aim but cannot be thrown as fast. Experiment and weigh the tradeoffs to find what works best for you.

The basic rabbit stick is about two inches in diameter and has all its edges rounded. This helps cut down on sound as it flies through the air and gives less warning to your prey. Rounding the edges takes little time either with a knife or by abrading on a rough stone. (A large stationary rock works better than a small movable one.)

Rabbit Stick Modifications

A host of other modifications can be made to improve the performance of the rabbit stick. The weighted rabbit stick is much like the basic rabbit stick except that one end is bulbous. When thrown, the stick spins. The bulbous end spins more slowly like a hub, and the handle spins like a spoke. This causes the end of the handle to spin more rapidly than other parts of the stick, making it capable of delivering a devastating blow to the target. This weapon is good for short distances in fairly open sections of woods and meadows, as well as in tall grass.

The boomerang, one of my favorites, has a natural curve in it and is carved so that a cross section is elliptical or winglike (one-half ellipse). This weapon does not return, as is commonly thought, but flies faster and more silently, as well as further and more flat, than any other rabbit stick I have ever used. (Most objects move in an arc when thrown, but due to the aerodynamics of the boomerang and its proximity to the ground, the arc is almost nonexistent.) The *best* terrain for the boomerang is in open

Boomerang

fields, using the sidearm throw for short or longer distances as described below.

Fire Hardening Your Rabbit Stick

Once you have modified your rabbit stick by carving or abrading, it is important to camouflage the carve marks to make it harder for the animal to pick up the stick's movement as it approaches. Camouflage of wooden tools can be done by "fire hardening," which will also increase the life span of your weapon. The best way to accomplish this is to thrust the rabbit stick into the sand close to, but not in, the fire. If you get the weapon too close to the fire, the wood will burn; too far and nothing will happen. You want the moisture to be driven out and the wood to be lightly browned. Smooth wood tends to become shiny as a result of this process, so you may want to scuff up such areas to aid in camouflage. In the absence of sand, the wood can be

held over the fire or just next to it, but you must closely monitor and rotate it almost constantly or you may char and weaken the weapon.

Throwing the Rabbit Stick

Throws can be made overhand, sidearm, and anywhere in between. Sidearm works well with the boomerang in open meadows or other areas where there is enough space between trees to allow for unhindered flight. Overhand works

Overhand throw

well in taller growth or in areas where there is little distance between trees.

The tricky part is preparing to release your weapon. You cannot stalk your quarry and then, when in range, rear back and hurl it. You must slowly position your body and throwing stick into launch position *as* you stalk.

For overhand throws, use your whole body—don't try to "muscle it" with just your arm. Slowly bring your stick and throwing arm back over your shoulder, and bend backward from your waist. Your body, now taut as a bow, is ready to contract, starting with your stomach muscles and ending with your arm and hand snapping forward like the cracking of a whip, hurling the weapon forward at your prey.

Sidearm throws are similar in that you use your whole body to launch

Sidearm throw

the stick. However, instead of bending backward (if you are right-handed), place your stick behind your neck and twist to the right until your left hand and shoulder are pointing at your target. Then, in a single motion, whip your body around, releasing the stick as your throwing hand comes to bear on the target. Be wary of nearby trees and low branches. Also, be sure to stalk into a fully cocked position to avoid giving yourself away by cocking back right before the throw.

It is wise to carry more than one weapon, as this allows you to immediately make a follow-up strike and ensure that the kill has been made. A stunned animal may appear dead, and then, as you approach, get up and hobble off to safety where it may die from its wounds out of your reach. A case in point: While hunting one day, I stalked a woodchuck and threw my boomerang, laying the animal out. I approached quickly with my spear at the ready and with ten feet to go saw the woodchuck get up and run. A good throw with my spear ensured meat for the evening meal.

THRUSTING SPEAR

The thrusting spear is designed to thrust directly into an animal without leaving your hands. Some animals, like rabbits and other small game, are struck from above.

Bone spearheads

Therefore, the spear must be able to withstand the force of being driven severely into the ground.

I prefer a stout sapling about five feet long for the shaft of the thrusting spear. It doesn't need to be straight, but the thin end should be sharpened and fire hardened (see "Fire Hardening," page159). I do not recommend using bone spearheads for small game, because you will likely stab through the animal and into the ground, breaking the tip that took such effort to create. For large game, a bone spearhead can be affixed to the shaft as described below.

THROWING SPEAR

The throwing spear is used for hunting animals at distances up to approximately fifteen feet.

Harvest a straight sapling about six feet in length with a diameter less than one and one-half inches. Sharpen the thicker of the two ends and fire-harden the tip.

Make bone spearheads as wide or wider than the shaft of the spear or arrow on which they are mounted. I use leg bones from deer, elk, or other large animals for spear tips. Smashing the bone leaves many shards of usable size that can be carved or abraded into the desired shape. Make the tang (the part of the spearhead that is connected to the shaft) as long as or longer than the tip, and flare it at the bottom. Bone can only be made so sharp; it is not a hard enough substance to create a razor-sharp edge. However, serrating the edge increases its ability to cut and takes little time with a good abrading stone.

To insert a bone spearhead, wrap strong cordage around the shaft

Spear tip ready for a bone point

eight inches from the pointed tip. Split the tip down to the cordage. Insert the spearhead tang, and pack around it with pitch and ash (see "Working with Pitch," page 68). Bind the head tightly with wet rawhide or sinew and let it dry. Once the hide has dried, slather the lashings with pitch and ash. To make a really solid seat for the spearhead, the inside of the split in the upper end of the spear shaft can be carved down to better accommodate the tang.

How to Throw a Spear

To throw a spear, first find the point in the middle of the shaft where the spear will balance if placed across an outstretched finger. Mark the balance point with charcoal and set the spear in your hand, with the mark in the center of your palm. Close your fingers around it and raise it over your shoulder as if preparing to throw. Note where the tip of your index finger touches the

spear, and carve a shallow groove all the way around the shaft. Every time you pick up your spear, your fingertip should be in that groove.

1. Start with a target about fifteen feet away, and if you are using a bone spearhead, be sure your target and the area around it are soft. The mechanics of throwing properly are worth learning even if the first few times you throw you feel awkward.
2. Face your target with your left arm out in front, pointing at the target.
3. Extend your right arm with the spear straight back, with the spearhead near your ear.
4. Shift your weight to your right foot as you lean back, and use your left foot as a counterbalance.

The next step should be done slowly a few times to ensure that you have the motion.

5. Keeping your eye on the target, begin moving the spear forward. As your hand moves toward the target, your elbow will move forward, too. During this movement, your elbow should point at the target and pass your shoulder *before* your hand does
6. As you release, follow through, with your index fingertip and the groove being the last point of contact with the spear. Your

throw should end with your finger pointing at the target.

BOLAS

The function of bolas is to hold prey long enough to allow you to approach and kill it with a thrusting spear or club. Primary bola game is large birds, such as turkey and geese, and long-legged animals like deer.

From three to seven weights of stone, wood, or leather pouches filled with sand are connected by equal lengths (about three feet) of cordage to another loop of cordage. When thrown, the weights fan out until one or more of the pieces of cordage hits an object, allowing the weights to continue to swing forward and wrap around the wings, legs, or branches of your target. This tangles and often temporarily stops any forward motion.

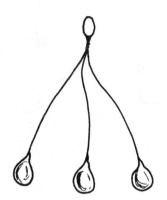

A bola with sand-filled pouches

A carved wood bola weight

Throwing the Bolas

Contrary to popular belief, bolas are not swung multiple times around your head prior to their release. This would only alert your prey. A more effective way is to start with your right index and middle fingers in the loop at about shoulder height. Meanwhile, your left hand provides tension on the cordage if you lace your fingers through the cordage and rest them on the weights, preventing any tangling. When you are in position to throw, release with your left hand while simultaneously whipping your right hand up and around your head once and following through until your right hand is pointing at your target.

There are many weapons and variations of each with which you can hunt. Some require less work and less practice than others, but the trade-off is that with less work comes less range; i.e., if you pick up a throwing stick, you can hunt immediately but with little range. If you take the time to make an effective hunting bow and the arrows to go with it, and spend more time practicing with your weapon, you can hunt a variety of game at greater distances. The upside of throwing sticks is that simple tools are easy to replace.

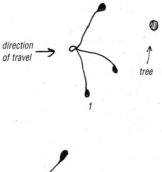 

direction of travel →

tree

1

2

3

top view

1

2

3

side view

Bola striking a target

(continued from page 157)

Hunting and harvesting can be performed in ways which are both sustainable and contribute to natural communities. Each life I take shapes the larger ecological system and has the potential to either hinder or foster the forest community. We have eaten woodchucks and deer to help balance their exploding populations. If two trees are physically competing for space, harvesting one stops both from dying in the long run. Removing another tree may bring light to four others. When you approach hunting and harvesting in this way, you develop a deeper relationship with the land. The land supports me and, in turn, I may caretake the land.

Hunting has a place within natural cycles. We recently explored the valley south of camp at dusk and heard a piercing, rhythmic cry. We followed it to the source and discovered a young cottontail. The rabbit had torn open its underside on a fierce hawthorn needle, and its innards hung from the surrounding twigs. We quickly moved away. Its call was not for its mother but for one who would efficiently end the pain and return its life to the natural cycles of nutrients.

I have also discovered another benefit in taking the life of an animal. When I hold its limp body and see up close the destruction I have delivered, I feel a great obligation to do good in my life, to be honest and true. When I eat a plant or an animal, that life joins with mine. I want my grandchildren to have the opportunity to choose experiences like I've had this summer and to be able to witness natural cycles without veils of plastic wrap and Styrofoam. Killing is real and necessary, and modern society seems bent on creating an illusion in which we'll all live some "happy" estranged existence.

David and I carried our honey loot as we filed out of the woods on an old logging road. We entered a field where deer silhouettes bounded around us, the sounds of their hooves echoing through the night.

An intense shooting star appeared to the north. It was so intense and large I thought it must have hit the earth. Were David and I the only ones to see that massive fiery ball with a long trailing tail?

Day 29

We sorted through the honeycomb this morning, marveling at the structural achievements of the bees. Most of the comb was a mixture of honey, pollen, and young bees. Occasionally, a section would be uniformly one of the above. There were many young bees; David had since done some research and told us that the queen bee lays about 2,500 eggs a day.

We tried different methods for extracting the honey, including pounding and dripping, and cutting and dripping. We rigged a drip set to take advantage of the heat of the day. We'll see what happens.

We all went fishing in the afternoon. Kayla speared her first fish! Although she was excited, she struggled with the actual killing of such a beautiful creature. Whether you hand fish or spearfish a trout, you must then hold it tightly, insert a thumb into its mouth for leverage, feel its raspy breaths and sharp teeth, and quickly snap its neck backward until it breaks.

Mike and I spearfished as a team in one pool. I waded in with the spear but the trout were beyond my field of vision. Mike crawled in behind a root system where he could see the fish. He directed me slowly. "Left a little. Now right. Deeper, lower. Okay, lunge!" Together, we pinned a massive trout to the wall of the pool. Mike grabbed it by the gills. This is community living; Mike and I work well together.

As the sun lowered to the west, we watched a pair of water snakes swim upstream to the pool where we had just been fishing. They seemed more brash than usual; they often slip out of sight with the approach of humans. Their dark bodies slithered along, fighting current, their heads just above water level, keeping an eye on us. The two of them slipped under the same root system where Mike had directed my spear.

We heard splashing, and the pair appeared holding a nine-inch trout between them. The two danced downstream, the smaller snake grasping the fish by the gills, and the larger snake holding the tail. Twisting and turning, the pair moved in tandem carrying the fish above water, like a shimmering baton between two runners. Neither let go, as they hauled out onto a gravel bar.

At first, the pair seemed to be working together, but snakes don't carry knives to split fish evenly. It soon became obvious we were witnessing a tug-of-war match, and the smaller snake had the better grasp. A third water snake came over to investigate, but, being the smallest of the three, it decided to move on to find food for itself. As the match continued, the smaller snake attempted to maneuver toward the front in order to swallow the trout whole. But to do this it needed to loosen its grasp. This may have been its greatest mistake, as the larger snake tore the fish away from the smaller snake and fell backward onto the gravel. Without further effort, the smaller snake abandoned the fish and glided downstream.

The fish flopped a bit, still alive. The winner held on tightly to the fish's tail. The water snake's prehistoric fangs were an obvious advantage for hunting slippery trout. As the fish quieted, the snake moved to the front and began to swallow the trout. We had learned from eating water snakes that the jaws are created by four separate bones that are connected by stretchy ligaments and muscles. The mouth slowly stretched, and we watched the head of the trout disappear. The enlarged head of

the snake repositioned with each surge of fish, which went deeper down its throat. There was no apparent rush, regardless of our presence. With time, only the trout's tail was visible, like a thick, massive snake tongue, and, of course, the bulge behind the snake's head.

The snake's body undulated and muscles rippled from front to rear, moving the fish further back into the snake's stomach. With the fish about one third of the way along the length of the snake, our water snake decided it was time to seek refuge from nosy humans. It slipped into the water and awkwardly made its way to a tussock, dragging itself across stones in shallow sections of the stream. Then it was gone. The snake was beginning a long rest to digest the meal. How long until it next needed to feed?

What a gift! We were able to witness the entire process. We fished, the snake fished, the snake ate, and we climbed our hill to digest trout—although ours would be cooked. We were active participants in natural ecology. In fact, we seemed to be eating water-snake style, gorging every few days with light grazing in between.

Day 30

Kayla left early this morning. She was soaked in last night's storm and was still wet when she left. I retired to my debris hut, where by morning my body's own heat had dried my clothes and spirit. I awoke to clear skies above the treetops and cool breezes pushing through the holes in my door.

Just below camp, Mike and I discovered what appeared to be a small town gathering of eastern newts. Eleven newts fed within several square feet of ground. Their brilliant orange bodies accented the forest floor among tiny maple seedlings. We watched them feed on insects, slowly climbing about above the forest debris. A few newts were in the transitional stage, in which they change from fluorescent orange "red efts" to olive creatures with orange spots.

Our honey extraction setup yielded very little pure honey. The comb we had collected was composed primarily of young bees, or brood comb. We were rather disappointed over the amount of honey and so decided to try to harvest the wax for candles. Our first chunk of comb refused to melt. We discovered that most of the brood comb was not made of wax. The comb was formed from a papery substance, more like the stuff of wasp nests. We did manage to melt a small amount of wax that seemed to hold honey rather than babies.

David's research outside of the woods revealed some interesting facts about honeybees. People who have collected honey claim that the area below the entrance in wild hives is generally the brood area. Our experience definitely supported this hypothesis. They also said that the honey stores were generally above the entrance. If this were true of our hive, we never even reached the honey stores.

I hunted woodchucks and rabbits from afternoon until sundown. Hunting always yields extraordinary experiences. Moving very slowly and really paying attention allowed me to witness what I would so often miss.

One particularly aware woodchuck stood to assess me thoroughly. I froze in midstep and the seconds turned into minutes. On and on the woodchuck stared, but I held steadfast. Another animal stalked to the edge of the field just several feet from me but was concealed by a wall of goldenrods. Woodchuck or rabbit? My mind raced. The animal must have sensed my busy thoughts or caught wind of my odor, as it backed away as cautiously as it had approached. By now, the leg that was supporting me was burning. I began to shift my weight slowly backward so that my weight could be shared by both legs. I waited a bit longer to see whether the animal would return to the edge of the field in front of me and emerge from the goldenrod. The first woodchuck had returned to grazing.

Grasses shook as another small creature approached. It was much too small to be a cottontail this time. A meadow vole entered the meadow and meandered between tufts of grass to a patch of red clover. It stood assessing the clover, which was exactly its height. Then the vole dropped down and cut each clover stem at its base to harvest and eat it in its entirety. Forgetting woodchucks, I tuned in on the meadow vole. I watched it feed for quite some time, until the small patch of clover was mowed clean. Then, as quickly as he'd appeared, the vole worked its way back to the goldenrod and was gone. An experiential gem. Such is the payoff of hunting.

As the sun faded and I stood watching the clouds, the doe I knew quite well entered the field. She used the same trails each evening and always fed alone. I had thought about sitting patiently and trying to touch her alongside that trail.

She eventually saw me and began to stalk closer to investigate. I stood still as she circled me, coming closer and closer. She snorted a bit and then, satisfied I was neither a threat nor interesting enough to pursue further, went about grazing. I slipped away. Before I entered the woods, I looked back at her. She was looking at me. I waved. She flicked her ears and went back to feeding.

I met Mike on the ridge and we stood for awhile, enjoying the calls of screech owls.

Day 31

We're practicing ancient skills on the edge of modern society. I can hear the highway at night and farm noises in the day, and I am constantly aware of other people in the woods. Sadly, I'd have to walk many, many days before I could find a plot of land large enough to yield sufficient food upon which to survive without crossing roads or seeing other people as I wandered. Our woodlands and our wilderness safe havens for our souls and fellow creatures are all islands amidst an ocean of industry and sprawling suburbia.

Generally, Mike, David, and I stay invisible by avoiding high-use trails and hiding from random hikers and explorers. It doesn't take much to disappear—just sitting several feet off-trail. Most people look down at the trail as they walk, because they don't trust their own feet to carry them. It took me awhile to build confidence in my feet.

Occasionally, people talk to themselves as they stride through woods and fields, and I hear what is said. It's completely unintentional eavesdropping. I hear about stresses in their lives or difficult decisions. Or sometimes it's singing or random mumbling that I'm unable to follow at all. So many people come to the woods to release their troubles.

Most people move unnaturally in the forest. Without concerns for food, shelter, or tools, they usually have no need to move slowly, or to see wildlife before the wildlife sees them. It is not necessary to look carefully. People can blunder along, wrapped in their own thoughts, much like dogs that crash through the woods knowing that Kibbles and Bits and a warm home await them.

Out of necessity and convenience, Mike, David, and I occasionally cross roads or follow short sections of pavement. Mike and I were recently held up by a flurry of country drivers. There we stood, a sight to behold: scruffy, dirty, both of us in camouflage pants, neither of us in shirts, and both armed with sticks. We studied people's faces as they drove past. There was a tremendous variation in response, but we found several patterns to hold true. There were those who didn't believe what they were seeing. Their eyes would become larger and larger, and their mouths would open wider and wider as they approached and passed. Then there were those who were completely disgusted and pushed to the far side of their seats while contorting their faces into ugly grimaces. They always accelerated as they passed us. There were also the confused drivers; their faces were blank slates that reflected their mental breakdown—they generally swerved. And then there were those people who were initially disgusted but were able to regain their regal, condescending expressions. To say the least, I felt neither welcome nor beautiful in their world of vehicles and deodorant. It all had to do with camouflage. In the woods, Mike and I blended well. In society, a different sort of camouflage is needed to blend: clean jeans, button-down shirt, and clean face and hands. Oh yeah—and we couldn't carry sticks. Well, maybe lumber.

(continued on page 176)

Camouflage

What does it take to move unseen through the land? Good camouflage! What is good camouflage? Let me break it down. Camouflage is intended to break up the outline of a person or object, because it is often the outline that attracts the eye and is recognized by the brain.

Good camouflage has two very distinct parts: physical and mental. The physical aspect of camouflage has to do with the blurring or changing of your outline and the distinctive body patterns that catch the eye, including the symmetry of your face or the series of parallel lines that make up your hands. The mental aspect has to do with the quieting of the mind and going into full-view vision in order to soften or diffuse your intent. As children, many of us found out in Hide-and-Go-Seek that intensely thinking "don't see me" or "I know they are going to find me" drew the attention of the seekers. Animals are far more sensitive in this area than humans.

Here you will be given pointers for physical camouflage, with an exercise at the end for mental camouflage.

PHYSICAL CAMOUFLAGE

Many types of camouflage are used by people the world over, but two of the most effective that we used were mud and charcoal. With mud, you camouflage to a specific area. With charcoal, you camouflage to shadow. Moving within shadow takes practice, as it often requires movement off-trail through thick and potentially noisy debris. You have to learn to trust your camouflage. Anyone can hide behind an object. The goal here is to be invisible while in the open.

Mud Camouflage

Mud camouflage is especially useful when you are not moving at all, or when you seldom move, as in the case of an ambush for game. Some pros of mud are its ability to decrease your scent, the non skin-like texture it gives your body, and the natural dappling it provides as it dries.

The cons are the potential for leaving a trail of mud smudges on leaves and the ground as you walk, and its lack of versatility; i.e., the type of mud you use—gray clay, for example—may be perfect camouflage for a streambed but will stick

Mud camouflage is very effective; here only the hand and fingers are discernible.

out clearly in the forest.

In a moist area or near water, you can make mud by pouring water onto the ground and digging in it with your hands or a stick. Once you have an adequate supply of mud, follow the two steps below to apply full mud camouflage. Take the time to see how the mud color compares to that of the area in which you plan to hide. And remember, mud changes color as it dries.

1. Liberally apply mud to your entire body while being careful not to get it into your inner ears or eyes. The consistency should be such that it sticks easily and does not readily run or fall off.
2. Pick up handfuls of dry debris and, with your eyes closed, gently toss them over your whole body. They should stick to the mud and provide a further breaking up of your outline.

Now you are ready to get to your hiding spot. A few points are worthy of note.

- Move carefully, because plants brushing you will give away your passage by way of mud on the leaves.
- Too much movement will result in much of your camouflage falling off.
- As you move, you generate heat and thus dry the mud faster.

Therefore, depending on what color the mud is when it is dry, it may require you to shift your hiding spot.

- Bring an extra handful of mud with which to cover the soles of your feet once you are in position or for touchup.
- Mud quickly cools the body. Even on warm days, a spot in the shade can quickly lead to shivering.
- If you have glasses, you can dip them in mud, then clean a line in the center of each lens to allow you to see with little reflective material exposed. Warning: Your glasses may sustain scratches.

Charcoal Camouflage

By far the warmer of the two camouflage techniques covered here, charcoal camouflage is also better for times when movement is required. The pros of charcoal are that it is dry and therefore warmer than mud, it does not brush off easily or leave obvious signs of your passage, it can be applied to blend with almost anything, and it is easily acquired. The cons are that it is harder to remove and can only be applied effectively to skin or light-colored clothing.

You can grind up charcoal from a wood fire and apply it as a powder, or with water, added as a paste. (White ash, *not charcoal*, when mixed with water makes lye, an alkali that will cause burns if it contacts your skin.)

Because your goal is to break up the outline of your body and the symmetry that easily defines parts of you, as a general rule it is best to lighten the hollows and darken the ridges. This does not mean that you should put a black line across your brow and down your nose. Mark your body with charcoal lines that run contrary to your body's natural contours. Soften the lines by gently rubbing your hands over them, smudging them. This softens the edges, dulls the sheen on your skin, and gives a dappled effect. Finally, dust and small debris can be sprinkled over your body. This may seem insignificant, as it does not appear to make much difference; however, your body's tiny hairs hold onto some of this debris and can help blend you with the background.

MENTAL CAMOUFLAGE EXERCISE

Sitting in the woods leaning against a tree or rock, or perhaps not leaning on anything at all, imagine your body growing into whatever it is in contact with. At the same time, imagine that whatever you are sitting on or leaning against is growing into you. Feel roots growing downward into the ground and bark creeping up and covering your body. Melt into the landscape. Maintain full-view vision, stretch your consciousness outward, and simply relax into your surroundings. Maintain this consciousness even when approached by animals and see what happens. Practice with birds first by having a friend sprinkle birdseed on you. Good luck, and long patience.

Can you spot the person in this photo?

(continued from page 172)

Anyway, the goal of this ramble is to report that Mike had asked the local camp residents if they would like to visit us and see for themselves what we were doing in the woods. Word of our encampment might have spread after our camp's discovery, and Mike felt that an invitation was a more proactive strategy than running away or allowing the local community to seek us out with questions, concerns, and potential misunderstandings. Our invitation was accepted, and a group of exuberant young boys and several staff were led up the steep ridge to our home. We showed them our debris huts, hunting weapons, canteens, cooking pots, cordage, fish hooks, and more. I told a story about fire, and Mike demonstrated the bow and drill. It went smoothly.

The counselors claimed the group had never been so attentive. It was easy. We were but a bridge to the fascinating world of nature; the woods did all the work. And it felt good to share what we were learning with others. It was reciprocity of sorts and a giving back to the cycles that sustain us all. Idealistic? Yes. I'm aware this may be my mind creating a scenario so that I can feel good about myself. I realize that the earth may be so powerful it does not need my help at all. Yet, I still choose to try to better our world. Perhaps this is optimism, rather than idealism.

This afternoon, I was overcome with the urge to make baskets, to work my hands. Until now, I have focused on skills that have utilitarian value for survival, such as cooking, hunting, and making containers for carrying water and collecting berries. I needed a break from function and therefore spent today on form. Function, of course, accompanies form, but these baskets were made for the pleasure of form rather than strictly for function. I worked as an artist rather than as a survivalist.

There is meditation in working with your hands, as well as working in art. I dug rootlets of hemlock and oak and felt the earth as I worked my fingers and forearms. I wove the rootlets together, enjoying the visual progression as much as the finished basket. While the hands work and the mind focuses on form, random mental gibberish, which so often clouds clarity, fades away. Art is a mantra, as effective as any.

(continued on page 180)

Baskets

Baskets are useful for a variety of tasks, such as carrying firewood, catching fish, storing foods, and holding fruits, seeds, and water. Many materials are available to make baskets of all shapes and functions. They can be loosely or tightly woven, rigid, or pliable. Loosely woven baskets can be lined with grass, leaves, or hides so that small objects can be carried without the risk of loss through the holes. Skins can be draped in the basket for rock boiling or carrying water. There are more basket types, weaves, shapes, and materials than I can cover, but here are a few basic baskets that can be adapted for many uses.

BASIC ROOTLET BASKET

Any pine, oak, or hemlock tree has many fine roots just below the surface of the soil. The rootlets are very flexible, making for easy weaving. The real bonus is that after a day or two, they dry and stiffen up, and the basket becomes fairly rigid.

1. By carefully working your hand into the dirt, you will find in the first half inch or so of soil, roots as thick as sturdy shoelaces. These can be dug and pulled up in three-foot lengths (or more), and when a quantity has been collected, the weaving can begin. Anytime rootlets are exposed, as in the case of storm-blown trees, make a point of collecting a supply.

2. Lay three, two-foot-long rootlets parallel on the ground and three more perpendicular to and on top of the first three at their mid-points. This spot is called the "hub," and the rootlets are called the "warps" or the spokes. The warps will be woven around by "woofs" of the same material.

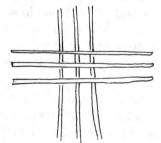

3. This is the hardest part of making this basket. Lay a rootlet under the bottom set of three warps. Moving clockwise around the hub, weave the woof over the top set of three and under the bottom set of three for two complete circuits. This will hold the warps together for the next step. Add in an additional warp by weaving it into the newly placed woof so there are thirteen warps radiating out from the hub. An odd number is required so that the woof falls first on one side of the warp, and in the next circuit it falls on the other side.

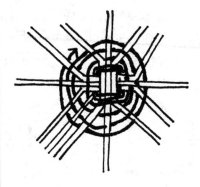

woof. Bend each warp over to the right and insert it into the woof alongside the neighboring warp.

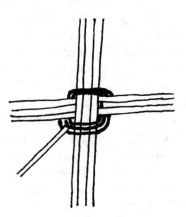

4. From here, it is just a matter of weaving around the hub by going over one warp and under the next with the woof. When a woof runs out, simply add another, making sure it overlaps for a few warps.

5. To finish off, stop weaving when about one and one-half inches of the warps are visible above the

BARK BASKETS

The beauty of bark is that it folds like paper when it is fresh, then hardens as it dries. Birch, tulip poplar, cedar, white pine, and elm are some of the best barks of which I am aware. (See "Cooking Containers," page 111, for tips on harvesting.) A fairly quick and functional bark basket is the "one-piece" or "single-fold" basket.

Step One
Lay out a piece of bark, cambium side (inside) up. The dimensions

are not important, but for the sake of clarity, I will use a piece ten inches wide by twenty inches long with the grain running along the twenty-inch axis. Draw a line *across* the center of the piece. The line marks the center of an ellipse, with the points ending just shy of the edges, as shown in the illustration.

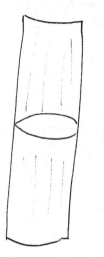

The wider you make the ellipse, the rounder the basket will be.

Step Two

Score along the ellipse line no more than one third of the way through the bark. Note: Baskets have been made with score marks on the outside when using bark that is more rigid, as in the case of rougher pine bark and elm. Additionally, with more pliable barks, I often will *not* score the bark at all, as it seems to bend into the desired shape without the risk of compromising the fibers.

Step Three

Fold the bark on either side of the ellipse upward, allowing one piece to overlap the other by an inch.

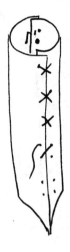

Step Four

Holes for stitching must be drilled or burned with either a hand or bow drill (either can be fitted with a bone or stone tip for boring through, or you can simply use a thin, tipped spindle to burn through; see "Fire Making," page 132). Making holes with an awl will often create a split. The placement of the holes depends on how you want to stitch the basket. Parallel holes, an inch from each edge, allow for a number of stitch patterns.

The rim piece is important in preventing splits from the top during regular use. Bore holes an inch from the top around the whole edge. Tie a knot or twig to the end of your stitching material

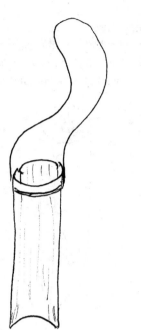

(cordage, rootlets, sinew, etc.) to keep it from passing through the holes. Run your cordage from the inside out; come over the rim piece and top edge back into the basket and through the next hole. Continue until you have gone through the last hole. Then, with the aid of a thin, blunt awl, push the cordage through the next hole from the outside in, and tie off.

Step Five

Adding a strap makes this basket far more useful. This can be done by threading a thong or cordage through the existing stitching on the sides and tying off.

(continued from page 177)

I stopped weaving to watch the debris about me ridge upward and move, like earth above a mole. I looked up to investigate the sounds, which were different from the sounds made by daddy longlegs spiders, which I've come to know very well this summer. I hear daddy longlegs all over the forest.

Any distraction by wildlife is fine with me. I watched the ridging debris, waiting for a glimpse of the creature below. I followed and followed, listening to jaws crunching, as the leaf litter rested. In time, a head wriggled free of the debris to assess the world about. A moment's glimpse and the short-tailed shrew withdrew back into the debris tunnel network to feed upon insects it had encountered.

I completed two baskets and have two more designs in mind. I felt refreshed and content. With my hands and spirit fed with art, I turned to fields to feed my stomach. Dewberries were exploding all over and I grazed on sorrels, plantains, clovers, and wild carrots.

A massive beetle as big as my thumb distracted me from journal writing. It crinkled leaves in a way I didn't recognize. These were not the sounds of daddy longlegs, small mammals, or feeding birds. David and I followed the beetle and watched her lay eggs periodically in the duff, just below the winter-fallen oak leaves. A thin tube projected from her abdomen into the ground, propping her body forward so much that her rear legs stuck straight out, parallel to the ground. Her body rose and fell—a very sexual movement that might have corresponded with the release of eggs.

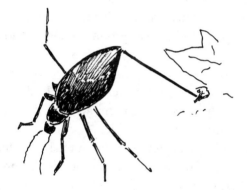

Day 32

Leaning against my debris hut early this morning, I watched a female hairy woodpecker. She hunted along branches of a chestnut oak, hopping backward while clinging upside down. This was amazing enough, but it was her liftoff that struck me even more. She let go and dropped like an arrow. Straight down she fell, wings tucked, completely aerodynamic. Just above ground, she opened her wings and toes for a perfect landing on the base of the trunk. She made a twenty-five-foot free fall before she spread her wings. It seemed a fun way to fly, and the grace of the landing was indescribable.

I set snares and wandered about during the morning. One of my new basket designs flopped and needs to be rethought. I hunted during the afternoon and evening. At one point, I was stalking a woodchuck while two deer were following me. Everything in nature moves in circles.

We hand fished for dinner. Our presence in one pool saved a green heron from the pursuing claws of a goshawk. Just about to be caught, the screeching heron plunged into the water right in front of Mike and me, and the goshawk veered upward, abandoning its attack. The heron swam about, neck extended, feathers ruffled, and for all purposes looked just like a grebe. It screamed and screamed, even though the goshawk had quickly disappeared downstream. When it regained composure, the heron flew away in the direction from which it had come.

The screech owls have spent their last few evenings around our fire circle. Tonight, the nearest owl and I called back and forth. I'd like to think we were communicating, that I was successfully producing screech-owl babble.

It's odd that humans claim animals are unintelligent just because they are unable to grasp and fluently produce a human language, such as English or American Sign Language. I have heard of no humans in modern societies who fluently communicate with an animal species in its own tongue. Have our egos influenced the creation of rules that govern languages to purposefully exclude animals?

Day 33

"Track Road" is an old 4x4 road that supports occasional farm equipment and holds excellent mud puddles. This morning's mud yielded a beautiful jumping mouse trail.

I cannot yet differentiate between the tracks of meadow and woodland jumping mice. I say "yet," for I feel that with a

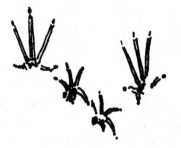

Jumping mice tracks

little research, a difference may emerge. The trail was a typical mix of patterns left by various bounds. Short bounds indicated the mouse was in no real hurry, although the animal did not feel safe enough to walk and explore the open road.

The tracks held tremendous detail. I stared at them, lying flat, protecting my track treasures from the hot, drying sun. Long toes with tiny ridges were present. Even individual palm pads registered. It was a beautiful picture: perfect tracks forming a trail across cracking mud, which produced an area between blocks of earth where tiny dewdrops clung to silken strands.

A great blue heron had walked the road, likely in search of frogs. Its tracks were the exact length of my hand, just as were bald eagle tracks along Oregon beaches earlier this summer. I also followed a cat for awhile. The flexibility of cat paws never ceases to amaze me. One moment the tracks are tiny, and the next moment, in the same substrate, the paw has expanded and left a track people might consider to be that of a bobcat. Several steps further and the cat's claws registered well; the tracks could have been mistaken for those of a gray fox.

I glimpsed a female mink race by across Track Road—possibly the same animal Mike and I had seen toward the start of the summer. A dash of dark brown and she was gone. She brought my attention to a shrew that had been killed by a cat, I believe, and abandoned next to the stream. Unfortunately, this is a common end for shrews; they are often abandoned after being killed.

I pressed the shrew's feet in mud. The palm-pad configuration matched my track plate research at home. I'd been working with a U.S. Forest Service biologist who captures small mammals. He allowed me to run the animals across sooted track plates. In this way I've been able to determine how to differentiate between the many small mammal tracks I find while wandering. But what struck me about the shrew's tracks was that they looked like tiny raccoon tracks: their long toes registered fully, connecting with the palm. Naturally, this may have to do with the pressure I was exerting, but it was something to keep an eye out for.

I was able to locate one of the screech owls this evening by following the alarm calls of wood thrushes and robins. I've begun to recognize the patterns of birdcalls that reveal the presence of screech owls—differences in the durations and intensities of the calls, differences between calls of alarm, and calls meant to harass the predator.

Our nights have been very dark and absolutely moonless. I'd missed the moon. Tonight, though, we were gifted to glimpse it again, a sliver low on the horizon. It had been so long since I had watched the moon, with all the complications of evening clouds, its positions in the sky, and its stages, that I decided to sit and watch. The moon was a dark yellow, like mustard. It did not spend much time with us this evening and moved lower on the horizon. The colors of the sliver changed from dark yellow to orange to blood red. It's an eerie thing to look at a blood-red sliver hung in the sky. It creates a mood, and you can't look away. It's not the feelings you get from horror movies, but of energy, raw power, which can certainly be frightening at times.

I sometimes wonder why the moon is red, and then I realize it's what's in the atmosphere. There must be a tremendous amount of pollution in the air. And that is a disturbing thought.

Day 34

Mike has decided he will begin a "vision quest" today. He'll stay out for four nights and four days. We've also all agreed upon an end for this adventure, which changes things dramatically. It looms on the horizon sooner than we expect. On the evening after Mike's return, I'll begin a solo of the same duration. Then I'll return and have two more days in the woods. On the third day after my return, we will eat breakfast at Mike's house. We will feast on smoothies and homemade waffles, which are Mike's culinary specialties.

It's not the end; David and Mike would like to bring in food and continue "camping" while practicing skills. Initially, this was also my plan, but now I feel it really is the end. I look forward to seeing Kayla again. I'll return to my apartment, fetch my camera, and photograph any animal signs I'd encountered over the summer that still persist. With an end scheduled, my mind has wandered a bit. I'm still present in the woods, but I've become more aware of the lifestyle that lies at the bottom of the hill.

Here, living with nature, my life is simple. It is this simplicity of survival that I sought this summer. I have felt the most connected to the world, and the most aware of a power greater than myself, when I have lived simply. Hiking, camping, and working with the land allow me this simplicity, but using survival skills has provided the greatest simplicity of all.

I remember a discussion I had with a woman from school. We were discussing spirituality, religion, and the countless "spiritual" options these days. She informed me she had about tried them all, yet she continued to feel frustrated, as no path had provided any proof of the existence of a "greater power." She assured me that just one miracle would make her loyal forever.

I, too, have read a great many books from philosophies around the globe and practiced various spiritual rituals. The place where I witness miracles is in nature. Life is intricate. Diverse organisms inhabit unique niches, and somehow each contributes to the overall ecosystem. Beautiful sunsets, cloud formations, horned moths, inchworms, and the bark of chestnut oaks are celebrated even by science. The difference, I've come to believe, is when you *choose* to see miracles in life, rather than take them for granted. Rather than spending my whole life searching for something, I'll hope to spend that time living.

I remember teaching a tracking class along a coastal beach this past spring. A participant discovered the egg casings of whelks and called the group together. I emptied a sack into my hand. There were hundreds and hundreds of tiny whelks, perfect replicas of the massive shells so many admire and collect. They were incredible. The woman pointed at the tiny whelks and said, "This is God."

Daily concerns have now become nonexistent. There is so much food in this bountiful area. The only food issues that persist are those I have created: I'd rather wander and explore than harvest all the time, and I still crave food from society even though I'm eating well. But there are no phones, no "bosses," no bills, no school, no stress at all. I haven't had a stress-induced headache since I arrived.

I began to practice survival skills years ago in the hopes of leaving society behind. I had rebelled against family, school, and society. But my final rebellion would be in leaving it all behind to undertake a mythic journey of man and nature. How my life has changed. I've come to peace with myself and with the demons of my past. I no longer have regrets. Well, maybe one— I do regret that there are people who remember me as an angry young man. I tripped and stumbled through early adulthood. As I look back, though, I must say I wouldn't change a thing. I am the culmination of my experiences and of the lives and experiences of my ancestors. All that has happened has led me to this place, and here, now, in this forest, I am surrounded by beauty. A breeze pushes north, raising goose bumps on my arms and swaying the hemlock canopy. A chickadee sings below me on the ridge and a veery sings in the trees above. Right now, in this place, I am happy.

In short, I have found that survival skills are not only functional in times of crisis, but also provide the opportunity to explore our true selves and what it means to be human. Survival skills also allow for a new relationship with the land. I walk in the woods and am more aware of the bounty that is present, the plants and animals which would sustain me if I so choose. Thus, each new understanding of how to harvest a plant or animal makes me more conscious of my environment and more aware of my relationship with natural systems.

I have witnessed people as they are struck by these skills. They look as if they have finally come home—holding their first fire, identifying their first fisher trail, or stalking barefoot across forest floor. So simple and grounded, yet so very powerful.

Mike left for the hill to the west in the evening and David has not yet returned from home. I gathered plants for dinner and checked a few wild pear trees. Mike and I found a tree with ripe fruit just yesterday. Wild pears are small, like plums, and have a crunchy, sweet bite. They were wonderful. I've missed eating fruit, other than, of course, berries.

I sat and enjoyed a fire as darkness closed around me. Fire, the perfect companion, offered light, cooking, and warmth. It's easy to dream while staring into a fire. The call of a close screech owl brought me back to my senses. I could see the owl's eyes flicker in the firelight as it perched in a nearby hemlock. One more call and the owl was off; I watched it go, mufflers of its feathers silencing its flight. I retired to bed soon after.

Mike has been compiling a list of meals or tastes he finds particularly wonderful. I have a new one for him: hemlock tea with a dash of honey. I also concocted a mint mix: spearmint, peppermint, wild mint, and honey.

There is something special about sitting around a fire at night. The dark enveloped me tightly, creating the sense of being in a room and sipping tea. It was peaceful.

Day 35

I'm still alone in camp. It's serene to be on your own. I strolled to check the traps. A snare had been run over and lay flattened in the trail. Maybe next time the animal will run through it, rather than over it.

On my way back, I looked at tracks. One mud puddle yielded some beautiful rat tracks. I may have been the only person excited to know they were here, but then again perhaps few would recognize their trails. The front tracks were like large mouse tracks and had a different shape than the prints of a red squirrel, which are similar in size. The front toes tended to splay, similar to the front tracks of opossum.

I also found beautiful cottontail, red fox, gray squirrel, jumping mouse, raccoon, opossum, and woodchuck trails on the way back. Tracks, tracks, tracks. I wish I had my camera for those rat tracks. Someday. This summer is about reveling in moving through the woods without camera gear.

David appeared when the sun was high, just in time for a quick rain shower and to try my acorn/black birch bark flour combo. Acorns weren't actually ripe yet, but I wanted to know what they offered this early in the season. The answer was less nut meat and a bitter flour. We tried ash cakes and gruel, then fried the flour in talo, or rendered fat. The fried flour had a welcome fried diner-like texture and flavor. All methods produced palatable food that was even pleasing with adequate quantities of honey.

(continued on page 191)

Acorn Flour

Of the many sources of food in the wild, acorns are a real boon to those willing to process them. Oaks can be divided into two basic types, red (or black) oaks and white oaks. They differ in a number of ways that are important to acorn harvest.

Red oaks, like the scarlet oaks, begin to bear fruit at about twenty years of age but don't reach their full potential until they are about fifty years old. Acorns take two years to mature and contain high amounts of tannins, giving the acorns a very bitter taste. They generally produce a good crop every three to five years. One tree may produce a good mast, while the tree next to it may be having a poor year.

White oaks can produce acorns every year, some with so little tannin that they can be eaten raw. According to the U.S. Forest Service, even though white oaks can produce high numbers of acorns, good years are sporadic, occurring once every four to ten years. Sometimes a few years will pass with no crop at all. In good years, not every tree will produce a heavy crop of acorns; therefore, when a healthy mast is available, it should be taken advantage of. The U.S. Forest Service further says that the best mast production occurs in years when the weather is warm for ten days during flowering and then cools down for the following thirteen to twenty days. It should be noted that white oak acorns germinate quickly upon falling to the ground, thus diminishing their nutritional value.

HARVESTING ACORNS

In the fall, any nuts in the Northeast—acorns, hickories, walnuts, butternuts, and beechnuts—are great sources of proteins and oils.

Acorns should be harvested in the fall when they are dropping nat-urally. Competition for acorns can be stiff, but in a good year, you should have no problem collecting more than you can deal with, especially if you are not against extra protein in the form of acorn weevils. When found on the ground with the cap still attached, acorns are almost certain to contain weevils, as are acorns that have a brown spot or a hole in them.

PREPARING ACORNS

You need to prepare acorns not only to remove the tannins but also to ensure that you don't lose your harvest to mold. Acorns should first be shelled (they are easily cracked when thumped with a stick). The tannins can then be leached out through cold or hot leaching.

In cold leaching, the shelled acorns are left in a bag or basket in flowing water until they can be eaten raw with little or no bitterness. This can take a few days; much depends on the flow of the water and the porosity of the bag. Shelled acorns are also subject to theft by critters, so beware.

In hot leaching, crushed or whole acorns are boiled in changes of water until the water remains clear or only lightly colored. According to Karen Sherwood of Earthwalk Northwest, the acorns must be immersed in *already* boiling water, and each successive change of water should be boiling prior to adding the acorns. Otherwise, the bitterness will stay even though the tannins are removed. The tea-brown water should not be thrown out, because it is an antiviral and antiseptic. This makes it a good wash for dermatitis and, according to Dan Fisher, an effective laundry detergent, although it will lightly stain white clothes. Mark Elbroch, after eating acorns for only a short while, discovered that his tolerance for the bitterness increased to a point where he found tasty what others could not stomach.

Once the tannins have been leached out, the acorns need to be roasted and pulverized into a fine powder. Store this flour in a cool, dry area.

UTILIZING ACORNS

Acorn flour lacks wheat's cohesiveness and produces a crumbly product unless it is cut 50/50 or 75/25 with another flour. Other possible additives are cattail pollen, bulrush or other ground seeds, and ground beechnuts, walnuts, and hickory nuts (nuts that need no treatment other than shelling). For porridge, a mixture of any of the above, in any ratio, can be made by adding hot water and stirring well.

Acorn ash cake is an excellent food. To make the dough, mix the flour and water so that it doesn't quite stick to your hands. Add water in small amounts, kneading the dough each time. Place fruit (reconstituted or fresh) in the middle of a quarter-inch-thick circle of dough, and fold the dough in half over the berries. Pinch the top edge together with the bottom edge to seal them. Bury this mixture in ashes near coals. The ashes serve as somewhat of a leavening agent, causing the outer dough with which the ashes are in contact to rise slightly. They are easily blown off the finished pastry.

Acorn bread is another outstanding food. You can use the following recipe to begin working with acorn flour while you are still at home. Many skills require practice before you can count on them in serious situations, so easing into some of the skills is fun and beneficial.

2 cups acorn flour
2 cups cattail or white flour
3 teaspoons baking powder
$\frac{1}{3}$ cup maple syrup or sugar
1 egg
$\frac{1}{2}$ cup milk
3 tablespoons olive oil
Bake in pan for 30 minutes or until done at 400 degrees

Utilizing acorns is truly an art. For those of you who want to take your skills beyond the simple scope of this discussion, we recommend, *It Will Live Forever: Traditional Yosemite Indian Acorn Preparation* by Beverly Ortiz and Julia Parker (Heyday Books, September 1996).

(continued from page 188)

I mentioned a massive beetle several evenings ago. I have continued to find identical species all over the woods, laying eggs in moss, duff, debris, and earth. It must be some sort of cyclic event, or I just haven't noticed. I've now tuned in to their sounds and movements and am able to recognize them amid the clamor of feeding birds, daddy longlegs, shrews, mice, and pine borers. It's quite amazing to recognize beetle footsteps in leaf litter.

I'm not sure I've mentioned how loud tiny pine borers are. I'd follow these grunt-like sounds to discover neatly piled shavings of wood under minuscule holes in recently felled or fallen pines. The noise was quite astonishing. I have waited to view the insects responsible on several occasions and seen such tiny black creatures I could scarcely believe it. I did not attempt to touch one in case it lashed out with hidden massive teeth and bored clear through my hand.

I had planned to begin my solo the evening after Mike returned, but unfortunately this would mean returning to camp when David would be celebrating his brother's birthday. This would leave Mike the burden of gathering food for a meal for two. If I left a day earlier, I might miss Mike's return, and I'm undecided about going a day later.

I'm looking forward to the experience. I'm excited about fasting and confining myself to a ten-foot circle for four days and nights. Some may find this odd.

I have begun to think about life after living in the woods. I've thought about what skills I will study and practice more in depth, such as collecting fall cordage materials and nuts, and I've thought about what foods I will eat. On the other hand, I realize I must find a job to make money to pay for my food and shelter, and for the courses that will help me attain new jobs, food, and shelters. We've made living so complicated.

In the woods the skills are direct. You learn to build shelters and harvest food from the land. In society there's this money stuff. You work and work to gain money to pay for shelter, food, and other commodities. The trick seems to be finding a job where you are feeding yourself (meaning body, mind, and spirit), without suffocating who you really are.

Most folks seem to think that earning cash to pay the bills isn't a waste of time. Yet, I have so many tracking and primitive skills projects going, and so many books I've started to read, that I feel constantly distracted by work to earn money to pay the bills. We've created an odd society. There are now new components to living, steps in the middle in order to survive. In all this complication, people are often misled and begin to feel that money is the *point* of living, rather than money being a means to really live.

I shared my hunting time in the lower field this evening with another predator. I had opted for a new hunting strategy, arriving early and waiting. I sat peacefully, watching the shadows grow longer. My shirt was pulled over my head and ears to keep the gnats at bay. Time passed as the sun dropped to the west. Then, I heard movement behind me. Something was stalking the edge of the field and was making quite a racket. I expected it to be the evening's first woodchuck, warily moving up to the field edge. I was glad to know that even animals have a hard time stalking quietly in goldenrod thickets.

Slowly, the animal approached, with long pauses between movements. One pause was so long, I almost forgot about the animal, because I had become distracted by a far-off woodchuck feeding. Suddenly, there was an explosive lunge to my left and a cottontail appeared at full gallop. With a quick twist of its body, it turned to follow the field edge and returned to the goldenrod about fifty yards away. The sound of the lunge had continued after the cottontail had appeared. A predator was still lingering. Then, I heard the stalking animal slowly move away. I don't know what it was. A fox? Coyote? Fisher? I didn't investigate either, because I was trying to retain a low profile. The stealthy predator remained anonymous.

DAY 36

David and I decided to do some fishing. Although I'd been eating regularly, I felt a little weak, especially on the hike up the ridge to camp. I felt I hadn't been eating enough—too much aimless wandering and too little harvesting. I love to wander. Anyway, we thought a sizable trout meal might be the cure.

We took the scenic route to fish via Track Road. There was a decent array of movement. One trail caught my interest. It was that of a young opossum, out on its own. I measured tracks and strides with the beaded bracelet Kayla had made for me. It's interesting to note that such a small animal might be encountered unaccompanied.

David and I lay next to the puddles and watched bobbing young wood and green frogs dive and burrow in the soft silt along the bottom. They created huge crevices in the earth, and a mound gave away their new whereabouts. They never stayed hidden long. They would bob back up to the surface and rest in shallow water. Their eyes and noses were visible along puddle edges, exposed to the open air.

We watched tiny insects navigate the pebble bottoms, following great valleys formed by the tracks of great blue herons on the hunt. Activity and life abounded in the puddles.

We devoted considerable time to watching mud daubers while lying in between muddy ruts in the road. They had large black bodies and golden legs and wings. Their abdomens bobbed up and down as they moved about the puddles. They would land and begin to probe various areas of the puddle with their mouths. They would dig in the moistest mud, very much like a dog, and create a perfect sphere of mud beneath them. Holding on to their work with their first four legs, they would rise, circling once or twice to gain altitude. Then they would fly directly through the stand of sumac to our south. We kept watching.

While we lay there, two great blue herons swooped in, nearly landing on us. Great grunting calls and flapping wings filled the air as they successfully diverted their direction at the

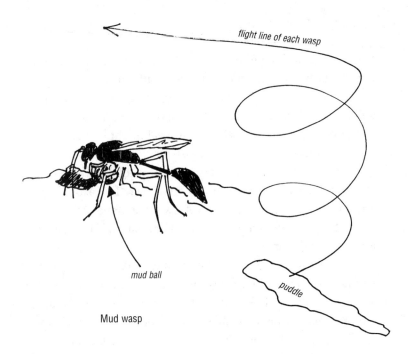

flight line of each wasp

mud ball

puddle

Mud wasp

last moment. They skimmed above our raised heads and headed back toward the stream.

Amidst the mud wasp activity, there was also a paper wasp—a larger, narrower version of a yellow jacket—which appeared to be returning to drink. Repeatedly it would land at one end of the puddle, insert its mouth, and be blown by the slight breeze to the other side. It was beautiful—a striking ship of yellow and black floating across the puddle.

These were the moments I wanted to last forever, the times I hoped I could meditate upon, pulling out of my memory banks to relive during hectic moments in society. We lay flat, like children, fascinated with absolutely everything. The sun beat down on my back and a light breeze played with my hair. Insects were tolerably low—a rare moment this summer. We just observed and learned. There was no other place in the world I wanted to be at that moment; I was content.

As we walked back to our fish spears, we approached and watched birds bathe in large puddles. A black and white warbler, tufted titmice, catbirds, and a scarlet tanager all shared one small puddle. As we walked in the woods over the summer, we alarmed fewer and fewer birds. They seemed to become more tolerant of us, or something about us has become less threatening. The tanager perched just above the puddle and completed a full body preen. His fluorescent red body, accented by black wings, tail, and plumage around the beak, were a sight to behold.

Whenever I look at tanagers, I remember my high school ornithology class and a time when we admired a tanager and a cardinal in the same tree. The red of the tanager is indescribably brighter than that of the cardinal. I don't know who was more excited, the professor or me. His passion was addictive, and that is how teachers should be.

DAY 37

I awoke in the morning, remembering the night's storm. I thought of stubborn Mike, who would sit through anything out there. As I sat next to my debris hut and cooled off, I spotted the gray squirrel that uses our camp. Our camp is surrounded by red squirrels, but we have a gray squirrel in our actual camp. It is a skittish animal and flees at any sound or movement.

The squirrel walked toward me, and when it was close, it began a ritual I had never witnessed before. The movements were extremely quick. There were two young chestnut oaks next to each other, surrounded by a bed of moss. The squirrel's movements alternated in rapid succession. It began to dig in the moss in a random pattern, throwing it up in the air. Then, it would leap about two feet up the tree and leap off, completing one and one-half flips to land on its head and shoulders in the moss. This was followed by more digging and more aerial diving with twists and flips from the two oaks. Then, flips and rolls from ground level were incorporated into the alternating antics of aerial flips, rolls, and digging. The squirrel would also rub its cheeks along the moss before leaping upward, or it would hang upside down and rub its face along the trunk or on the moss at the base of the tree, if he could reach it. The event lasted five minutes. The moss looked like a battlefield, and without any cue I was able to discern, the squirrel began walking slowly away. It bounded a few times. It walked up to a large mushroom, plucked the entire thing, and devoured it. That squirrel had to be dizzy!

What had I just witnessed? I don't know. Possibly a scenting behavior I may never fully comprehend. The moss was spread about, pulled up almost completely. Upon closer inspection, I noticed the area was covered in gray squirrel hairs.

I decided to look for similar signs in areas I knew were occupied by gray squirrels. I looked at the moss at the base of trees for signs of disturbance. I eliminated any moss patches that were affected by traveling animals and only included disturbed areas where I found a minimum of ten squirrel hairs. By the end of the day, I had found six such areas. I was beginning to believe it really was a scent-marking behavior.

There is a rhythm to my days—not a rote schedule, but a rhythm that I enjoy. I check traps after the sun has reached the valley floor and investigate tracking spots along the way. Most often the traps produce no prey, and I spend considerable time

Coyote tracks

Red fox tracks

rearranging them to attempt to catch what animals tripped them and weren't caught. Just a few days ago, I caught a wood-chuck that escaped the snare because the sapling I had bent to form the trap had lost its spring while being held in position for several days. I vary my route to visit different areas. Today there were coyote tracks near my northern snares, which worried me a bit. I didn't want to have a meal stolen before I found it.

I tend to spend late mornings working on skills, such as making cordage or containers. Sometimes I write. I start my days peacefully, often stopping to listen to the wind in the canopy and to reflect on our time here.

Early afternoon is my personal time to wander and watch. During the late afternoon and into the evening, Mike and I hunt independently and then gather dinner. I check the traps again before sitting by the fire and drinking an evening tea. I watch the sunset, the moon, and the stars wherever I am at the time.

There is natural variation, and there is nothing to hold me to what I wrote about the rhythm of my days. If we should snare an animal in the morning, we would eat our big meal for brunch. We prefer to fish earlier in the day so that we can hunt in the evening. Hunting is connection time—more personal time. The goal is to watch and experience; the kill is secondary.

(continued on page 203)

Cordage

With no nails or screws for building in the wild, the value of cordage is clear. Cordage is the nuts and bolts, the nails and screws, the very twine in the yarn of the land. Cordage is used, among other things, for bowstrings, snowshoe bindings, basket handles, bolas, snares, nets, fishing line, lashings, bags, and belts. It is also used for sewing, weaving, making a fire with a bow drill, and building shelters. Of the many cordage options available, most fit into one of three categories.

First are the annuals. Plants such as milkweed, dogbane, stinging nettle, and hemp have a pithy center and strong fibers that grow on the outside of the stalk. Harvesting the fibers is done when the plant is dead in the fall but has not yet had the chance to start decomposing. I have harvested stalks in the winter and spring from still standing plants, but the fibers were weak.

The second type of good-quality fiber can be found in the meaty leaves of yucca and agave located throughout much of the West, as well as in plantings in the East, or in the bark of basswood (American linden), cedar, aspen, cottonwood, ash, hickory, tamarack, willow, and juniper found in the East. Fibers within this category can be harvested anytime, yet require more work to gather and prepare.

Third, cordage can be made from almost any plant, although the quality, or lack thereof, will vary considerably. Velvet leaf, fireweed, evening primrose, cattail, wild grape, bulrush, grasses, conifer rootlets, and green sapling bark (pounded with a mallet) are a few. Cordage can also be made from animal products like sinew, rawhide, and hair.

HARVEST AND STORAGE

Many fibrous annuals, including milkweed and dogbane, tend to grow in large patches and, once recognized, can easily be found during the summer and early fall when they are still alive and easy to distinguish from other similar plants. Harvest the dry, dead stalks in late fall by breaking them off at the ground and bundling them together for transport and storage. I prefer to harvest after the seeds have dispersed (or I sprinkle them myself) to ensure that the following year I am able to harvest in the same area. Keep the stalks in a dry place out of direct sunlight until needed.

Basswood and yucca offer up

their fibers in different ways. When harvesting yucca and agave, carefully cut a few leaves from the base of the plant (the tips are very sharp). If you are traveling, wrap the cut ends in wet towels or paper and cover them with plastic. If you are going to work with the fibers nearby, then they can remain uncovered.

Basswood trees can be found from eastern North Dakota, south to eastern Texas, and east to the Atlantic. When harvesting basswood, the bark can be peeled easily from a live tree or branch. Large trees (eighteen inches or more in diameter) can have bark removed with no ill side effects. (I am not a tree surgeon, so please check with one prior to removing bark if you are concerned about parasites or adversely affecting a given tree.) My rule of thumb is to take a piece no wider than one quarter of the diameter of the tree. Example: If I have a tree with a twenty-four-inch diameter, I will take a six-inch-wide strip of bark.

Cut the width of your intended strip horizontally through the bark, then pry the cut section upward with a stick or sturdy knife. Once you have enough bark freed from the tree, take hold of it with your hands and pull while walking backward from the tree. The strip will run up the trunk, getting narrower as it climbs until it tapers to a point and breaks. In general, the longer

the strip, the better, as this will define the length of the fibers with which you will be working.

The bark must now ret, or soak, submerged in water. Soaking in running water, as in a cold creek, will require a longer ret time (four to six weeks) than in a warm pond (two to four weeks). The soaking begins the breakdown process in the bark, which is made up of many layers of fine, paperlike material. Pieces left too long in the water are still useful; although the exposed layers may have rotted, there may remain plenty of good material under them.

PREPARING THE FIBERS
Annuals

1. With milkweed or dogbane, crush the stem with your fingers, or between two hard objects, and

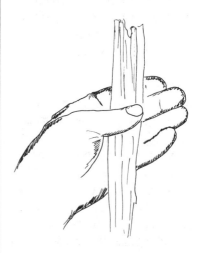

Preparing to break a milkweed stalk

open it by sliding your thumb down one of the cracks until the stalk is lying with the inside up and open to the sky. Remember, the fibers you seek are on the outside of the plant and now sit in your hand, facing the ground.

2. With the stalk under your right arm, and your right palm supporting the plant, extend the open stalk three inches past your palm (see illustration on previous page) and break downward. Should you break upward, you may sever the fibers. Pull off the woody portion. This should leave you with a papery, fibrous material or skin still attached to the stalk on one end. Extend the stalk another three inches beyond your hand and repeat. Once the stalk has been treated thus, rub the weak and wispy bit of "skin" between your hands until it feels softer and the woody bits and outermost skin crack away. You're now ready to spin the fibers into cordage, as described below.

Yucca

A smooth, round stone the size of a dinner plate near flowing water is optimal for this task. You will also need a wrist-thick stick. Dip the yucca in the water and lay it on the rock. Pound on it for about twenty strokes before dipping it in the water again. As you alternate between pounding and dipping, you will notice that not only are you making a frothy mess of natural soap on the rock, but also, all the green meat of the plant is dissipating and white fibers are being revealed. Soon, that is all that will remain. These fibers can be left attached to the very sharp point of the leaf and stored for later use, or you can cut all but three or so fibers and use the pointed leaf tip as a natural needle and thread. Proceed to the section below on spinning the fibers into cordage.

Basswood

Pull the retted bark from the water and peel up layers of fibers. Stiffer sections can be pounded in fashion similar to that of yucca (see above),or the bark can be left to ret longer. The fibers are then ready to be worked into cordage.

SPINNING FIBERS INTO CORDAGE

1. Hold the fibers near the middle of their length, with the thumb and forefinger of each hand about four inches apart. Begin twisting the material by rolling it between your right thumb and forefinger while holding firmly with your left.
2. This continued twisting will cause a loop or kink to form in the area between your hands. Grasp the loop or kink between the left thumb and forefinger, letting both "bundles" of fiber hang down.
3. With your right thumb and fore-

finger, twist the strand on the right (strand A) counterclockwise, or away from you, then wrap the twisted strand A toward you, or clockwise, around strand B.

4. Releasing strand A, grasp strand B and repeat what you have just done with strand A. This method, while slow, will make for a tight and consistent string suitable for bows and snare lines.

You can do this process faster:

1. Hold the fibers near the middle in your left hand and lay them across your right thigh, with the two strands separated by a few inches.
2. Place your right hand on the strands, with the pad of your middle finger on the forward strand and the other strand just below it closer to your palm.
3. Slide your right hand forward, rolling both strands, still inde-

Set-ups for reverse-wrapping of long fibers

pendent of each other, until the near strand reaches the base of your palm.

4. Now pull your hand back, bringing both strands together where they will wind about one another. Grasp the strands where they meet, then repeat.

This method is especially useful for rapid production of weaving materials or for making string that is not intended for heavy work.

For bundles of long fibers like basswood, one end can be attached to an object, and a large loop of thin cordage, placed at the center point, can be attached to another object, such as a tree.

With the bundle forming a straight line from the anchored end through the loose loop, the free end is twisted until a kink is formed in the middle. Then, while maintaining some tension, the free end is brought to the anchored end, which is then freed. Both bundles are allowed to wrap around each other. The loose loop is untied and removed from the cordage. There are many variations of this method, and I encourage you to discover them as you experiment on your own.

SPLICING

Often, the fibers used are not long enough to create a rope of a usable length. Therefore, you'll need to splice in additional fibers. Two tech-

A full lay-in

niques are commonly used, and I have found both satisfactory.

1. If both fiber bundles below the spun cordage are of the same length, then a "full lay-in" is an option. To clarify, when two inches or more of unspun fibers are left remaining to be wrapped, a new fiber bundle is grasped at its center and laid with the center point at the last wrap. The new lengths are now wrapped along with the old. To avoid the bulge that the full lay-in leaves in the cordage, you can trim one of the unspun fiber bundles hanging below the cordage by five inches, then proceed as described below.

2. If the fiber bundles below the spun cordage are uneven, a splice is required. When two or more inches are left on one fiber bundle, a new bundle is laid on the remaining two inches, and you continue to reverse-wrap once again.

There is no substitute for practice when making cordage. Your speed and quality will improve quickly once you have the basic concept down. Pay attention to how tightly or loosely you are wrapping, then note the quality. Too loose a wrap will result in weak cordage, and too tight a wrap will compromise the flexibility and therefore the longevity of the cordage (tight fibers rubbing hard against one another will weaken and break). Try for an even width and don't get discouraged if it takes you ten or more feet to produce a nice section of cordage.

(continued from page 197)

I move much more slowly and notice a great deal more when I move with the intention of hunting; slowly moving and paying close attention seems to release intuitive depths. I feel out potential trails, hunting areas, and the whereabouts of animals.

It was Mike who came up with a hypothesis correlating daydreaming and hunting woodchucks. He noticed that while he hunted and then suddenly began to daydream, he was actually near a woodchuck. Over time, daydreaming became a flag for paying greater attention and noting animal presence.

I tested the hypothesis myself and found tremendous supporting evidence. Over and over again, I'd be silently moving along, and when I began to daydream, I'd catch myself and freeze. Upon closer inspection of the area, an animal would either be in sight, but not moving, or literally be just around the next bend. It is as if some ancient part of me has hunted before.

My natural rhythms allow for personal time, reflection, and peace of mind. In society, I keep schedules more than rhythms. I wake up to go to work, not when my eyes open. I use an alarm clock rather than trusting my internal timepiece. I go to bed after the commute back from night classes, not when I am tired. I schedule personal time for tracking when I can; I'm not always able to stop and fully appreciate when tracking presents itself to me. I often can't stop and marvel at what I encounter, because I'm late for this or that. Here, I have no obligations, and when I feel like watching or listening, I can. When an opportunity for learning presents itself, I take it.

I'll miss the freedom and the flexibility of rhythms when I return to schedules. The challenge, of course, is to allow for rhythms in society. I remind myself, life is to be lived, not endured.

Each night the moon grows larger and spends more time reflecting light in our neck of the woods. What a gift to be able to move without apprehension at night. Of course, moving slowly, sensing your way off-trail in pitch black, has its benefits.

I crawl up the ridge on all fours, catching blotchy green flashes as my hands and arms move into peripheral vision. Could this be what's called aura? Or the light surrounding tree trunks which illuminates their shapes in the blackness?

But, I appreciate the light the moon lends. The walk to my debris hut was less treacherous.

DAY 38

David and I made a pilgrimage miles downstream to a place we refer to as "the gorge." We went in quest of rumored large trout for Mike's feast this evening, to celebrate the end of his fast and time alone.

We wandered the stream along the way. Waters became wider and deeper. The stream where we fished and played had joined others, gaining volume and strength. Trout darted for deep waters or under banks as we passed numerous pools. There is so much life in these streams. We kept moving for the most part, stopping to watch cedar waxwings catch flies and to admire a massive old pine, saved from logging only because it had fallen across the stream.

Our arrival at the gorge was sudden; each bend in the river looked similar to the last, but then there it was. The gorge lay before us, a massive bedrock of shale carved over many lifetimes by moving water.

Similar to the waterfall we visited to the north, the walls of shale were carpeted by moss at water level and up higher by lichens and ferns. The shallow root systems of hemlocks hugged the edges of the walls, and behind them, white oaks anchored in deeper soils. Like the waterfall, this place was stunning, breathtaking; it was a sacred place. But in contrast to the waterfall, it seemed that many people knew about this spot and had visited and discarded scraps of our current culture amidst piles of beer cans. I managed to maintain my focus on the natural surroundings rather than the trash.

The gorge was a long, connected series of carved bowls of

water. The crystal clear, light blue water reached depths of fifteen feet and slid through without a ripple. I lay, head hanging over the ten-foot walls, watching trout and suckers dart about over the smooth, sandy floor.

We stripped down and slowly entered the frigid water. We had hoped to hand fish the depths but found it difficult. I wasn't sure whether I was stalking rock, log, or fish, and the cold water diverted my attention.

I climbed out and told David I'd prefer to spearfish above the gorge. David had another idea. He wanted to dash back to camp, pick up goggles he had there, and, with his car, drive back to rejoin me. He was worried about leaving me for so long, but I assured him I'd be fine.

I don't know how long David was gone—many hours, for sure. I sat most of the time, absorbing sun and attempting to memorize every crack and plant along the far wall. I wanted to remember this place; I hoped to carry it with me.

I also lay gazing into the pools, watching how the trout moved and where they stopped to rest, and where the sandy, rocky floor and shale walls met. This was how David found me upon his return.

In society, I live a hectic schedule of daily events. To sit and do nothing is borderline uncomfortable, a sure sign of a lifestyle that needs changing. Here, I am changed. I often sit "unproductively" and feel that these are the most productive parts of my day. Waiting for others or animals or sitting for no reason at all is no longer uncomfortable or a chore, but rather a blessing. I have slowed down.

David appeared with a fascinating primitive mask he'd acquired someplace else. It was formed from plastic and rubber. With it, you could go under water and see as clearly as if you were in the air. Such perfect vision and so many fish distracted me from the icy water. I caught three large trout with my hands before turning the mask over to David for a go.

I sat in the sun and violently shivered for ten minutes before settling into light shivers for another fifteen. Eventually, the sun warmed even my bones and I had another go with the mask in the depths of the gorge. It was beautiful below the surface. Fish floated in sunlit waters, their movements so easy, their bodies so light. I stayed under water for as long as I could to stare at a tiny sunfish that hung about mid-depth in one of the carved bowls. Every detail shone so clear. The fish was stunning.

Upon our return to the field below camp, David and I watched a family of chipping sparrows. The two young were fully grown and capable, yet had brown caps, not having yet developed their rusty crowns. The mother hopped about, pulling insects from plantains and clover. She fed her young in between their own individual forays among the low vegetation. They pecked randomly, chasing moths and other insects as they were flushed from the grass. Many young birds were leaving their nests throughout the area. Summer is coming to an end. Soon, I too, would be leaving the security of this nest, our lush hillside, and the surrounding valleys.

Mike returned as the sun began to drop to the west, and we feasted. He told horrendous tales of relentless swarms of mosquitoes and gnats, as well as a series of nights, each one colder than the previous. His eyes were clear, though—his smile real. Mike was so happy to be back. I was next. David said he'd have to hear directly from the "Creator" before he did another solo and fast. And apparently he hasn't heard, yet.

DAY 39

Mike and I checked the snares together. No catch this morning, although the snares were being moved by passing woodchucks. We talked about tracks in all the mud puddles that we encountered as we walked.

While walking through a field of flowering cinquefoils and clovers, I was stung by a honeybee. I was moving quickly—my mind was somewhere else—trying to catch up with Mike. I stepped on the bee as it worked, and it retaliated with a nasty sting to the arch of my foot; the bee died.

It was quite an intense burn indeed. I brushed the stinger

off and limped about four steps before I spotted the leaves of common plantain, renowned for extracting the poisons of bee stings. I chewed a few leaves and applied a poultice. No lie—within ninety seconds the burn had disappeared. I continued to sit for a few minutes with the poultice. Then I caught up with Mike over the next rise and reapplied a poultice for five minutes. The sting barely swelled; the pain never returned. If I continue to study plants, all culinary and medicinal worries might fade away. Nature provides what we need.

I interpreted the sting as a reminder to slow down. I had blocked out the background buzz of working bees for a moment and had been reminded that they, too, exist. Walking barefoot forces me to pay attention and slow down. Where and how are my feet landing? With a subtle roll, my feet mold to the earth, and in my imagination I see the natural contours within landscapes.

With shoes, I'm able to blunder through the woods. They are armor, protecting me from my own sloppiness. Feet may land wherever they fall, mind may race a mile a minute, and the result is a crashing fool who notices nothing. Not much of a sales pitch for my Adidas. They have their place, though—down the ridge, across the stream, through the fields, and to the nearest flat, hot asphalt.

There is nothing like walking quietly and slowly through the woods. Vision alters, and you notice every movement. Gut feelings emerge to fill the space abandoned by mental garbage. Shift your weight from your center, rather than from your head, just as is emphasized in martial arts, and the bounce of modern gaits is removed. Walking in dry leaf litter and stepping on a soft cushion of moss, which holds the moisture from the last rain, is as refreshing as a dip in the stream.

I remember my first few days in the woods this summer; I was in transition. Shoes were off, feet were here, but mind and focus had not yet arrived. I beat myself up a bit. Luckily, cuts and scrapes heal, and with time I slowed down to match the rhythm of the forest.

(continued on page 211)

Hygiene

Keeping clean and healthy in the wild is not as tough as it might seem. Once your diet of natural foods has pushed out all the toxins and other super-processed food of society, you will find that your body odor and oily hair fade away and plaque appears less on your teeth.

BRUSHING YOUR TEETH

A black birch twig with one end chewed to a frayed tip works well as a toothbrush and tastes good, too. Oak twigs are also popular, because the tannins help kill bacteria and remove their cavity-causing by-products.

CLEANING YOUR BODY AND CLOTHING

Soapwort, sometimes called bouncing bet, is found in disturbed soil, on riverbanks, and in streambeds. It has leaves that can be briskly rubbed between your hands, creating a green lather that works very well as a soap and deodorizer. Yucca leaves and roots (found naturally in the Southwest, but also a common ornamental plant) can be dipped in water and beaten with a stick alternately to create good washing suds. *Do not use agave*, as the sap is acidic and will give you a burning rash as well as burn holes in your clothes. Sand and stones are great washboards for scrubbing out clothes and scouring hands.

WASHING YOUR HAIR

One of the best hair washes is mud from a hot spring. Clay does a somewhat inferior job and requires a second wash with a deodorizing soap or plant such as soapwort or mashed mint. Either one should be mixed with water until it is a just pourable mixture. Apply it to your hair, working it in so that it is thoroughly soaked. Leave it in for ten minutes or more and rinse well.

MENSTRUAL PADS

The absorbent quality of moss makes it a great natural substitute for soaking up women's menstrual flow. Burn discarded moss to deter large predators from becoming interested, or bury it far from camp.

DEFECATING

This is a tender subject for many people, yet an important one. Many nervous poopers have refused to give in to the urge due to their lack of comfort with primitive toiletries. Holding a bowel movement back results in constipation and, if not tended to, can lead to impaction, a condition requiring medical attention. It is liberating indeed to walk into the woods and know that at any time, in any environment, *you* can drop your trousers and comfortably take care of business. With that in mind, most public lands have strict guidelines concerning this very subject, so be sure you familiarize yourself with local protocols.

Most people who defecate in the woods will dig a six-inch hole, complete their business, fill it in, and cover it with a rock. After years of pooping in the woods, I have come to the conclusion that leaving poop on the surface allows it to disappear far faster than if you put in the ground, given that store-bought toilet paper is *not* used. Additionally, if poop is visible, you are less likely to step in it; if it is cleverly "buried" under two inches of soil, you end up with something akin to a minefield and develop a fear of picking up rocks. When you are in areas that receive few visitors, and you leave your poop on the surface, defecate in out-of-the-way places where people are not likely to go, such as thickets, next to thornbushes, and the like.

The following are eight ways in which to wipe yourself. The position you use can minimize the need for extensive wiping, so it is best to poop in a squat. It helps in voiding the bowels, as well as in spreading your buttocks, keeping them safely out of harm's way. Sitting over a log, straight or forked, is more comfortable for some, while others prefer to partially squat while holding onto a tree to keep from falling over backward.

- Snow is a tad chilly, yet very effective, as it melts and conforms to your personal shape, allowing for a good cleaning.
- Sand works very well, too! While squatting, wipe lightly with a handful of dry sand. The second wipe can be a little harder. The sand soaks up any moisture, sticks to other remnants, and is then easily brushed off with a final handful of sand. This method is not as uncomfortable as it may sound.
- Stones, rounded and slightly rough, are very effective. Be careful in temperature extremes. It is possible to injure yourself with very hot or very cold stones.
- Pinecones should first be checked for pitch. If any is found, discard it. If not, wipe from the stem to the tip. Most pinecones are comfortable to use and effective.
- Sticks can be used, although they're not the best choice. They require a little more effort to get yourself really clean.

- Leaves are better doubled up, but don't press too hard or you will "pop" through. Use the rough side of the leaf—the ribbed side—to catch all wipeables. Watch out for poison oak, poison ivy, and stinging nettle leaves. These would cause *great* discomfort.
- Grass and moss are fantastic for wiping. Wad them up into a clump like a little green scrub brush and wipe away.
- Water, of course, is great, but it's best to use it after first using one of the above. If water is to be used, carry a container away from the water source to avoid contamination.
- Be imaginative—nature is full of potential toiletries.

CARING FOR INFECTED WOUNDS

Wounds need careful care. Any infection may kill you if you do not tend to it properly.

While on an excursion, a friend got a small cut on his foot. A few days later, I saw two red streaks originating from the cut and running up his leg to his calf. I immediately sent him to see a doctor. Those red lines were acute lymphangitis, or blood poisoning. If left untreated, the bacteria causing the infection would multiply rapidly along the lymphatic vessel, causing red streaks. It may invade the bloodstream and could cause septicemia, a serious and potentially deadly illness.

Prompt care of wounds is of utmost importance. Any cut should be cleaned with clean or boiled water and monitored for redness, tenderness, or swelling. By far the best natural treatment I have encountered is broadleaf plantain. Four to five tender leaves chewed to a pulp (a rather bitter mouthful) should be applied to the wound and held in place for three to five hours. This works miracles for even the most painfully infected cuts. The improvement should be very noticeable after five hours.

Note that this is not a substitute for professional medical care. Your body and mind are the most valuable of survival tools, so take good care of them. Don't try to "tough it out" if there is any question as to the severity of an injury or illness. Leaving the woods to get a wound or illness looked at by a healthcare professional is a good idea. Besides, if it turns out not to be serious, you can return to the woods with no questions regarding your health.

(continued from page 207)

On our way back, I discovered one very exciting trail, that of a bounding short-tailed shrew. I would have never been able to recognize the trail without my ongoing studies of live-trapped small mammals. I was able to identify the animal by foot pad configuration and the number of toes. The shrew was in an atypical bounding pattern, which we may learn with time is its preferred gait at high speeds. We'll have to wait and see.

I remember a dream from earlier in this adventure. I was walking down a hill to the north. The sun was shining brightly and hung in the sky straight overhead. Near the mailboxes of local houses, which were clustered together along the dirt road, sat a rabbit. My shirt was tucked in, and I held my throwing stick over my shoulder. I approached closer and closer, aimed, released, and missed the cottontail, shooting off to the left. I remember searching for my throwing stick, chest deep in brambles.

The dream had struck me as a bit odd, because I never expected to be in that location without Mike, who knew folks in the vicinity. Nor did I expect to be hunting cottontails mid-day along a road near clustered mailboxes. But I didn't pay it much heed.

Today, that scenario occurred perfectly. I was chest high in brambles when it struck me, and I remembered the dream. I had hiked up there with Mike to explore, then we had separated. I never found my throwing stick.

These sorts of dreams, snippets of reality that come true, occur frequently. *Deja vu,* I suppose. The mind and spirit are remarkable. Whenever one of my dreams comes true, I always plan to pay more attention to my dreams. But I have so many dreams every night and fall quickly behind. What is our human potential?

Tomorrow evening, I'll begin my solo. I hope to clarify my path in life and learn more about myself. I have so many different interests right now, and I worry that the decisions I make while in the thick of society might be skewed or impulsive. I think I want to remain an environmental educator, but I'm feeling pulled in new directions. And, I really enjoy American Sign Language. How do these two fit together? Then there's wildlife tracking and the primitive skills, both of which feed me and I enjoy. I'm also in a relationship with a woman I care for deeply and who needs to be supported on her path. Yet I would also like to further my own education and broaden my experiences. I feel pulled in six directions at once and wonder which way to go. Will these paths all weave together, or pull me apart like some archaic torture device? And then the niggling question: Do I really have a "path" at all, or is this some mental trickery to feel better about myself, to feel special? Perhaps there's no place to be except right here, right now. These are the thoughts I bring to the solo.

Day 40

Last night was hot. I awoke groggy, mouth dry, and body overheated sometime after the moon had disappeared over the horizon. I rolled out of my debris hut and stumbled to the fire circle where I had left water. Mouth quenched and body cooling, I then began to hear them. My body and mind had distracted me from the ongoing concert on the other side of the hill. Coyotes howled in unison, and their music flowed down the ridge like water. Barks, yips, and howls wound together to create song. The woods were silent otherwise; all listened to the coyotes. I sat for awhile, an attentive audience. Gradually, I drifted to sleep, with their beautiful voices filling my shelter.

As morning became midday, David led us to an old overgrown orchard he had explored a few days before. The pear tree in the middle of the tangles of goldenrod, *ribes*, grasses, and blooming soapwort had begun to drop fruit. Several species of animals were eating the pears, and David wanted confirmation of his observations.

The entire area was ideal for voles. Tunnel entrances spotted the area, giving us a hint of the lengthy network upon which we walked. Tunnels and vole scat surrounded the fruit. Pears were being devoured, tiny incisions creating intricate textures.

Deer were also visiting the tree and eating the fruit. Both voles and deer seemed to investigate each pear by biting in different areas and on multiple pieces of fruit before feeding on a selected few. Most of the fruit, however, was being eaten by insects. Black ants were the most visible.

I continued to wander the hill with Mike until early afternoon. It was time to begin my solo; I was ready.

I've decided to sit on the hillside just below where I killed the fawn near the beginning of our time here. Solos are often described as mini "deaths," an exchange for which you gain greater insights or connections with self and spirit. I will experience my "death" where I took the life of another. It is a gesture. I take so much from this hill and would like to think I gave something back as a participant in natural cycles rather than just an observer.

I've been thinking about the next four days and nights for some time. No doubt this time will be challenging, requiring a further surrender of mind, body, and spirit. You have to really let go of what you think you need in order to remain steadfast in a solo.

DAY 44

I left in the late afternoon, sun to the west, four days ago, and returned with the sun to the west on this day. It seems an odd time to enter and exit a solo, but it gave the others time to fish and gather for dinner. I am thankful I don't have to rush out and gather. I'm drained. The long walk down one ridge, along another ridge, and up a third ridge to camp took tremendous effort.

This was my third such solo in my life, and each provided unique challenges. The first I attempted while I was building trails in California five years ago. I hadn't a clue what I was doing, and after staying awake for thirty-six hours, I managed to persuade myself that it wasn't the right time for me to solo. As a result, I stopped and returned to camp. The mind plays terrible tricks; I would have liked to have stuck out the duration.

My second solo was in a remote corner of Utah and provided wonderful wildlife experiences and deep insights into then-current decisions; I went ahead and acted on every one of them. I was ready for my mind to try to tell me I wasn't prepared and talk me out of the experience, and therefore recognized and did not acknowledge those particular mental obstacles. But food became a concern and distraction. I thought about every item I wanted to eat and about the meal I planned to have when I reached a nearby town.

This time, it was the duration that challenged me. Time seemed to pass so slowly. Yet, in retrospect, the experience seemed to have zipped by.

I'll start from the beginning. I strolled up the long, broken logging road holding a bundle of clothes and water. Wildlife abounded along the way, from shrews to birds to deer. I will attempt to keep from being anthropomorphic, but the animals did seem to behave differently that afternoon.

There was a buck in the trail as I turned a bend. He looked in my direction and stepped just off-trail. He stared at me as I approached. He must have known I was a human, because without pause, I walked closer and closer. I also looked him straight in the eye, an act that usually sends animals fleeing. Not this one. His large, deep, dark eyes held my stare. His moist, black eyes and nose shone; his ears were held erect below beautiful antlers in velvet. His entire head was accented by the sun, which made the scene even more stunning and surreal.

When I was about fifteen feet away, I wanted to stop. My mind said I'd scare off the buck if I stopped, but I did anyway. We stared at each other. I said "thanks" aloud, as his behavior seemed so out of place that I counted it as a gift. The deer was undaunted by my pause less than ten feet away and watched me go up the trail. Perhaps I was putting out a different vibe or intention as I approached my solo spot, and the animals were able to pick up on the shift.

Just around the next bend I came upon a flock of wild turkeys. Anyone who knows turkeys knows that at the slightest whiff or sight of people, they are off like bullets. They either run along the forest floor or crash through the canopy, their massive wings and bodies colliding with as many branches as possible. I wonder how they don't hurt themselves.

Not this flock. They moved to the upside of the trail and turned to watch as I passed. Sunlight accented the red and blue skin of the massive gobbler as he eyed me. He held his head high, jerking it to the left to follow me up the trail. It was a good start to be sure.

Throughout most of the solo, I simply thought. I thought about my questions, and when I felt I was done with them, I thought about the past and future. For the whole summer, I have explored the physical environment, but here I explored my inner self. It's sort of like dealing with old clothes. You sort out what belongs to you from what belongs to other people and to our culture (realize that not every thought in your head is truly yours—many are thrust upon you without your taking the time to really decide whether you agree with them). Then you choose what still remains useful. If it's still good, you clean it off and neatly put it somewhere you can find it again. Here's an example. "Yes, animal tracking still feeds me and I do it because I want to." So I keep that one. If it's old and ugly or no longer useful, you get rid of it. Guilt is often a product of trying to live in a way that pleases other people. My way of dealing with guilt is to seek it, make peace with it, then toss it out. All of this is an internal cleansing process, a refurbishing act that brings clarity to your purpose and actions.

Perhaps the belief system with which I struggled most was this idea of "following your path." The concept of following your path is not my own, but one I've acquired somewhere in years past. It has a Buddhist ring to it, but as I sit with what it means to me, it seems more related to New Age movements and psychotherapy. Do we each have a purpose? Do we each have a life path? I don't know. It would certainly be easier to believe we do, because then everything could be divided into right and wrong—either contributing to the path, or working against it. But dichotomies worry me, and I still have many questions. I believe each of us is special. I believe in following my heart, and it does seem as if opportunities align when I do so. Life just seems easier when I remain true to myself. Perhaps this is what is meant by staying on one's path.

I also absorbed the natural environment. When I sit for an extended period in nature, something happens. While moving, I often witness nature in reaction to myself. I see little of the wildlife, and what I do see is running away. Sitting over time allows the natural rhythm of the forest to resume around me, and I am allowed a privileged view of natural cycles at work.

My first dawn brought all sorts of wildlife. The cardinal started singing very early and was eventually joined by the pee-wee, followed by the rest. A doe came upon me very early, when the light was so low the air appeared thick, like soup. She saw me and began the ritualistic snorts, stamps, and false charges. Eventually, she passed by. I watched the dark silhouette of a great horned owl fly south just overhead to roost for the day. But what excited me the most was above me on the ridge.

The alarm calls of birds brought my attention uphill to see a fisher looking at me. We didn't look at each other long before the fisher loped, in typical mustelid fashion, up a log lying with the slope of the hill. Then it was gone. Fishers are just returning to this area. To see one here, where they are rare, was a real gift. Actually, it's only the third time I've ever seen a fisher in the wild.

The first time is a story worth telling. I was living in southern New Hampshire at the time, in a rural area along a very narrow road. During the snow season, I followed my animal neighbors four to five days each week. Whatever trail I began with, I switched to those of fishers as soon as I crossed their trails.

Nobody walked this land I tracked, which consisted of private lots, a granite quarry, an abandoned railroad line, and a poorly managed tree farm with a few beaver ponds, streams, and natural ponds. Yet, wildlife abounded. One mile up the road, in the "nature reserve," a scenic spot with a large pond and picnic tables, I'd venture to say one-fifth of the wildlife activity occurred. (If those making decisions back in the day had practiced tracking, perhaps I'd have been tracking in the reserve, and the rock quarry would have been up the way.)

I followed the fishers for many hours and many miles. I learned so much. There were two females within my range, and their trails did not overlap. There also was a massive male that roamed the entire area. The male was so large, his track dimensions were larger than every published parameter I've read. This male was the animal whose trail I followed relentlessly.

In the beginning, I noticed the fisher held relationships with three kinds of animals: raccoons, porcupines, and red fox. It was these animals the fisher scented and followed for short durations. It is a common misconception that fishers live almost entirely on porcupines. I remember a working naturalist assuring me I hadn't tracked a fisher on the hill in his town in New York. He said I had been mistaken, as there were no porcupines in his area. He was right about the porcupines.

However, I often see signs of fishers scenting, following, and killing raccoons, and this fisher was no exception. He also kept in touch with a large porcupine, which lived fifty yards from his den. Fifty yards separated two boulder jumbles; one housed a pair of fishers and the other a porcupine. The fisher constantly entered the porcupine den, circled the boulders, and left scat on the rock in the middle of the den. This would all happen while the porcupine was present. The first time I saw this, I expected to enter and find porcupine remains scattered about, but instead, I was chased out by the porcupine. I've been revisiting the area for several years now, and the two animals continue to be neighbors.

My fisher also heavily scented red-fox trails. These two animals had an unusual relationship. Both would raid each other's caches when opportunities presented themselves. I also tracked the male fisher chasing the local red fox, which narrowly escaped. Fishers are known to kill fox, but I also know people who have watched a red fox fight off a fisher. Apparently, there is no sure winner if the two species tangle.

I followed this male fisher for months, finding and picking apart caches in trees and buried under snow. I tracked him after he'd taken one of the neighbor's chickens, as well as cats, raccoons, grouse, hares, and gray, red, and flying squirrels. Fishers are perfectly engineered for hunting; their rear feet are able to turn 180 degrees, which enables them to run up and down trees at the same speed. No one is safe.

After about a month of tracking this animal, he took interest in a fourth animal species. He began to scent and follow my old trails as he crossed them. We had entered into a relationship. We were both taking notice of the other on a regular basis. I knew his patterns and whereabouts, and I have no doubt that he knew mine.

During the winter, I was enrolled in night classes four nights a week. Each night, I'd drive along and reach my little winding road where I knew the fisher crossed on a regular basis. I'd turn the radio off, turn on the high beams, and think, "Maybe tonight's the night—the night I'll see my fisher." My actions became so ritualized I began to wonder if they had become a hindrance to seeing the fisher. So, I'd approach the road and think, "Don't say tonight's the night," which of course meant it was already too late. I was in a serious rut.

One night, no different from the rest, I approached my turn. I said to myself, "Try not to think about it," which meant I already had. I reached for the radio, which hummed softly in the background, and thought, "Don't worry about the radio. He'll hear the car, not the radio." So, I left it on. When I turned onto my road and the forest came in close, arching in from both sides, I felt it. My gut, my intuition, twinged, and I knew something was different. It wasn't the sort of knowing that comes from the head. I drove, more aware than ever. I had been told to notice something. All the way down the road, winding around until I reached the gate of my driveway, I waited patiently. Nothing. I couldn't believe it. That particular feeling had never failed me before.

I turned into the long, wide, gravel drive, which sloped up at the far end. The drive was surrounded on the left by the house, and horse fields lay straight ahead and to the right. As I turned in, something jumped in front of the car. It loped up the drive in front of me and ran up the hill at the far end. I did not think; I allowed my body to absorb recognition. The animal ran along the top of the incline and into the horse fields. I kept turning, keeping the beautiful, loping fisher in my headlights, and watched as he faded into darkness to my right. I found his tracks on my steps.

That is what tracking is all about—gaining a relationship with wild creatures and connecting on a level deeper than intellect and logic. It took time, but I earned that relationship and eventually a private sighting of the animal itself. He'd never visited the horse fields before, and he never visited again for the remainder of winter, at least as far as I know.

My solo spot lay within a cusp between bird habitats on the hillside. The rose-breasted grosbeaks flew low on the hill, and the scarlet tanagers generally stayed high. There, I watched both, as well as mingling orioles, all of which provided colorful feasts for the eyes. Birds are curious creatures and come close to inspect what's odd and new in their environment. They would hop on branches, coming closer and closer to inspect me, reaching five or six feet away. They took turns—first the hairy woodpecker, then the black-and-white warblers, the ovenbirds, the juncos, the chickadees, the flickers—the list goes on and on. I enjoyed those moments when the birds were so close I could really admire their beauty.

The scarlet tanager varied the routine. The male spotted me from afar and began to approach. He came to the edge of my circle and inspected me thoroughly. Then he flew off and I sat alone for a few minutes. He reappeared with his mate and they both gave me a thorough inspection. These two birds did everything together. Where one sang or fed, the other was surely nearby. They were a lesson in commitment—a lesson I felt I needed to learn.

I was sitting and watching as one dusk settled upon the landscape when I was pulled from my thoughts by the rapid approach of alarming robins. I looked up and watched as a female great horned owl landed on a branch not twenty feet away. It was still light, and I was able to admire this striking bird with her brilliant oranges, rusts, browns, and creams. Her incredible feathered talons gripped the branch. Unfortunately, a small sprig of hemlock blurred her face, and I began to crane my neck to gain a better view. The owl also spotted my movement and began to crane her neck to better inspect me. Both of us tried to be subtle.

Finally, she'd had enough craning. She dropped off her perch, which was level with my head, and glided directly at me. She turned about five feet from my head, one wing facing the earth, the other the sky. Her talons pointed and flexed toward me, and her intense eyes scrutinized me up and down. She hung there, suspended for a moment with one wing up and the other down, then silently flapped north along the ridge. No doubt my mouth hung open and my eyes were wide.

Jon Young once told me how to decipher whether crows you hear are harassing a red-tailed hawk or a great horned owl by listening to the movement of their calls. If they suddenly drop off, aiming downward, the bird of prey dropped off its roost, which is typical behavior of great horned owls. Should the calls rise and become louder, they are following a hawk, which launches up and out. It was crystal clear this evening. Even from as low as ten feet, as the owl dropped, the raucous robins followed, and there was a quick dropoff in their calls.

I spent time on my solo also watching and connecting with a male rufous-sided towhee. I knew each of his calls and the feeding circuit he followed. One time I was lying flat, and the bird was feeding so close, I could see my own reflection in his ruby red eyes.

A small raptor appeared to perch on a low snag at the top of the drainage in which I sat. I couldn't quite make it out— merlin or sharp-shinned hawk? It sat for perhaps fifteen minutes, then swooped down directly at my head. It spread its wings, tail, and talons right before my eyes and landed not four feet behind me, taking my rufous-sided towhee away. The towhee made one last call, a call I hadn't heard before, and then there was silence. I was deeply disturbed and became absolutely certain that I or someone close to me was going to die. (But no one close to me died, and I can chuckle to myself now.)

(continued on page 226)

Rawhide and Sinew

Rawhide is animal skin that has merely had the flesh side scraped to remove any fat and meat left on during the skinning process. The hair is often removed as well. Rawhide is great for making lashings; hard cases for items like bone hooks, needles, or pemmican; shoe soles; cordage; and more. The great value of rawhide is that when it is wet, it is elastic and can be tied around objects like the head of a stone hammer or snowshoes. As it dries, it shrinks and hardens. Of course, the reverse is also true. When rawhide gets wet, it softens and stretches. Methods for protecting rawhide from the effects of moisture will be addressed shortly.

To make rawhide, you will need a green (fresh), or soaked wet hide, which can be prepared using either the racked hide method *(dry scrape) or the skinned log method (wet scrape).

RACKED HIDE METHOD

Racking a hide is merely a way of supporting a hide within an external framework, like an artist framing a canvas. Most commonly, four poles are laid out on the ground in a rectangle and lashed at the corners.

1. Size the poles so there is a one-foot margin between the hide and the rack all around; this will allow for stretching.
2. Place the hide, while it is still green, in the middle of the framework, and make holes in the edges about every three inches or less and about one and one-half inches in from the edge. All holes should be a one-half-inch slit parallel to the nearest edge.
3. To be sure the hide is centered in the rack, tie the four corners first—not tightly, just snugly for now.
4. Lace the hide to the rack by starting at the bottom. (To make your own lacing material, see "Cordage," page 198.)
15. Tie the lacing or cordage to the frame, then run it through the corresponding hole in the hide and back to the frame again.
6. Continue this process all the way around the hide, lashing each side more tightly than the last so that the fourth side tightens the hide. As it dries it will tigten further and become

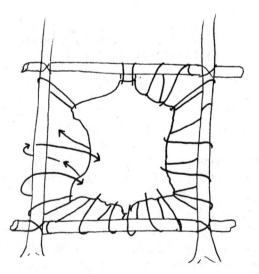

drum-like. Be careful not to overtighten or the holes in the hide may tear out.

7. Due to stretching, you will need to snug up some of the lashings during the scraping process. It is also advisable when lacing to run all ties from the back of the hide to the back of the frame, around the frame to the front, thence through the hole in the front of the hide. This will keep the hide on a single plane rather than having one tie pulling the hide toward the back of the frame and the next tie pulling toward the front.

8. Lean the racked hide against a tree and, starting with the stake scraper (see "Making Camp," page 32) perpendicular to the hide, scrape downward from the neck. All flesh and fat should peel away and run down the hide. Be careful not to slide the scraper sideways and slice the hide.

9. To remove the hair, soak the hide in water until the hair "slips" (comes out when gently pulled). Soak times vary. In cold, clear, flowing water, it can take three weeks. In a bucket of water, changed once daily, it

Dry scraping

takes half that time or less. Water containing a lot of tannins (such as from boiling acorns) makes the time even shorter.

10. Once the hair slips, the above process can be repeated for the hair side of the hide. I prefer to soak hides until the hair slips prior to fleshing. This helps me avoid having to rack the hide twice. Once the hair is removed, the hide can be dried and stored indefinitely. It's rawhide ready to go.

SKINNED LOG METHOD

You will need a smooth, peeled log and a broad scraper (see "Making Camp," page 32).

1. Lay the hide hair side down on the log, leaving a bit of the hide hanging over one raised end.
2. Leaning against the log, pinching the overhanging hide between the log and your body, scrape downward, using the scraper like a squeegee. All fat and meat should run down the hide.
3. Work your way from side to side on the top portion, then pull the hide further up the beam and continue until you are done.

WORKING WITH RAWHIDE

To make lashings or laces, you can cut a circle from the hide, then cut a continuous spiral into it like you are peeling an apple without breaking the skin. One effective method is to

Wet scraping

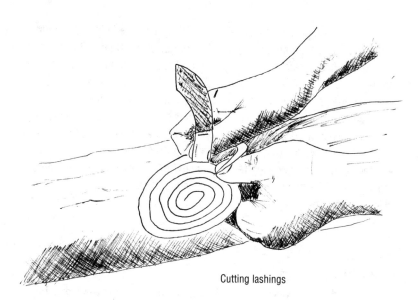

Cutting lashings

stick a knife in a log and, while grasping the disk in both hands, pull it into the blade in a spiral pattern. To use the lashings, soak them until they are elastic (a few hours), tie them, and let them dry. If the lashings get wet, they will loosen and be pliable again. One method for lessening this effect of moisture is to tie one end of the wet rawhide to a tree, stretch it taught, tie the other end to another tree, and let the rawhide dry.

Some waterproofing is possible for binding items like hammerheads that need to remain tight: Cover them with a light layer of pine pitch and sprinkle the pitch with ash.

SINEW

Sinew or tendon is found on the legs or along the back straps of

animals (the long muscles on either side of the spine). Let me use a deer as an example. In a deer's legs, there is a white, flexible bundle on the back side of the leg bones. Smaller bundles can also be found on the front side.

Deer leg sinew

In the back, sinew is on the surface of the muscle, is more silver in color, and is flat instead of in a bundle.

Harvest the back sinew as you would skin a section of hide. Leg sinew just needs to be cut out, and the clear sheath needs to be removed (done by slicing lengthwise, then opening the bundle and pulling out the fiber bundles).

Hang harvested sinew to dry in a spot out of direct sunlight. When dry, the sinew should be beaten between a smooth rock and a piece of wood or chewed to separate the fibers. Once it is partially separated, rub it briskly between your hands to finish the job. The fibers are now ready to be twisted into cordage or used as thread.

(continued from page 221)

Perhaps it was a lesson about routines. In a short time, I had completely memorized the towhee's feeding routine. Many teachers discuss falling into routines, or "ruts," when we operate automatically—driving, walking, eating, sleeping, marrying, and raising children without paying attention. Yet our modern society seems to encourage the creation of "ruts." Perhaps the death of the towhee was a reminder not to become attached? Or perhaps the towhee would have been killed regardless of whether I was present or not, and the "lesson" is just gibberish I've made up in my head.

The animals I watched most were my immediate neighbors, a family of southern red-backed voles. I'd never seen a red-backed vole in the wild. I had only read about how much time they spend underground and had looked at drawings and photos. This family spent a great deal of time running about above ground. They used fallen logs as highways, quickly covering distances in search of mushrooms. They'd chop the massive mushrooms into little pieces to begin with and make numerous trips back and forth to their holes. When a manageable chunk remained, they'd carry the whole thing along their log highways back to their burrows.

They were beautiful creatures. Once, in the middle of the day, I looked over to investigate a rustle of leaves. A vole was perched on a log, back lit perfectly by the sun, looking at me. Its rusty fur gleamed in the sun and quivered in the breeze. Its rounded ears were accented by the backlight, while its black eyes studied me. The vole looked like a miniature pika, a small lagomorph, which I spent time observing exactly this time last year in the Cascade Mountains.

You think and think out there until you can think no more. As the third day ended, my mind stopped. It broke down, I suppose, or ran out of things to ponder. It didn't last long at first, but I was able to call upon this state for the remainder of the solo. I sat without thought, just existing, absorbing my place. Perhaps it was then that I was truly living in the moment.

These precious experiences were the goal of fasting and sitting. When the commentator in the back of my mind stops, when I don't have to name every birdcall and track, I feel more peaceful and present. These moments also provide the greatest insights. Perhaps I'm just suddenly able to hear what some part of me knew and was trying to communicate all along. It's in these moments you just decide what to do or know the answer to some question, or very often a new set of questions emerges to replace the old.

I was happy to also see a female fawn on my solo trip. She wandered through and bedded down about twenty yards from me. Here, where I had taken a fawn, another was thriving. On the last day, the fawn walked right up to my area. We spent an awkward ten minutes as the fawn decided what to do about this new and unusual lump leaning against the chestnut oak in her area. She was stunning—very healthy indeed. Her coat had a youthful sheen, her eyes the innocence of life. With the alarm of a hairy woodpecker, she'd had enough and moved back down the ridge. I wished her well.

I planned and thought about my future through and through. How would things work out? Where do survival skills and American Sign Language fit into my future? The largest unknown was Kayla. What would she choose to do? But this time made it very clear that our relationship would require our full commitment if it were to continue to blossom. We needed to support and enjoy each other as we both stumbled into careers.

There is one last wildlife observation worth mentioning. John McCarter, friend and tracker, and I have been studying squirrel marking behaviors. We believed we had differentiated certain gray squirrel signs from red squirrel signs on trees. I had witnessed two counts of gray squirrels working on vertical chewed stripes on tree trunks. We strongly believed red squirrels created similar stripes along the dead, lower branches of dominant conifers. Yet, neither of us had witnessed their creation. That is, until now.

The hemlock I watched stood at the corner of two red-squirrel home ranges. I watched one chase the other away, then visit the tree. It walked out on the branch, a typical location for chewed stripes I had seen in the past, and slowly began to smell. The procedure was smell, bite, smell, and bite, again and again, and then the red squirrel was off. I watched this squirrel return to check this branch every so often over the four days, slowly smelling the branch's entirety before heading off. I was thrilled. Finally, I had verification of our beliefs. There is still so much to understand.

I felt guilty about killing mosquitoes when I was sitting out there. I was there to give and give, yet I took and took. It was a great relief to discover that the carpenter ants were carrying dead mosquitoes back to their nest. For hours, I watched the ants find and carry the mosquitoes away. From then on, I put the squashed bloodsuckers closer to the ants. Nothing out here is wasted; everything is recycled back into the system.

Then it was time to return to camp. As I sat against my oak tree near the fire circle, it was difficult to "sum up" what was revealed during this solo. It's as if what you receive is in code, and it takes time to translate into what the conscious mind understands. But several things were clear. First, my relationship with Kayla was stalled by my inability to commit fully; I was afraid of taking the next step. Second, I felt confirmed in my feelings that this experience would be an end to my studying survival skills, or at least for some time. But now, I did not feel guilty or strange about it. I was ready to fully embrace a new life and devote myself fully to studying and researching animal tracking. Perhaps it would be in tracking that I'd have something to contribute. I also knew that I no longer wanted to teach kids—I felt more like an entertainer than a teacher. So many folks pressure me into teaching wilderness skills to young people and preach that this is how to save the earth from human destruction. "Not to teach young people is to turn one's back on the future of the planet," they say. Well, I'm glad to be rid of that manipulative train of thought, as well as the guilt I was feeling for wanting to move on to new things. There are numerous ways to contribute to conservation.

I was still not sure how American Sign Language would fit into my future, but I knew that I loved the practice and the people and would continue to participate in the community. And if I wasn't sure before, I was certain now that I would do everything in my power to avoid working at a job I didn't like. I did not want to end up living only for the weekends. My heart would decide where I worked, and it would be in a field I enjoyed.

Day 45

I returned last evening to a wonderful meal. Trout and wild pears were offered, which I'd requested. I relished their flavors and textures. David and Mike had also been modernized in my absence; both were clean shaven and fresh back from town. They added cheese and bread and a bakery-fresh cookie to my bark slab. I ate well.

Today was for reflection, journal writing, and a last bit of wandering. Mike and I found a perfect deer skull, with every tooth still intact; there wasn't even any sign of rodents gnawing the bone. Mike said I should take it, which I did.

Tomorrow morning we leave for Mike's house to have smoothies and, if our shrunken stomachs allow, waffles with fruit. Kayla, too, will be waiting. Our time here has come to a close.

Our camp, set into a western slope, did not allow for proper appreciation of sun or moon rises. Out and about this evening, we watched the moon rise over our hill. The moon was full, the night clear. The moon hung low in the sky, a massive yellow ball, a mellow hue. As it rose, it became brighter and brighter until it was difficult to look directly into its face. A few small clouds passed through. So light were the clouds and so bright the moon, the clouds appeared to pass behind the moon and move away. The moon was stunning; out here I was so aware of its cycles.

We strolled up familiar trails and reached camp. My last night in my debris hut. I'll miss its conforming comfort and coziness.

Day 46

I awoke, comfortably cool in my debris hut. The time to move on had arrived. I began to return my shelter to the earth, scattering debris and sticks randomly. I thanked my spot. There were things to look forward to, and there was so much I would regret leaving behind. I piled my accumulated wealth in a basket of pine roots and began to wander down the hill.

Kayla was waiting for us where we stepped from meadow to gravel. We had too many stories to start gibbering away; over time, they would all emerge. Each of us weighed ourselves. I had lost twenty-two pounds, Mike fifteen, and David two. We then gorged on waffles and fruit. And just as when David's girlfriend had visited, I was knocked out by eating modern foods. I felt ill, yet Mike, once again, was energized from overeating. Such different bodies we have.

It has become clear how my body reacts to modern foods. I feel bloated and lethargic for many hours after a meal. My body also begins to overheat, which contributes to the feelings of nausea and potential vomiting. All this and more, I experienced from the end of the meal to the evening, culminating in my laying in a fetal position, poised to be sick.

I think the problem may lay in the complexity of foods. Over the summer, we ate meat, or meat and greens, or meat, carbohydrates, and greens. We didn't mix and match, combining ten to twelve items at one time. Read a label for waffle batter and you'll know what I mean. We'll see how long these feelings last.

My vehicle still worked and started up without problems. Slipping behind the wheel was not difficult, and I was off for home. Kayla had gone ahead of me. I hadn't driven more than five minutes when a black Monte Carlo loomed in my rearview mirror. I could feel the driver's tension in my own neck and shoulders. A deep breath and I was able to protect myself from his stress. I pulled over to let him roar past.

When I first started to drive again, I kept to just below posted speeds; it felt fast enough. I'd like to say this lasted forever, or at least a week, but the truth is, within an hour I had slipped into speeding along with the others in transit.

I have, however, so far managed to keep from becoming stressed. I still have nowhere to be and no time to be there. I drove and moved as the road and conditions allowed.

Kayla arrived home ahead of me. Our cabin was barren, as our possessions were stored in the basement so that we could sublet the place while we were both away. A stack of mail awaited our return, and in it a dreaded bill: $832. I put all the mail away and relaxed. Too much reality, too quickly. I'd look at the mail in a few days, bit by bit.

We decided to sleep in a tent.

A Few Days Later ✒

I've been reflecting on our summer. Although we did eat pizza and Leah brought us a meal, I'm not concerned that we weren't as strict as we planned to be at the start of the experience. It was an important lesson in letting go and allowing the experience to become what it was; it was also a reminder than we are and forever will be students of the natural world, and not experts.

Mike and I are confident we had achieved what we set out to do—we were neither dependent upon modern foods nor modern technologies, excepting knives and clothes, for our survival. Rather, we had survived off the land and learned indescribable amounts about survival, primitive skills, and ourselves in the process. We realized there would have been much work to complete before we would have been able to continue through the winter, including the arduous tasks of storing foods and making winter clothes. It was because we weren't planning to stay away that long that our summer was so carefree.

If one word could be used to express what we did this summer, it would be "roam." This word incorporates the freedom with which we moved. I've thought of animals roaming, but until now, never people. We had no place to be and no schedule to keep. It was this ultimate freedom that I will miss.

Many teachers around the world say that if you touch real truth, you can never go back to living any other way. This summer, I touched real freedom, and I now find myself comparing everything in society to what I had this summer. Life will never be the same.

I cherish the pace to which my body and mind slowed, and I can only hope to hold onto it as I dive back into a hectic schedule of work and school. I will still walk in the woods. I will sit behind the farm where I live and absorb nature. I will still track animals and create hand-drill fires.

I've been full since I left the woods about five days ago. I no longer feel sick after every meal, but I'm always rather uncomfortably bloated. Now that I've eaten all the meals I hoped to, perhaps I'll allow my stomach to finish one project before I give it another. And I must mention something I've been told by several reliable sources since exiting the woods: One should never end a fast or an experience such as ours with a massive meal of complex foods. The shock to your body can be dramatic and may even be fatal. We're lucky we didn't die! Experts say to start with simple foods, such as broths and fruits and such, and then gradually work up to a modern-day meal over several days.

10 DAYS LATER

Time is moving slowly back into my life. As I look back at our summer, the closest thing to time I witnessed was in the passing of the berry crops we foraged. When I think of berries, I think of my grandfather, who passed away several years ago. He gathered blackberries and raspberries every year, and I used to place mounds of vanilla ice cream on those piles of berries during my visits. My grandfather was a remarkable naturalist. We would take long walks through the countryside and he'd tell stories, teach me about flowers and birds, and recite poetry about wild creatures. His passion and support may be the reason I took the journey this summer. He may have been the inspiration behind my love for the natural world. It may be my grandfather to whom I owe thanks for my ability to truly discover myself.

Thank you, Daddidar.

Blackberry

Epilogue

Much has changed in the decade since Mike, David, and I undertook this adventure. Mike has married and has two sons, two exuberant black labs, and a house in rural New York. He continues to practice wilderness living skills and tests them in natural settings. Mike now runs his own educational programs under his company, Woodland Ways, teaching wilderness survival skills to children and adults. He did quit smoking.

David continued to practice survival skills but slowly transitioned into modern pottery and new crafts. I've lost touch with him in recent years but wish him well wherever he might be.

After our summer, I practiced survival skills less and less; instead, I devoted my life to animal tracking. I do miss making fires and primitive shelters; perhaps someday those skills will play a larger role. Kayla and I separated a year after the experience, and it has been many years since I've seen her. She married someone else.

I've spent years reflecting on our adventure, for it remains among the most powerful experiences in my life. After so many years, our time in the woods continues to shape who I am, how I think, and what I do. It will remain a reservoir of strength and peace from which I can draw during hectic times in my life, or when I need a boost. Living survival also allowed us to glimpse certain truths. I will never think of time and schedules in the same way; we trick ourselves into believing we must follow culturally imposed timetables and expectations. I will never look at berries and trout in the same way, or food markets and plastic-wrapped, processed resources. And I am more comfortable with myself than ever before. Thinking back on our summer makes me smile. I regret nothing. And I would do it again in a heartbeat.

Our summer in survival was a turning point in my life. The experience taught me much about letting go and going with the flow. Most of all, I learned about energy efficiency. Efficiency is predominant on your mind when you live in a survival situation. You cannot afford to waste energy; every action must have purpose. I've carried that lesson from the woods, and it has made my life easier; it has governed my decision-making and focused my intentions and behaviors. Our summer also taught me much about the relationship between function and purpose.

I had some initial trepidation about releasing a journal written so many years ago, because in some ways I've changed so much, and I was concerned about misrepresenting who I am today. When I reread my journal this past year, I became aware that the words I used to describe certain scenarios, to offer thanks and talk of spirit were not my own. They were taught to me by those who led the workshops on survival skills which I attended, most of whom had never taken a survival trip themselves. It's taken me years to realize that at times in my journal, I expressed myself unnaturally; I wrote in a language and about certain concepts because I thought I was supposed to. For instance, at that time I unconsciously believed that good people gave thanks frequently and bad people did not. Nearly ten years later, I feel that *good* and *bad* are not helpful labels at all.

Survival schools, like tracking schools, can be split into two large categories. One group emphasizes form over function, meaning an emphasis on an experience which provides an avenue for self discovery, connection with place and/or a spiritual path. Mastery of survival skills is secondary. The second group emphasizes function over form—the practical of skills which keep you alive in natural environments. When we undertook our adventure, I was naïve to this division, and to the fact that I was a product of the schools which interwove spiritual dogma with survival skills.

For example, during our summer we found that working with pine pitch and building bark containers were two critical skills needed for our survival. Yet I knew of no school at the time which taught those particular skills. Most taught how to build containers which require too much energy to create, or relied on materials that couldn't be found under normal conditions—cut rounds of wood, for example. Without a metal saw, it's very difficult to find rounds of wood in a natural setting. The courses we attended prior to our adventure were also filled with unnecessary rituals and routines. Yet the leap Mike, David, and I took when we attempted to utilize the skills in an actual survival setting forced us to prioritize function before form, and to refine skills and behaviors in such ways as to promote energy efficiency.

As I shifted my emphasis to the application of primitive skills in a survival situation and the application of wildlife tracking in monitoring and research, my relationships with nature, people, and language began to evolve. I'm still thankful for life, but I no longer need to voice it all the time. Rituals have dissolved into direct experience. And whereas during our summer I still struggled with really knowing that we as humans are as equally connected to natural systems as coyotes and deer, I feel that now. Even prayer seems unnecessary when remaining true to yourself; active participation in natural systems seems prayer enough.

You might say I've switched "camps" in the last ten years with regards to primitive skills and animal tracking schools. For now I promote function before form; in this way form is dictated by rate of success. If a skill doesn't find animals, make fires under any circumstance, keep you warm, feed you, or answer some purpose, then why practice it? To practice survival and tracking skills which do not work, or lack application, is to lose the very skills we seek to protect and practice.

Application is of paramount importance in keeping these skills real and useful; application also keeps our egos from making the skills into something they aren't.

What is the purpose of learning survival skills if not to apply them in natural settings? That is their function. Yes, the beneficial byproducts of practicing survival and tracking skills are endless, and their educational value for children and adults is indisputable. Yet survival skills evolved with humankind through countless generations of humans living as hunter-gatherers. That's what these skills are for, and thus in their application are revealed true insights into what it means to be human, to be animal.

Some folks argue that one should learn survival skills to plan for worst case scenarios, but they should not be practiced without dire need. This is fear-based thinking, and in my opinion the polar opposite of what these skills are truly about—survival and tracking skills are about embracing living, not fearing death.

We killed many animals during our summer, but never flippantly or for pleasure. After ten years, I have this to say: Survival in the natural ecosystems of the northeast of North America is impossible without killing animals. A vegetarian existence is a luxury borne of modern convenience and privilege. And even as a vegetarian or vegan, you still kill plants, fungi, and other life forms. To deny that you are responsible for deaths every day is to deny your connection to natural systems; it is an illusion. Yet conscious participation in natural systems won't make you mean or cold-hearted. It just makes you honest, which often stimulates humility. Death is natural. Be thankful for life.

During our summer we also disregarded every law to do with hunting and fishing. We are not proud of breaking laws, but it was a necessary step in order to experience what we did. It was never our intention to undermine a system which fosters conservation. Practicing primitive hunting and fishing techniques requires you to break most current hunting and fishing regulations, and killing game animals out of season is poaching. We wanted to experience survival; we ate what we killed and tried our best to be respectful. Judge us as you will. Today Mike and I support hunting and fishing laws, recognize their importance and respect those who are models of excellent hunting and fishing etiquette. Yet I will also add that when I question the function behind specific laws, I'm not always sure of their purpose. Are they to conserve natural resources, minimize the possibility of people being injured, and protect animals from inhumane deaths? Or, are they about making money and exerting government control? Are the laws helping to protect and foster hunting, trapping, and fishing in American culture, or to polarize viewpoints and create divisions in voter polls and regional populations? I think it's a combination of all these things. Hunting should never be allowed to become a red versus blue debate.

But perhaps the greatest question of all is this: Did Mike and I succeed in *surviving* that summer? Did two slices of pizza, a handful of granola, and a portion of Leah's Mexican pie provide the nutritional needs required to fuel my body for forty-six days in the woods while building shelters, wandering, and weathering storms and cold fronts? I would argue that I would not have walked out of the woods as healthy as I did if that were all I had eaten. Though inconsistent with our original goals, we adapted, we let go of expectations, and we ended the experience feeling we had achieved a lifestyle which was not dependent upon modern society. We also let go of our concerns over how you the readers would judge our inconsistencies, preferring instead to tell a story of learning rather than expertise. Our summer was nothing short of amazing, and the greatest gift we could have given ourselves. I also believe that it marked my transition into manhood.

I hope you, too, will be generous enough to award yourselves your own adventures, whatever form they may take. Practice your skills, take short trips, and bring a sleeping bag as backup. Slowly transition into a longer, less technology-dependent experience. Then do us all a favor and rejoin us to tell *your* stories. The loose community of those who have an interest in survival skills will benefit from real tales filled with mistakes and laughter. Mike and I believe achievable stories are the most inspirational.

Appendix

WILDERNESS LIVING AND SURVIVAL SCHOOLS

There are numerous schools that provide workshops for wilderness living and survival skills in North America and beyond. Thomas J. Elpel teaches wilderness skills at Hollowtop Outdoor Primitive School in Montana and runs a website where schools may post their contact information. With his permission, we've reprinted that list here. He warned us that at any given time 5% to 10% of the information is likely incorrect due to people constantly moving, starting and stopping programs, and other variables. With this in mind, it might be worth checking the school list on his website at http://www.hollowtop.com/schools.htm. We should also mention that each school will have its own character, strengths, and weaknesses and likely will teach a limited set of skills. Shop around as you consider taking workshops and ask lots of questions to make sure you find the school that is best suited to your personal goals. Enjoy.

WITHIN THE UNITED STATES

Alabama

Randall's Adventure Training
Mike Perrin
PO Box 51
Blaine, TN 37709
856-932-9111
mike@jungletraining.com

Arizona

Aboriginal Living Skills School, LLC
Cody Lundin
PO Box 3064
Prescott, AZ 86302
520-636-8384
abodude@alssadventures.com

Arizona (continued)

Ancient Pathways, LLC
Tony Nester
1931 E. Andes
Flagstaff, AZ 86004
928-774-7522
anester@apathways.com

Arizona Outdoor Institute
Dave Ganci
4753 Gloria
Prescott, AZ 86301
928-778-2567
canyon@hotmail.com

Native American Self-Awareness
    Institute
Dr. John Standingbear
    Hoopingarner & Molly Swan
2422 N. 72nd Place
Scottsdale, AZ 85257
480-970-8811

Randy Kinkade
141 W. Forrest Feezor
Corona, AZ 85641
520-360-6868
randy@willowriverwilderness.com

Raven's Way Traditional School
Vince Pinto
PO Box 16261
Portal, AZ 85632
520-403-5085

Reevis Mountain School
Peter Bigfoot
HC 02, Box 1534
Roosevelt, AZ 85545
520-467-2675

Arkansas

Cedar Creek Nature Studies
Randy & Susie Teague
1796 Cedar Creek Road
Hot Springs, AR 71901
501-262-0567
ccns@cedarcreeknaturestudies.com

California

Earth-Heart
Malcom & Deborah Ringwalt
PO Box 926
Topanga, CA 90290
310-967-1336
mail@earth-heart.net

Headwaters School
Tim Corcoran
PO Box 1698
Santa Cruz, CA 95061-1690
831-423-3830
info@hwos.com

Lifesong Wilderness Adventures
(Classes in northern California)
Mark Wienert Jr.
PO Box 135
Idleyld Park, OR 97447
541-496-0496
lifesongwild@yahoo.com

Oldways Workshops
Norm Kidder
Sunol Regional Wilderness
PO Box 82
Sunol, CA 94536
925-862-2600
svisit@ebparks.org

California (continued)

Paleotechnics
Tamara Wilder and Steven Edholm
PO Box 876
Boonville, CA 95415
707-793-2287
ts@paleotechnics.com

Sasquatch Way
Nachshon Rose
PO Box 137
Lakehead, CA 96051
530-945-1929
abospirit@excite.com

School of Self Reliance
Christopher & Dolores Nyerges
PO Box 41834
Eagle Rock, CA 90041
323-255-9502

Colorado

Boulder Outdoor Survival School
Josh Bernstein
PO Box 1590
Boulder, CO 80306
800-335-7404

Cottonwood Institute
Ford Church
1076 Grant Place
Boulder, CO 80302
303-447-1076
info@cottonwoodinstitute.org

Earth Knack
Robin Blankenship
PO Box 508
Crestone, CO 81131
719-256-4909

Nature Knowledge
"Mountain Mel" Deweese
1825 Linden Street
Grand Junction, CO 81503
907-242-8507
mtnmel@youwillsurvive.com

Outdoor Wisdom and Living Skills
 (OWLS)
Fire Mountain & Aaron Huey
5745 Olde Stage Road.
Boulder, CO 80302
720-231-9389
aaronhuey@earthlink.net

Primitive Skills & Braintanning
Michael Foltmer
1330 Brantner Road
Evans, CO 80620
970-339-5608

Wilderness Institute of Survival
 Education
Don Davis
8415 Coyote Run
Loveland, CO 80537-9665
970-669-9016
dondavis@frii.com

Florida

Global Principles Survival School
653 West 23rd St. #294
Panama City, FL 32405
850-722-7870
president@globalprinciples.com

Georgia

Hofunee Programs
Scott Jones
2550 Elberton Road
Carlton, GA 30627
706-743-5144
scottj@arches.uga.edu

Medicine Bow Wilderness School
Mark Warren
104 Medicine Bow
Dahlonega, GA 30533
medbow@alltel.net

Idaho

Backtracks, LLC
Dave & Paula Wescott
PO Box 905
Rexburg, ID 83440
208-359-2400
Dwescot@aol.com

Salmon Outdoor School
Joe & Denise Bigley
PO Box 17
Tendoy, ID 83468
208-756-8240
school@aboman.com

Illinois

Ancient Lifeways Institute
John & Ela White
Michael Hollow Road
Michael, IL 62065
618-576-9255
AncientL@aol.com

Center for American Archeology
PO Box 366
Kampsville, IL 62053
618-653-4316
CAA@caa-archeology.org

Nature Education Programs, Ltd.
3030 Warrenville Rd., Suite 215
Lisle, IL 60532
630-955-9550
natedpro@aol.com

Northwest School of Survival
Brian Wheeler
800 W. 5th Ave., Suite 103-B
Naperville, IL 60563
603-305-9717
Info@nwsos.com

Maine

Beartraks Schools of Wilderness
    Living
Dan Fisher
99 Woodside Road
Brunswick, ME 04011
207-729-8616
info@beartraks.com

Earthways
Ray & Nancy Reitze
RR2, Box 2700
Canaan, ME 04924
207-426-8138

Maine Primitive Skills School
Michael Douglas
716 Church Hill Road
Augusta, ME 04330
207-623-7298
info@primitiveskills.com

Sandy River Outdoors
Adam Cates & Coby Leighton
PO Box 164
Solon, ME 04979
207-431-4729
207-578-2437
info@sandyriveroutdoors.com

Maine (continued)

Sunrise Wilderness Skills
Matt and Kate Pinkham
3 Gladd Lane
Milo, ME 04463
207-943-5710
mkpink@surfglobal.net

Michigan

Willow Winds
Jim Miller
962 F-30
Mikado, MI 48745

Missouri

First Earth Wilderness School, LLC
Bo Brown
3425 N. FR 209
Strafford, MO 65757
bo@firstearth.org

Montana

A Naturalist's World
Jim Halfpenny & Diann Thompson
PO Box 989
Gardiner, MT 59030
406-848-9458
trackdoctor@tracknature.com

Hollowtop Outdoor Primitive
  School
Thomas J. Elpel
12 Quartz Street
Pony, MT 59747-0697
406-685-3222
www.hollowtop.com

Four Seasons Prehistoric Projects
Lynx Vilden (aka. Lynx Shepherd)
1501 Dodge Creek
Rexford, MT 59930

The Artisan
Melvin Beattie
PO Box 9736
Helena, MT 59604-9736
406-458-5493

Nebraska

Spirit in the Wind
Rick & Doris Hamilton
87255 464th Avenue
Stuart, NE 68780
402-924-3180
hamilton@elkhorn.net

New Hampshire

Jack Mountain Bushcraft, LLC
Tim Smith
PO Box 61
Wolfeboro Falls, NH 03896-0061
603-569-6150
timsmith@jackmountainbushcraft.
  com

New Jersey

Primitive Industries
Jack Cresson
40 E. 2nd Street
Moorestown, NJ 08057
856-234-3286
jackcresson@juno.com

The Tracker, Inc.
Tom Brown, Jr.
PO Box 173
Asbury, NJ 08802-0173
908-479-4681

New Jersey (continued)

Wild Food Company
Linda Runyon
PO Box 83
Shiloh, NJ 08353
856-234-3286
lrunyon8@yahoo.com

New Mexico

The Earthen Spirituality Project
Jesse Wolf Hardin & Loba Hardin
PO Box 516
Reserve, NM 87830
505-533-6446
earthway@concentric.net

The Tracking Project
John Stokes
PO Box 266
Corrales, NM 87048-8788
505-898-6967

New York

Ancient Skills School
Joe Longshore II
357 Cowan Road
Canton, NY 13617

Gibbons' Woodfolks
PO Box 35
Plattsburgh, NY 12901
518-578-4124
Woodfolks@westelcom.com

Hawk Circle
Ricardo Sierra
PO Box 506
Cherry Valley, NY 13320
607-264-3396
Ricardo@hawkcircle.com

Ndakinna Wilderness Project
23 Middle Grove Road
Greenfield Center, NY 12833
518-583-9980
jim@ndakinna.com

The Wilderness Center
Marty Simon
435 Sandy Knoll Road
Chateaugay, NY 12920
518-497-3179

Wilderness Way School
Mike Head
744 Glenmary Drive
Owego, NY 13827
607-687-9186

Wildman Steve Brill
320 Palmer Terrace, 2A
Mamaroneck, NY 10543
914-835-2153
wildmansteve@bigfoot.com

Woodland Ways
Mike Pewtherer
PO Box 228
Philmont, NY 12565
845-486-7092

North Carolina

Earth School
Richard Cleveland
PO Box 777
Tryon, NC 28782
866-504-3199
info@lovetheearth.com

Skills Alive
Mac Maness
103 Briarpatch Lane
Boone, NC 28607
828-262-9629
mac@abotech.com

North Carolina (continued)

Turtle Island Preserve
Eustace Conway
1443 Lonnie Carlton Road
Triplett, NC 28618
828-265-2267
mail@turtleislandpreserve.com

Windsong Primitives
Benjamin Pressley
1403 Killian Road
Stanley, NC 28164
benjamin@perigee.net

Yonah Earthskills Programs
Steven "Snowbear" & Mary Taylor
901 S. Carter Cove Road
Hayesville, NC 28904
828-389-9336

Ohio

Goosefoot Acres Center for
    Resourceful Living
Peter Gail, Ph.D
PO Box 18016
Cleveland, OH 44118
216-932-2145
PETERGAIL@aol.com

Midwest Native Skills Institute
Tom Laskowski
PO Box 31764
Cleveland, OH 44131
Toll Free: 888-886-5592
tom@survivalschool.com

Oregon

Dancing Hawk Native Lifeways
    School
Tony "Kerrke" Yu
2520 Kingsley Road
Hood River, OR 97031
541-806-0898
kerrke@dancinghawk.com

Northwest School of Survival
Brian Wheeler
2870 NE Hogan Road, Suite E, #461
Gresham, OR 97030
503-668-8264
Info@nwsos.com

Wild Food Adventures
John Kallas, Ph.D
4125 N. Colonial Avenue
Portland, OR 97217-3338
503-775-3828
mail@wildfoodadventures.com

Pennsylvania

Earth Star Survival
Bob Collins
224 Trinity Avenue
Ambler, PA 19002
215-654-9164
bobcollins@earthstarsurvival.com

South Carolina

Windwalker Outdoor School
Landy Young
142 Grapevine Road
Summerville, SC 29483
843-871-3272
windwalkersc@yahoo.com

Tennessee

Big Oak Wilderness School
Lisa & G.T. Sanford
7616 Nolensville Road
Nolensville, TN 37135-9458
615-776-2147
gtsan@edge.net

Spirit Bow Wilderness School
Doug Jones
2024 Blue Ribbon Downs
Lebanon, TN 37087
doug_jones@spiritbow.com

Utah

Lifeways Earth Living School
Holly Stokes
PO Box 70
Spring City, UT 84662
435-787-3732
lifewaysschool@hotmail.com

Vermont

Camp Wihakomwi
Bull Run Road
Northfield, VT 05663
802-485-4321

Vermont Wilderness School
Steve Young and Mark Morey
67 Main Street, Suite 13
Brattleboro, VT 05301
802-257-8570
steve@VermontWildernessSchool.org

Virginia

Cliffside Workshops
Errett Callahan
2 Fredonia Avenue
Lynchburg, VA 24503
434-528-3444

Earth Connection
Tim MacWelch
PO Box 32
Somerville, VA 22739
540-270-2531
econnect@earth-connection.com

Earth Quest
David Dabbs & Steve Sims
506 Wilson Lane
Stuart, VA 24171
540-930-3340

Nature Awareness School
Del & Lynne Hall
PO Box 219
Lyndhurst, VA 22952
540-377-6068

Two Suns Earth School
Route 1, Box 318
Fulks Run, Virginia 22830

Washington

Earthwalk Northwest, Inc.
Frank & Karen Sherwood
PO Box 461
Issaquah, WA 98027
425-746-7267

Simply Survival
Greg & Kim Davenport
PO Box 449
Stevenson, WA 98648
509-427-4022

Wilderness Awareness School
Jon Young
26425 NE Allen Street, Ste 203
Duvall, WA 98019
425-788-6155

Washington (continued)

WOLF School of Natural Science
Chris Chisholm &
    Melva van Schyndel
PO Box 1108
Monroe, WA 98272
360-319-6892
info@wolfjourney.com

Wisconsin

Medicine Hawk Wilderness Skills,
    Inc.
PO Box 07482
Milwaukee, WI 53207
630-955-9550
natedpro@aol.com

Native Ways School
Gregg Weiss
PO Box 133
Cornucopia, WI 54827
715-742-3281
nativeways@hotmail.com

Teaching Drum Outdoor School
Tamarack Song
7124 Military Road
Three Lakes, WI 54562
715-546-2944
balance@teachingdrum.org

Tracks & Trees Learning Center, LLC
Doug Gaulke
N7597 County Highway Y
Watertown, WI 53094
920-699-3217
dugtracs@execpc.com

OUTSIDE THE UNITED STATES

AUSTRALIA

Dundalli Art & Culture
Rick Roser
PO Box 247
Fortitude Valley, QLD 4006
(07) 3358 5455
mavericktrading@optusnet.com.au

Wilderness Survival Training Center
Bob Newcomer
9 Tanbark Circuit, Suite 1426
Werrington Downs, NSW 2747
1426@coverage1.com

BELIZE

Jabiru Lodge
Bruce Carroll
PO Box 127
Ashuelot, NH 03441 USA
jabirulodge@yahoo.com

CANADA

Alberta

Karamat Wilderness Ways
Randy & Lori Breeuwsma
Box 483
Wildwood, AB TOE 2M0
780-325-2345
randy@karamat.com

The Trapper
Ross Hinter
PO Box 246
Tomahawk, AB TOE 2H0
780-797-3808

British Columbia

Survivors Edge
Jackson Wagner
3127 Robinson Road
Sooke, BC VOS 1NO
250-642-0628
survivorsedge@shaw.ca

Wild Awakening
Sherene C. Djafroodi
PO Box 442
Atlin, BC, VOW 1A0
403-651-0214
info@wildawakening.com

Windwalker
Wes Gietz
2205 Walnut Avenue
Comox, BC V9M 1N6
250-339-3197
wgietz@windwalker.ca

WOLF School of Natural Science
Chris Chisholm &
    Melva van Schyndel
Box 434, 1641 Lonsdale Ave
North Vancouver, BC, V7M 2J5
604-418-8900
info@wolfjourney.com

Ontario

Alba Wilderness School
Chad & Barry Clifford &
    Tania Marsh
R.R.#4
Lanark, ON, KOG-1KO
613-259 3236
alba@magma.ca

FINLAND

Finland Survival Guild
Petri Heinonen
Heikinkuja 4 C 24
F-13800 Katinala
Finland

GERMANY

ARVEN
Naturopathic Medicine &
    Outdoor Skills
Susanne Fischer-Rizzi
Postfach 24
D-87475 Sulzberg
Germany
Tel: 08376 1777

NETHERLANDS

EXTRA Survival Courses
Rene Nauta
De Bree 27
8381 BS VLEDDER
The Netherlands
Tel: 0031 521 381110
Fax: 0031 521 380130
info@extrasurvival.nl

FYLGJUR
Christo Motz
PO Box 4285
3006 AG Rotterdam
The Netherlands
Tel: +31 10 453 23 79
+31 615 08 09 73
info@fylgjur.nl

SWEDEN

Davaj Northern Bushcraft &
  Trekking
Geerd de Koning
Ystasjon 188
84050 Gallo
Sweden
Tel: 0046069320206
dekoning@telia.com

Swedish Survival Guild
Spelmanshöjden 13
174 50 Sundbyberg
Postgironummer: 282901-8
message@survive.nu

The Institute for Ancient
  Technology
S. Strandv·gen 7
832 43 FROSON
Tel: 063-10 63 20
nevka@telia.com

UNITED KINGDOM

Backwoods Survival School
Patrick McGlinchey
9 Loanend Cottages
Cambuslang
Glasgow G72 8YD
Scotland, UK
Tel:. 0141 641 2055
info@backwoodsurvival.co.uk

Bison Bushcraft
Roger Harrington
No. 3 Beech Farm Cottages
Bugsell Lane
Robertsbridge
East Sussex
TN32 5EN
UK
Tel: +44 01580 882194
Info@bisonbushcraft.co.uk

Breakaway Survival School
Mick Tyler
17 Hugh Thomas Avenue
Holmer
Hereford
HR4 9RB
UK
Tel: 01432-267097
mick@breakawaysurvival.co.uk

Cambrian School of Survival
PO Box 82
Aberystwyth
Ceredigion
SY23 1WH
UK
Tel: 01970 612969
info@cambriansurvival.co.uk

United Kingdom (continued)

Natural Pathways
PO Box 824
Canterbury
CT4 6YQ
UK
Tel:. 44 01304 842045
naturalpathways@onetel.net.uk

Outdoor World Survival School
7 Highland Court
Bryncethin
Bridgend
Mid Glamorgan
South Wales
UK
CF32 9US
Tel: 01656 725532
admin@outdoorworldactivities.co.uk

South West Survival School
Nigel Startin
Hollybush Bungalow
Fore Street
Tintagel
Cornwall
PL 34 ODE
UK
Tel: 08700 755763
nigel@i-survive.co.uk

Survival School
Jonny Crockett
Northwood
Poltimore
Exeter
Devon
EX4 0AR
UK
Tel: +44 01392 460312
jonnycrockett@survivalschool.co.uk

The UK Survival School
Seymour House
24 East Street
Hereford
HR1 2LU
UK
Tel: 00 44 (0)1432 376751
info@uksurvivalschool.co.uk

Wild-Live
PO Box 4
Newry
BT34 5WY
Northern Ireland, UK
Tel: 02843 771 446
info@wild-live.org

Woodlore Ltd.
Ray Mears
P.O. Box 3
Etchingham
TN19 7ZE
UK
Tel: 01580 819668
info@raymears.com

Woodsmoke
Ben McNutt
PO Box 45
Cockermouth
Cumbria
CA15 9WB
UK
Tel: 01900 821733
info@woodsmoke.uk.com

INDEX